THE LONELY CROWD

3—
5c

DAVID RIESMAN was originally trained as a lawyer. Upon graduation from the Harvard Law School, he became law clerk to Justice Brandeis and later was deputy assistant district attorney of New York County. He also was a teacher of law at the University of Buffalo. He is now professor of social science at the College of the University of Chicago.

NATHAN GLAZER is an associate editor of *Commentary* magazine.

REUEL DENNEY is a professor of social science at the College of the University of Chicago.

THE LONELY CROWD and its successor *Faces in the Crowd* were the product of several years of research under the sponsorship of the Yale University Committee on National Policy. THE LONELY CROWD was originally published by the Yale University Press in 1950.

THE LONELY CROWD

~~~~ A STUDY OF THE CHANGING

AMERICAN CHARACTER ~~~~~~

BY DAVID RIESMAN

WITH NATHAN GLAZER AND REUEL DENNEY

ABRIDGED BY THE AUTHORS

DOUBLEDAY ANCHOR BOOKS

DOUBLEDAY & COMPANY, INC., GARDEN CITY, NEW YORK.

PREFACE

THIS book was written during 1948 and 1949 under a grant from the Committee on National Policy of Yale University. While engaged in writing it, we were also conducting interviews with Americans of different ages, both sexes, from various social strata, and in many parts of the country. These interviews—not intended to be representative of the enormous diversity of America, but rather to be a source of illustrative data—were drawn on to only a slight extent for the writing of this book. Besides conducting interviews, we visited and observed schools, studied poll data and the vast range of other information about contemporary America social scientists have made available, and read histories, biographies, and novels. Mainly, however, this book is based on our experiences of living in America—the people we have met, the jobs we have held, the movies we have seen. This book, therefore, represents an effort to interpret and organize our experience of contemporary America and its relation to the past and the prospective future. However, the fact that we were simultaneously conducting interviews and planning several community studies forced us towards the clarification and systematization of our ideas, which then served to guide interviewing and the analysis of interviews. Some of the later phases of this work are reported in a sequel to this volume, *Faces in the Crowd* (Yale, 1952).

We are greatly indebted to the Yale Committee on National Policy for the freedom it gave us, and to the Carnegie Corporation, which financed the Committee; we are also indebted to a number of colleagues who read and criticized various sections of this book: these are listed in the preface and footnotes of the original edition of *The Lonely Crowd* which is published by the Yale University Press.

The present edition is about four fifths as long as the original edition. It is not only an abridgment, but to some extent a new edition, for many passages have been rewritten and others rearranged. However, in editing, we have aimed only at greater clarity and conciseness: we have not tried to take into account the criticisms made of the original work because we believed it would be more helpful to our readers to be loyal to our original errors than to try to conceal them. Consequently, the reader may be assured that any critique he may read of the original work will hold for this one, and what we have taken out has been removed for his convenience in understanding, and not to protect him from controversy.

CONTENTS

PART II: POLITICS

PART III: AUTONOMY

PART I: CHARACTER

I

SOME TYPES OF CHARACTER
AND SOCIETY

. . . nor can the learned reader be ignorant, that in human nature, though here collected under one general name, is such prodigious variety, that a cook will sooner have gone through all the several species of animal and vegetable food in the world, than an author will be able to exhaust so extensive a subject.

Fielding, TOM JONES

I speak of the American in the singular, as if there were not millions of them, north and south, east and west, of both sexes, of all ages, and of various races, professions, and religions. Of course the one American I speak of is mythical; but to speak in parables is inevitable in such a subject, and it is perhaps as well to do so frankly.

Santayana, CHARACTER AND OPINION
IN THE UNITED STATES

THIS is a book about social character and about the differences in social character between men of different regions, eras, and groups. It considers the ways in which different social character types, once they are formed at the knee of society, are then deployed in the work, play, politics, and child-rearing activities of society. More particularly, it is about the way in which one kind of social character, which dominated America in the nineteenth century, is gradually being replaced by a social character of quite a different sort. Just why this happened; how it happened; what are its consequences in some major areas of life: this is the subject of this book.

But just what do we mean when we speak of "social character"? We do not speak of "personality," which in current social psychology is used to denote the total self, with its inherited temperaments and talents, its biological as well as psychological components, its evanescent as well as more or less permanent attributes. Nor even do we speak of "character" as such, which, in one of its contemporary uses, refers to only a part of personality—that part which is formed not by heredity but by experience (not that it is any simple matter to draw a line between the two): Character, in this sense, is the more or less permanent socially and historically conditioned organization of an individual's drives and satisfactions—the kind of "set" with which he approaches the world and people.

"Social character" is that part of "character" which is shared among significant social groups and which, as most contemporary social scientists define it, is the product of the experience of these groups. The notion of social character permits us to speak, as I do throughout this book, of the character of classes, groups, regions, and nations.

I do not plan to argue over the many ambiguities of the concept of social character—whether it may properly be ascribed to experience rather than to heredity; whether there is any empirical proof that it really exists; whether it is "more important" than the elements of character and personality that bind all people everywhere in the world together, or those other elements of character and personality that separate each individual from every other, even the closest. The assumption that a social character exists has always been a more or less invisible premise of ordinary parlance and is becoming today a more or less visible premise of the social sciences. It will consequently be familiar under one name or another to any of my readers who are acquainted with the writings of Erich Fromm, Abram Kardiner, Ruth Benedict, Margaret Mead, Geoffrey Gorer, Karen Horney, and many others who have written about social character in general, or the social character of different people and different times.

Most of these writers assume—as I do—that the years of childhood are of great importance in molding character. Most of them agree—as I do—that these early years cannot be seen in isolation from the structure of society, which affects the parents who raise the children, as well as the children directly. My collaborators and I base ourselves on this broad platform of agreement, and do not plan to discuss in what way these writers differ from each other and we from them.

I. Character and Society

What is the relation between social character and society? How is is that every society seems to get, more or less, the social character it "needs"? Erik H. Erikson writes, in a study of the social character of the Yurok Indians, that ". . . systems of child training . . . represent unconscious attempts at creating out of human raw material that configuration of attitudes which is (or once was) the optimum under the tribe's particular natural conditions and economic-historic necessities."[1]

From "economic-historic necessities" to "systems of child training" is a long jump. Much of the work of students of social character has been devoted to closing the gap and showing how the satisfaction of the largest "needs" of society is prepared, in some half-mysterious way, by its most intimate practices. Erich Fromm succinctly suggests the line along which this connection between society and character training may be sought: "In order that any society may function well, its members must acquire the kind of character which makes them *want* to act in the way they *have* to act as members of the society or of a special class within it. They have to *desire* what objectively is *necessary* for them to do. *Outer force* is replaced by *inner com-*

[1] "Observations on the Yurok: Childhood and World Image," *University of California Publications in American Archaeology and Ethnology,* XXXV (1943), iv.

pulsion, and by the particular kind of human energy which is channeled into character traits."[2]

Thus, the link between character and society—certainly not the only one, but one of the most significant, and the one I choose to emphasize in this discussion—is to be found in the way in which society ensures some degree of conformity from the individuals who make it up. In each society, such a mode of ensuring conformity is built into the child, and then either encouraged or frustrated in later adult experience. (No society, it would appear, is quite prescient enough to ensure that the mode of conformity it has inculcated will satisfy those subject to it in every stage of life.) I shall use the term "mode of conformity" interchangeably with the term "social character"—though certainly conformity is not all of social character: "mode of creativity" is as much a part of it. However, while societies and individuals may live well enough—if rather boringly— without creativity, it is not likely that they can live without some mode of conformity—even be it one of rebellion.

My concern in this book is with two revolutions and their relation to the "mode of conformity" or "social character" of Western man since the Middle Ages. The first of these revolutions has in the last four hundred years cut us off pretty decisively from the family- and clan-oriented traditional ways of life in which mankind has existed throughout most of history; this revolution includes the Renaissance, the Reformation, the Counter-Reformation, the Industrial Revolution, and the political revolutions of the seventeenth, eighteenth, and nineteenth centuries. This revolution is, of course, still in process, but in the most advanced countries of the world, and particularly in America, it is giving way to another sort of revolution—a whole range of social developments associated with a shift from

---

[2] "Individual and Social Origins of Neurosis," *American Sociological Review*, IX (1944), 380; reprinted in *Personality in Nature, Society and Culture*, edited by Clyde Kluckhohn and Henry Murray (New York, Alfred A. Knopf, 1948).

an age of production to an age of consumption. The first revolution we understand moderately well; it is, under various labels, in our texts and our terminology; this book has nothing new to contribute to its description, but perhaps does contribute something to its evaluation. The second revolution, which is just beginning, has interested many contemporary observers, including social scientists, philosophers, and journalists. Both description and evaluation are still highly controversial; indeed, many are still preoccupied with the first set of revolutions and have not invented the categories for discussing the second set. In this book I try to sharpen the contrast between, on the one hand, conditions and character in those social strata that are today most seriously affected by the second revolution, and, on the other hand, conditions and character in analogous strata during the earlier revolution; in this perspective, what is briefly said about the traditional and feudal societies which were overturned by the first revolution is in the nature of backdrop for these later shifts.

One of the categories I make use of is taken from demography, the science that deals with birth rates and death rates, with the absolute and relative numbers of people in a society, and their distribution by age, sex, and other variables, for I tentatively seek to link certain social and characterological developments, as cause and effect, with certain population shifts in Western society since the Middle Ages. It seems reasonably well established, despite the absence of reliable figures for earlier centuries, that during this period the curve of population growth in the Western countries has shown an S-shape of a particular type (as other countries are drawn more closely into the net of Western civilization, their populations also show a tendency to develop along the lines of this S-shaped curve). The bottom horizontal line of the S represents a situation where the total population does not increase or does so very slowly, for the number of births equals roughly the number of deaths, and both are very high. In societies of this type, a high proportion of the population is young, life expectancy is low, and the turnover of generations is extremely rapid. Such societies are said to be in the phase of "high growth potential"; for should something happen to decrease the very high death rate (greater production of food, new sanitary measures, new knowledge of the causes of disease, and so on), a "population explosion" would result, and the population would increase very rapidly. This in effect is what happened in the West, starting with the seventeenth century. This spurt in population was most marked in Europe, and the countries settled by Europeans, in the nineteenth century. It is represented by the vertical bar of the S. Demographers call this the stage of "transitional growth," because the birth rate soon begins to follow the death rate in its decline. The rate of growth then slows down, and demographers begin to detect in the growing proportion of middle-aged and aged in the population the signs of a third stage, "incipient population decline." Societies in this stage are represented by the top horizontal bar of the S, again indicating, as in the first stage, that total population growth is small—but this time because births and deaths are low.

The S-curve is not a theory of population growth so much as an empirical description of what has happened in the West and in those parts of the world influenced by the West. After the S runs its course, what then? The developments of recent years in the United States and other Western countries do not seem to be susceptible to so simple and elegant a summing up. "Incipient population decline" has not become "population decline" itself, and the birth rate has shown an uncertain tendency to rise again, which most demographers think is temporary.[3]

It would be very surprising if variations in the basic conditions of reproduction, livelihood, and survival chances, that is, in the supply of and demand for human beings,

---

[3]The terminology used here is that of Frank W. Notestein. See his "Population—The Long View," in *Food for the World*, edited by Theodore W. Schultz (University of Chicago Press, 1945).

with all it implies in change of the spacing of people, the size of markets, the role of children, the society's feeling of vitality or senescence, and many other intangibles, failed to influence character. My thesis is, in fact, that each of these three different phases on the population curve appears to be occupied by a society that enforces conformity and molds social character in a definably different way.

The society of high growth potential develops in its typical members a social character whose conformity is insured by their tendency to follow tradition: these I shall term *tradition-directed* people and the society in which they live a society *dependent on tradition-direction.*

The society of transitional population growth develops in its typical members a social character whose conformity is insured by their tendency to acquire early in life an internalized set of goals. These I shall term *inner-directed* people and the society in which they live a society *dependent on inner-direction.*

Finally, the society of incipient population decline develops in its typical members a social character whose conformity is insured by their tendency to be sensitized to the expectations and preferences of others. These I shall term *other-directed* people and the society in which they live one *dependent on other-direction.*

Let me point out, however, before embarking on a description of these three "ideal types" of character and society, that I am not concerned here with making the detailed analysis that would be necessary before one could prove that a link exists between population phase and character type. Rather, the theory of the curve of population provides me with a kind of shorthand for referring to the myriad institutional elements that are also—though usually more heatedly—symbolized by such words as "industrialism," "folk society," "monopoly capitalism," "urbanization," "rationalization," and so on. Hence when I speak here of transitional growth or incipient decline of population in conjunction with shifts in character and conformity, these phrases should not be taken as magical and comprehensive explanations.

My reference is as much to the complex of technological and institutional factors related—as cause or effect—to the development of population as to the demographic facts themselves. It would be almost as satisfactory, for my purposes, to divide societies according to the stage of economic development they have reached. Thus, Colin Clark's distinction between the "primary," "secondary," and "tertiary" spheres of the economy (the first refers to agriculture, hunting and fishing, and mining; the second to manufacturing; the third to trade, communications, and services) corresponds very closely to the division of societies on the basis of demographic characteristics. In those societies which are in the phase of "high growth potential," the "primary" sphere is dominant (for example, India); in those that are in the phase of "transitional" growth, the "secondary" sphere is dominant (for example, Russia); in those that are in the phase of "incipient decline," the "tertiary" sphere is dominant (for example, the United States). And of course, no nation is all of a piece, either in its population characteristics or its economy—different groups and different regions reflect different stages of development, and social character reflects these differences.

HIGH GROWTH POTENTIAL: TRADITION-DIRECTED TYPES

The phase of high growth potential characterizes more than half the world's population: India, Egypt, and China (which have already grown immensely in recent generations), most preliterate peoples in Central Africa, parts of Central and South America, in fact most areas of the world relatively untouched by industrialization. Here death rates are so high that if birth rates were not also high the populations would die out.

Regions where the population is in this stage may be either sparsely populated, as are the areas occupied by many primitive tribes and parts of Central and South America; or they may be densely populated, as are India, China, and Egypt. In either case, the society achieves a Malthusian bargain with the limited food supply by killing off, in one way or another, some of the potential surplus of births over deaths—the enormous trap which, in Malthus' view, nature sets for man and which can be peaceably escaped only by prudent cultivation of the soil and prudent uncultivation of the species through the delay of marriage. Without the prevention of childbirth by means of marriage postponement or other contraceptive measures, the population must be limited by taking the life of living beings. And so societies have "invented" cannibalism, induced abortion, organized wars, made human sacrifice, and practiced infanticide (especially female) as means of avoiding periodic famine and epidemics.

Though this settling of accounts with the contradictory impulses of hunger and sex is accompanied often enough by upheaval and distress, these societies in the stage of high growth potential tend to be stable at least in the sense that their social practices, including the "crimes" that keep population down, are institutionalized and patterned. Generation after generation, people are born, are weeded out, and die to make room for others. The net rate of natural increase fluctuates within a broad range, though without showing any long-range tendency, as is true also of societies in the stage of incipient decline. But unlike the latter, the average life expectancy in the former is characteristically low: the population is heavily weighted on the side of the young, and generation replaces generation far more rapidly and less "efficiently" than in the societies of incipient population decline.

In viewing such a society we inevitably associate the relative stability of the man-land ratio, whether high or low, with the tenacity of custom and social structure. However, we must not equate stability of social structure over historical time with psychic stability in the life span of an individual: the latter may subjectively experience much violence and disorganization. In the last analysis, however, he learns to deal with life by adaptation, not by innovation. With certain exceptions conformity is largely given in the "self-evident" social situation. Of course nothing in human life is ever really self-evident; where it so appears it is because perceptions have been narrowed by cultural conditioning. As the precarious relation to the food supply is built into the going culture, it helps create a pattern of conventional conformity which is reflected in many, if not in all, societies in the stage of high growth potential. This is what I call tradition-direction.

A definition of tradition-direction. Since the type of social order we have been discussing is relatively unchanging, the conformity of the individual tends to be dictated to a very large degree by power relations among the various age and sex groups, the clans, castes, professions, and so forth—relations which have endured for centuries and are modified but slightly, if at all, by successive generations. The culture controls behavior minutely, and, while the rules are not so complicated that the young cannot learn them during the period of intensive socialization, careful and rigid etiquette governs the fundamentally influential sphere of kin relationships. Moreover, the culture, in addition to its economic tasks, or as part of them, provides ritual, routine, and religion to occupy and to orient everyone. Little energy is directed toward finding new solutions of the age-old problems, let us say, of agricultural technique or "medicine," the problems to which people are acculturated.

It is not to be thought, however, that in these societies, where the activity of the individual member is determined by characterologically grounded obedience to traditions, the individual may not be highly prized and, in many instances, encouraged to develop his capabilities, his initiative, and even, within very narrow time limits, his aspirations. Indeed, the individual in some primitive societies is far more appreciated and respected than in some sectors of modern society. For the individual in a society dependent on tradition-direction has a well-defined functional relationship to other members of the group. If he is not killed off, he "belongs"—he is not "surplus," as the modern unemployed are surplus, nor is he expendable as the unskilled are expendable in modern society. But by very virtue of his "belonging," life goals that are *his* in terms of conscious choice appear to shape his destiny only to a very limited extent, just as only to a limited extent is there any concept of progress for the group.

In societies in which tradition-direction is the dominant mode of insuring conformity, relative stability is preserved in part by the infrequent but highly important process of fitting into institutionalized roles such deviants as there are. In such societies a person who might have become at a later historical stage an innovator or rebel, whose belonging, as such, is marginal and problematic, is drawn instead into roles like those of the shaman or sorcerer. That is, he is drawn into roles that make a socially acceptable contribution, while at the same time they provide the individual with a more or less approved niche. The medieval monastic orders may have served in a similar way to absorb many characterological mutations.

In some of these societies certain individuals are encouraged toward a degree of individuality from childhood, especially if they belong to families of high status. But, since the range of choice, even for high-status people, is minimal, the apparent social need for an individuated type of character is also minimal. It is probably accurate to say that character structure in these societies is very largely "adjusted," in the sense that for most people it appears to be in tune with social institutions. Even the few misfits "fit" to a degree; and only very rarely is one driven out of his social world.

This does not mean, of course, that the people are happy; the society to whose traditions they are adjusted may be a miserable one, ridden with anxiety, sadism, and disease. The point is rather that change, while never completely absent in human affairs, is slowed down as the movement of molecules is slowed down at low temperature; and the social character comes as close as it ever does to looking like the matrix of the social forms themselves.

In western history the Middle Ages can be considered a period in which the majority were tradition-directed. But the term tradition-directed refers to a common element, not only among the people of precapitalist Europe but also among such enormously different types of people as Hindus and Hopi Indians, Zulus and Chinese, North African Arabs and Balinese. There is comfort in relying on the many writers who have found a similar unity amid diversity, a unity they express in such terms as "folk society" (as against "civilization"), "status society" (as against "contract society"), "*Gemeinschaft*" (as against "*Gesellschaft*"), and so on. Different as the societies envisaged by these terms are, the folk, status, and *Gemeinschaft* societies resemble each other in their relative slowness of change, their dependence on family and kin organization, and—in comparison with later epochs—their tight web of values. And, as is now well recognized by students, the high birth rate of these societies in the stage of high growth potential is not merely the result of a lack of contraceptive knowledge or techniques. A whole way of life—an outlook on chance, on children, on the place of women, on sexuality, on the very meaning of existence—lies between the societies in which human fertility is allowed to take its course and toll and those which prefer to pay other kinds of toll to cut down on fertility by calculation, and, conceivably, as Freud and other observers have suggested, by a decline in sexual energy itself.

TRANSITIONAL GROWTH: INNER-DIRECTED TYPES

Except for the West, we know very little about the cumulation of small changes that can eventuate in a breakup of the tradition-directed type of society, leading it to realize its potential for high population growth. As for the West, however, much has been learned about the slow decay of feudalism and the subsequent rise of a type of society in which inner-direction is the dominant mode of insuring conformity.

Critical historians, pushing the Renaissance ever back into the Middle Ages, seem sometimes to deny that any decisive change occurred at all. On the whole, however, it seems that the greatest social and characterological shift of recent centuries did indeed come when men were driven out of the primary ties that bound them to the western medieval version of tradition-directed society. All later shifts, including the shift from inner-direction to other-direction, seem unimportant by comparison, although of course this latter shift is still under way and we cannot tell what it will look like when—if ever—it is complete.

A change in the relatively stable ratio of births to deaths, which characterizes the period of high growth potential, is both the cause and consequence of other profound social changes. In most of the cases known to us a decline takes place in mortality prior to a decline in fertility; hence there is some period in which the population expands rapidly. The drop in death rate occurs as the result of many interacting factors, among them sanitation, improved communications (which permit government to operate over a wider area and also permit easier transport of food to areas of shortage from areas of surplus), the decline, forced or otherwise, of infanticide, cannibalism, and other inbred kinds of violence. Because of improved methods of agriculture the land is able to support more people, and these in turn produce still more people.

Notestein's phrase, "transitional growth," is a mild way of putting it. The "transition" is likely to be violent, disrupting the stabilized paths of existence in societies in which tradition-direction has been the principal mode of insuring conformity. The imbalance of births and deaths puts pressure on the society's customary ways. A new slate of character structures is called for or finds its opportunity in coping with the rapid changes—and the need for still more changes—in the social organization.

A definition of inner-direction. In western history the society that emerged with the Renaissance and Reformation and that is only now vanishing serves to illustrate the type of society in which inner-direction is the principal mode of securing conformity. Such a society is characterized by increased personal mobility, by a rapid accumulation of capital (teamed with devastating technological shifts), and by an almost constant expansion: intensive expansion in the production of goods and people, and extensive expansion in exploration, colonization, and imperialism. The greater choices this society gives—and the greater initiatives it demands in order to cope with its novel problems—are handled by character types who can manage to live socially without strict and self-evident tradition-direction. These are the inner-directed types.

The concept of inner-direction is intended to cover a very wide range of types. Thus, while it is essential for the study of certain problems to differentiate between Protestant and Catholic countries and their character types, between the effects of the Reformation and the effects of the Renaissance, between the puritan ethic of the European north and west and the somewhat more hedonistic ethic of the European east and south, while all these are valid and, for certain purposes, important distinctions, the concentration of this study on the development of modes of conformity permits their neglect. It allows the grouping together of these otherwise distinct developments because they have one thing in common: *the source of direction for the individual is "inner" in the sense that it is implanted early in life by the elders and directed toward generalized but nonetheless inescapably destined goals.*

We can see what this means when we realize that, in societies in which tradition-direction is the dominant mode of insuring conformity, attention is focused on securing external *behavioral* conformity. While behavior is minutely prescribed, individuality of character need not be highly developed to meet prescriptions that are objectified in ritual and etiquette—though to be sure, a social character *capable* of such behavioral attention and obedience is requisite. By contrast, societies in which inner-direction becomes important, though they also are concerned with behavioral conformity, cannot be satisfied with behavioral conformity alone. Too many novel situations are presented, situations which a code cannot encompass in advance. Consequently the problem of personal choice, solved in the earlier period of high growth potential by channeling choice through rigid social organization, in the period of transitional growth is solved by channeling choice through a rigid though highly individualized character.

This rigidity is a complex matter. While any society dependent on inner-direction seems to present people with a wide choice of aims—such as money, possessions, power, knowledge, fame, goodness—these aims are ideologically interrelated, and the selection made by any one individual remains relatively unalterable throughout his life. Moreover, the means to those ends, though not fitted into as tight a social frame of reference as in the society dependent on tradition-direction, are nevertheless limited by the new voluntary associations—for instance, the Quakers, the Masons, the Mechanics' Associations—to which people tie themselves. Indeed, the term "tradition-direction" could be misleading if the reader were to conclude that the force of tradition has no weight for the inner-directed character. On the contrary, he is very considerably bound by traditions: they limit his ends and inhibit his choice of means. The point is rather that a splintering of tradition takes place, connected in part with the increasing division of labor and stratification of society. Even if the individual's choice of tradition is largely determined for him by his family, as it is in most cases, he cannot help becoming aware of the existence of competing traditions—hence of tradition as such. As a result he possesses a somewhat greater degree of flexibility in adapting himself to ever changing requirements and in return requires more from his environment.

As the control of the primary group is loosened—the group that both socializes the young and controls the adult in the earlier era—a new psychological mechanism appropriate to the more open society is "invented": it is what I like to describe as a psychological gyroscope.[4] This instru-

---

[4] Since writing the above I have discovered Gardner Murphy's use of the same metaphor in his volume *Personality* (New York, Harper, 1947).

ment, once it is set by the parents and other authorities, keeps the inner-directed person, as we shall see, "on course" even when tradition, as responded to by his character, no longer dictates his moves. The inner-directed person becomes capable of maintaining a delicate balance between the demands upon him of his life goal and the buffetings of his external environment.

This metaphor of the gyroscope, like any other, must not be taken literally. It would be a mistake to see the inner-directed man as incapable of learning from experience or as insensitive to public opinion in matters of external conformity. He can receive and utilize certain signals from outside, provided that they can be reconciled with the limited maneuverability that his gyroscope permits him. His pilot is not quite automatic.

Huizinga's *The Waning of the Middle Ages* gives a picture of the anguish and turmoil, the conflict of values, out of which the new forms slowly emerged. Already by the late Middle Ages people were forced to live under new conditions of awareness. As their self-consciousness and their individuality developed, they had to make themselves at home in the world in novel ways. They still have to.

INCIPIENT DECLINE OF POPULATION: OTHER-DIRECTED TYPES

The problem facing the societies in the stage of transitional growth is that of reaching a point at which resources become plentiful enough or are utilized effectively enough to permit a rapid accumulation of capital. This rapid accumulation has to be achieved even while the social product is being drawn on at an accelerated rate to maintain the rising population and satisfy the consumer demands that go with the way of life that has already been adopted. For most countries, unless capital and techniques can be imported from other countries in still later phases of the population curve, every effort to increase national resources at a rapid rate must actually be at the expense of current standards of living. We have seen this occur in the

U.S.S.R., now in the stage of transitional growth. For western Europe this transition was long-drawn-out and pain-
ful. For America, Canada, and Australia—at once beneficiaries of European techniques and native resources—the
transition was rapid and relatively easy.

The tradition-directed person, as has been said, hardly
thinks of himself as an individual. Still less does it occur to
him that he might shape his own destiny in terms of personal, lifelong goals or that the destiny of his children
might be separate from that of the family group. He is not
sufficiently separated psychologically from himself (or,
therefore, sufficiently close to himself), his family, or group
to think in these terms. In the phase of transitional growth,
however, people of inner-directed character do gain a feeling of control over their own lives and see their children
also as individuals with careers to make. At the same time,
with the shift out of agriculture and, later, with the end of
child labor, children no longer become an unequivocal economic asset. And with the growth of habits of scientific
thought, religious and magical views of human fertility—
views that in an earlier phase of the population curve made
sense for the culture if it was to reproduce itself—give way
to "rational," individualistic attitudes. Indeed, just as the
rapid accumulation of productive capital requires that
people be imbued with the "Protestant ethic" (as Max
Weber characterized one manifestation of what is here
termed inner-direction), so also the decreased number of
progeny requires a profound change in values—a change so
deep that, in all probability, it has to be rooted in character
structure.

As the birth rate begins to follow the death rate downward, societies move toward the epoch of incipient decline
of population. Fewer and fewer people work on the land
or in the extractive industries or even in manufacturing.
Hours are short. People may have material abundance and
leisure besides. They pay for these changes however—here,
as always, the solution of old problems gives rise to new
ones—by finding themselves in a centralized and bureaucratized society and a world shrunken and agitated by the

contact—accelerated by industrialization—of races, nations, and cultures.

The hard enduringness and enterprise of the inner-directed types are somewhat less necessary under these new conditions. Increasingly, *other people* are the problem, not the material environment. And as people mix more widely and become more sensitive to each other, the surviving traditions from the stage of high growth potential—much disrupted, in any case, during the violent spurt of industrialization—become still further attenuated. Gyroscopic control is no longer sufficiently flexible, and a new psychological mechanism is called for.

Furthermore, the "scarcity psychology" of many inner-directed people, which was socially adaptive during the period of heavy capital accumulation that accompanied transitional growth of population, needs to give way to an "abundance psychology" capable of "wasteful" luxury consumption of leisure and of the surplus product. Unless people want to destroy the surplus product in war, which still does require heavy capital equipment, they must learn to enjoy and engage in those services that are expensive in terms of man power but not of capital—poetry and philosophy, for instance.[5] Indeed, in the period of incipient decline, nonproductive consumers, both the increasing number of old people and the diminishing number of as yet untrained young, form a high proportion of the population, and these need both the economic opportunity to be prodigal and the character structure to allow it.

Has this need for still another slate of character types actually been acknowledged to any degree? My observations lead me to believe that in America it has.

A definition of other-direction. The type of character I shall describe as other-directed seems to be emerging in very recent years in the upper middle class of our larger cities: more prominently in New York than in Boston, in Los

---

[5]These examples are given by Allan G. B. Fisher, *The Clash of Progress and Security* (London, Macmillan, 1935).

Angeles than in Spokane, in Cincinnati than in Chillicothe. Yet in some respects this type is strikingly similar to the American, whom Tocqueville and other curious and astonished visitors from Europe, even before the Revolution, thought to be a new kind of man. Indeed, travelers' reports on America impress us with their unanimity. The American is said to be shallower, freer with his money, friendlier, more uncertain of himself and his values, more demanding of approval than the European. It all adds up to a pattern which, without stretching matters too far, resembles the kind of character that a number of social scientists have seen as developing in contemporary, highly industrialized, and bureaucratic America: Fromm's "marketer," Mills's "fixer," Arnold Green's "middle class male child."[6]

It is my impression that the middle-class American of today is decisively different from those Americans of Tocqueville's writings who nevertheless strike us as so contemporary, and much of this book will be devoted to discussing these differences. It is also my impression that the conditions I believe to be responsible for other-direction are affecting increasing numbers of people in the metropolitan centers of the advanced industrial countries. My analysis of the other-directed character is thus at once an analysis of the American and of contemporary man. Much of the time I find it hard or impossible to say where one ends and the other begins. Tentatively, I am inclined to think that the other-directed type does find itself most at home in America, due to certain unique elements in American society, such as its recruitment from Europe and its lack of any feudal past. As against this, I am also inclined to put more weight on capitalism, industrialism, and urbanization—these being international tendencies—than on any character-forming peculiarities of the American scene.

[6]See Erich Fromm, *Man for Himself*; C. Wright Mills, "The Competitive Personality," *Partisan Review*, XIII (1946), 433; Arnold Green, "The Middle Class Male Child and Neurosis," *American Sociological Review*, XI (1946), 31. See also the work of Jurgen Ruesch, Martin B. Loeb, and co-workers on the "infantile personality."

Bearing these qualifications in mind, it seems appropriate to treat contemporary metropolitan America as our illustration of a society—so far, perhaps, the only illustration—in which other-direction is the dominant mode of insuring conformity. It would be premature, however, to say that it is already the dominant mode in America as a whole. But since the other-directed types are to be found among the young, in the larger cities, and among the upper income groups, we may assume that, unless present trends are reversed, the hegemony of other-direction lies not far off.

If we wanted to cast our social character types into social class molds, we could say that inner-direction is the typical character of the "old" middle class—the banker, the tradesman, the small entrepreneur, the technically oriented engineer, etc.—while other-direction is becoming the typical character of the "new" middle class—the bureaucrat, the salaried employee in business, etc. Many of the economic factors associated with the recent growth of the "new" middle class are well known. They have been discussed by James Burnham, Colin Clark, Peter Drucker, and others. There is a decline in the numbers and in the proportion of the working population engaged in production and extraction—agriculture, heavy industry, heavy transport—and an increase in the numbers and the proportion engaged in white-collar work and the service trades. People who are literate, educated, and provided with the necessities of life by an ever more efficient machine industry and agriculture, turn increasingly to the "tertiary" economic realm. The service industries prosper among the people as a whole and no longer only in court circles.

Education, leisure, services, these go together with an increased consumption of words and images from the new mass media of communications. While societies in the phase of transitional growth begin the process of distributing words from urban centers, the flow becomes a torrent in the societies of incipient population decline. This process, while modulated by profound national and class differences, connected with differences in literacy and loquacity, takes place everywhere in the industrialized lands. Increasingly, relations with the outer world and with oneself are mediated by the flow of mass communication. For the other-directed types political events are likewise experienced through a screen of words by which the events are habitually atomized and personalized—or pseudo-personalized. For the inner-directed person who remains still extant in this period the tendency is rather to systematize and moralize this flow of words.

These developments lead, for large numbers of people, to changes in paths to success and to the requirement of more "socialized" behavior both for success and for marital and personal adaptation. Connected with such changes are changes in the family and in child-rearing practices. In the smaller families of urban life, and with the spread of "permissive" child care to ever wider strata of the population, there is a relaxation of older patterns of discipline. Under these newer patterns the peer-group (the group of one's associates of the same age and class) becomes much more important to the child, while the parents make him feel guilty not so much about violation of inner standards as about failure to be popular or otherwise to manage his relations with these other children. Moreover, the pressures of the school and the peer-group are reinforced and continued —in a manner whose inner paradoxes I shall discuss later— by the mass media: movies, radio, comics, and popular culture media generally. Under these conditions types of character emerge that we shall here term other-directed. To them much of the discussion in the ensuing chapters is devoted. *What is common to all the other-directed people is that their contemporaries are the source of direction for the individual—either those known to him or those with whom he is indirectly acquainted, through friends and through the mass media. This source is of course "internalized" in the sense that dependence on it for guidance in life is implanted early. The goals toward which the other-directed person strives shift with that guidance: it is only the process of striving itself and the process of paying close attention to the signals from others that remain unaltered throughout life. This mode of keeping in touch with others* permits a close behavioral conformity, not through drill in behavior itself, as in the tradition-directed character, but rather through an exceptional sensitivity to the actions and wishes of others.

Of course, it matters very much who these "others" are: whether they are the individual's immediate circle or a "higher" circle or the anonymous voices of the mass media; whether the individual fears the hostility of chance acquaintances or only of those who "count." But his need for approval and direction from others—and contemporary others rather than ancestors—goes beyond the reasons that lead most people in any era to care very much what others think of them. While all people want and need to be liked by some of the people some of the time, it is only the modern other-directed types who make this their chief source of direction and chief area of sensitivity.[7]

It is perhaps the insatiable force of this psychological need for approval that differentiates people of the metropolitan, American upper middle class, whom we regard as other-directed, from very similar types that have appeared in capital cities and among other classes in previous historical periods, whether in Imperial Canton, in eighteenth- and nineteenth-century Europe, or in ancient Athens, Alexandria, or Rome. In all these groups fashion not only ruled as a substitute for morals and customs, but it was a rapidly changing fashion that held sway. It could do so because, although the mass media were in their infancy, the group corresponding to the American upper middle class was comparably small and the elite structure was extremely reverberant. It can be argued, for example, that a copy of The Spectator covered its potential readership more thoroughly in the late eighteenth century than The New Yorker covers its readership today. In eighteenth- and nine-

---

[7] This picture of the other-directed person has been stimulated by, and developed from, Erich Fromm's discussion of the "marketing orientation" in Man for Himself, pp. 67–82. I have also drawn on my portrait of "The Cash Customer," Common Sense, XI (1942), 183.

teenth-century English, French, and Russian novels, we find portraits of the sort of people who operated in the upper reaches of bureaucracy and had to be prepared for rapid changes of signals. Stepan Arkadyevitch Oblonsky in *Anna Karenina* is one of the more likeable and less opportunistic examples, especially striking because of the way Tolstoy contrasts him with Levin, a moralizing, inner-directed person. At any dinner party Stepan manifests exceptional social skills; his political skills as described in the following quotation are also highly social:

Stepan Arkadyevitch took in and read a liberal newspaper, not an extreme one, but one advocating the views held by the majority. And in spite of the fact that science, art, and politics had no special interest for him, he firmly held those views on all subjects which were held by the majority and by his paper, and he only changed them when the majority changed them—or, more strictly speaking, he did not change them, but they imperceptively changed of themselves within him.

Stepan Arkadyevitch had not chosen his political opinions or his views; these political opinions and views had come to him of themselves, just as he did not choose the shapes of his hats or coats, but simply took those that were being worn. And for him, living in a certain society—owing to the need, ordinarily developed at years of discretion, for some degree of mental activity—to have views was just as indispensable as to have a hat. If there was a reason for his preferring liberal to conservative views, which were held also by many of his circle, it arose not from his considering liberalism more rational, but from its being in closer accord with his manner of life . . . And so liberalism had become a habit of Stepan Arkadyevitch's, and he liked his newspaper, as he did his cigar after dinner, for the slight fog it diffused in his brain.

Stepan, while his good-natured gregariousness makes him seem like a modern middle-class American, is not fully other-directed. This gregariousness alone, without a certain sensitivity to others as individuals and as a source of direction, is not the identifying trait. Just so, we must differentiate the nineteenth-century American—gregarious and subservient to public opinion though he was found to be by Tocqueville, Bryce, and others—from the other-directed American as he emerges today, an American who in his character is more capable of and more interested in maintaining responsive contact with others both at work and at play. This point needs to be emphasized, since the distinction is easily misunderstood. The inner-directed person, though he often sought and sometimes achieved a relative independence of public opinion and of what the neighbors thought of him, was in most cases very much concerned with his good repute and, at least in America, with "keeping up with the Joneses." These conformities, however, were primarily external, typified in such details as clothes, curtains, and bank credit. For, indeed, the conformities were to a standard, evidence of which was provided by the "best people" in one's milieu. In contrast with this pattern, the other-directed person, though he has his eye very much on the Joneses, aims to keep up with them not so much in external details as in the quality of his inner experience. That is, his great sensitivity keeps him in touch with others on many more levels than the externals of appearance and propriety. Nor does any ideal of independence or of reliance on God alone modify his desire to look to the others —and the "good guys" as well as the best people—for guidance in what experiences to seek and in how to interpret them.

The three types compared. One way to see the structural differences between the three types is to see the differences in the emotional sanction or control in each type.

The tradition-directed person feels the impact of his culture as a unit, but it is nevertheless mediated through the specific, small number of individuals with whom he is in daily contact. These expect of him not so much that he be a certain type of person but that he behave in the approved way. Consequently the sanction for behavior tends to be the fear of being *shamed.*

The inner-directed person has early incorporated a psychic gyroscope which is set going by his parents and can receive signals later on from other authorities who resemble his parents. He goes through life less independent than he seems, obeying this internal piloting. Getting off course, whether in response to inner impulses or to the fluctuating voices of contemporaries, may lead to the feeling of guilt.

Since the direction to be taken in life has been learned in the privacy of the home from a small number of guides and since principles, rather than details of behavior, are internalized, the inner-directed person is capable of great stability. Especially so when it turns out that his fellows have gyroscopes too, spinning at the same speed and set in the same direction. But many inner-directed individuals can remain stable even when the reinforcement of social approval is not available—as in the upright life of the stock Englishman isolated in the tropics.

Contrasted with such a type as this, the other-directed person learns to respond to signals from a far wider circle than is constituted by his parents. The family is no longer a closely knit unit to which he belongs but merely part of a wider social environment to which he early becomes attentive. In these respects the other-directed person resembles the tradition-directed person: both live in a group milieu and lack the inner-directed person's capacity to go it alone. The nature of this group milieu, however, differs radically in the two cases. The other-directed person is cosmopolitan. For him the border between the familiar and the strange—a border clearly marked in the societies depending on tradition-direction—has broken down. As the family continuously absorbs the strange and so reshapes itself, so the strange becomes familiar. While the inner-directed person could be "at home abroad" by virtue of his relative insensitivity to others, the other-directed person is, in a sense, at home everywhere and nowhere, capable of a rapid if sometimes superficial intimacy with and response to everyone.

The tradition-directed person takes his signals from others, but they come in a cultural monotone; he needs no complex receiving equipment to pick them up. The other-directed person must be able to receive signals from far and near; the sources are many, the changes rapid. What can be internalized, then, is not a code of behavior but the elaborate equipment needed to attend to such messages and occasionally to participate in their circulation. As against guilt-and-shame controls, though of course these survive, one prime psychological lever of the other-directed person is a diffuse anxiety. This control equipment, instead of being like a gyroscope, is like a radar.[8]

The Case of Athens. Could other civilizations, such as the ancient Hebrew, Greek, and Roman, also be characterized at successive stages in their population-subsistence development as tradition-directed, inner-directed, and other-directed? In all likelihood the tremendous growth of world population since about 1650—and consequently the S-curve of population growth—is unique in the history of mankind and the consequence of an altogether new (industrialized) type of technological, economic, and social organization. Nonetheless, the fact that every society has some form of organization and some "technology," be it the most unscientific ritual, constitutes proof of an effort, more or less successful, to bring down the death rate and improve the standard of living over that of mere animal existence. And an exploratory study of the Athenian empire suggests that there, too, a correlation between population growth and social character of the type we have described for the recent West may be discerned.[9]

What scant evidence we have of the long-term trend of population growth in the empire must be derived from the patient studies of present-day demographers and from the remarks of ancient Greek authors. The Homeric epics depict a volatile society in which the institution of private property had already disrupted the tradition-directed com-

---

[8]The "radar" metaphor was suggested by Karl Wittfogel.

[9]The following discussion draws on an unpublished monograph by Sheila Spaulding, "Prolegomena to the Study of Athenian Democracy" (Yale Law School Library, 1949).

munal organization of tribe, phratry, and clan. Revolutionary improvements in cultivation of the soil, made possible by continued settlement in one place, increased the standard of living and, as a corollary, initiated a phase of population growth that was to continue for several centuries. Private ownership, the development of an exchange economy, and the patrilineal inheritance of property encouraged the concentration of wealth and produced economic and social inequality. A new, three-fold social stratification interpenetrated the traditional organization and not only loosened the hold of the clan upon its members but also encouraged the coalescence of individuals with like economic status from different tribes and phratries. The reform measures taken by Solon and others in succeeding generations also clearly imply that some individuals and families were far more successful than others in achieving the new economic goals of leisure and material wealth.

During the five hundred years after the founding of the Athenian state there seems to have existed an expanding "frontier" economy, based in part upon the exploitation of internal resources, made possible by technological improvement and the institution of slavery, and in greater part upon the conquest of other peoples and the incorporation of their wealth into the domestic economy. One might well adduce as indications of inner-direction during this period the changing attitudes toward the family and the upbringing of children; the laws which enhanced the freedom of the individual, for example, the significant reforms which permitted the free alienation of property and the initiation of a criminal prosecution by a "third party"; the multiplication of opportunities for profitable employment in commerce, agriculture, and industry; the drift from country to city; the enthusiasm for exploration and conquest; and the increasing interest in philosophic speculation and science.

By the turn of the fifth century the Athenian empire had reached the zenith of its power; and the Greeks of this period were familiar with the idea of an expanding population. Both Plato and Aristotle advocated a stationary population. Two centuries later we find that the problem has radically shifted and the fear of overpopulation has been replaced by the fear of depopulation. Polybius, writing in the second century, declared that the population of Greece was dying out because of the practice of infanticide. This is undoubtedly an overstatement; infanticide was confined, as contraception tends to be today, largely to the upper and upper middle classes. Nevertheless, it indicates the trend toward artificial limitation of the size of the family and suggests that the population had reached the period not only of incipient but of actual decline. It is as an expanding population begins to reach its peak that we see the rise of social forms that seem to indicate the presence of the other-directed mode of conformity.

For example, the institution of ostracism, introduced as a means of preventing tyranny, became in the fifth century a formidable weapon of public opinion, wielded capriciously as a means of insuring conformity of taste and "cutting down to size" those statesmen, playwrights, and orators of markedly superior ability. In addition, the common people produced a numerous brood of informers "who were constantly accusing the better and most influential men in the State, with a view to subjecting them to the envy of the multitude." In *The Jealousy of the Gods and Criminal Law in Athens* Svend Ranulf has meticulously traced the incidence and development of the "disinterested tendency to inflict punishment" which, based upon a diffuse characterological anxiety, could perhaps be described as the ascendancy of an omnipotent "peer-group."

All this was accompanied by a decline in inner-directed dutifulness toward the political sphere. In spite of the deference shown by many authors to Athenian "democracy" of the fifth century, one is struck by the apathy of the voting population. What had earlier been a hard-won privilege of the lower classes—attendance at the ecclesia or popular assembly—became during the rule of the demos an obligation. Various punitive measures were introduced to insure a quorum; and when these failed, the "right to vote" became a paid service to the state.

Here in the history of the Athenian empire we have an area in which more detailed research and analysis might very profitably be undertaken; obviously, no more has been done in these remarks than to suggest certain problems that would be relevant for such research. Similarly, the problems of Rome during the reign of Augustus suggest the emergence and ascendancy of the other-directed character type as the population reached the phase of incipient decline. The importation of a new poetic language legitimating the importance of subtle states of personal feeling, in the Alexandrian-influenced work of such poets as Catullus, and probably Gallus, may evidence shifts toward other-direction in the dominant classes.

Some necessary qualifications. The limitations of language lead me to speak as if I saw societies as always managing to produce the social organization and character types they need in order to survive. Such an assumption, raising the image of a separate body, "society," making certain demands on people and testing out various processes, would introduce an unwarranted teleology into social change. What seems to happen is that by sheer "accident" any of a number of ways of insuring characterological conformity may exist in a given society. Those which have been successful in preserving a coherent society are transmitted as unconsciously as they arose; but, since by their historical success they present themselves for study and investigation, it appears as if some teleological force, serving the interest of society, has introduced the successful—or fairly successful—mode of insuring conformity. Yet we must recognize that societies do disintegrate and die out despite what may appear to be successful methods of insuring character perpetuation. Correspondingly, we must not deny the probability that societies can tolerate, even without disintegration, much more disorganization and even ruin than many people recognize.

We must not overestimate the role of character in the social process. It is not a sufficient explanation, for instance, to say, as some students have said, that the German army held together because "the Germans" had an authoritarian character, since armies of very diverse character type do in fact hold together under given conditions of battle and supply. Nor will it do to assume, as American aptitude-testers sometimes do, that certain jobs can be successfully handled only by a narrowly limited range of character types: that we need "extrovert" or "oral" salesmen and administrators, and "introvert" or "anal" chemists and accountants. Actually, people of radically different types can adapt themselves to perform, adequately enough, a wide variety of complex tasks. Or, to put the same thing in another way, social institutions can harness a gamut of different motivations, springing from different character types, to perform very much the same kinds of socially demanded jobs. And yet, of course, this is not to say that character is merely a shadowy factor in history, like some Hegelian spirit. Character will affect the style and psychic costs of job performances that, in economic or political analysis, look almost identical.

Thus we are forced to take account of the possibility that people may be compelled to behave in one way although their character structure presses them to behave in the opposite way. Society may change more rapidly than character, or vice versa. Indeed, this disparity between socially required behavior and characterologically compatible behavior is one of the great levers of change. Fortunately we know of no society like the one glumly envisaged by Aldous Huxley in Brave New World, where the social character types have been completely content in their social roles and where consequently, barring accident, no social change exists.

Finally, it is necessary to point out that social character types are abstractions. They refer back to the living, concrete human being, and in order to arrive at them, as we saw at the beginning of this chapter, it is necessary first to abstract from the real individual his "personality," then to abstract from that his "character," finally to abstract from that the common element that forms "social character."

In fact, the discerning reader may already have realized that in the nature of the case there can be no such thing as a society or a person wholly dependent on tradition-direction, inner-direction, or other-direction: each of these modes of conformity is universal, and the question is always one of the degree to which an individual or a social group places reliance on one or another of the three available mechanisms. Thus, all human beings are inner-directed in the sense that, brought up as they are by people older than themselves, they have acquired and internalized some permanent orientations from them. And, conversely, all human beings are other-directed in the sense that they are oriented to the expectations of their peers and to the "field situation" (Kurt Lewin) or "definition of the situation" (W. I. Thomas) that these peers at any moment help to create.[10]

Since, furthermore, each of us possesses the capacity for each of the three modes of conformity, it is possible that an individual may change, in the course of his life, from greater dependence on one combination of modes to greater dependence on another (though radical shifts of this kind, even when circumstances encourage them, are unlikely). For, unless individuals are completely crazy—and, indeed, they are never *completely* crazy—they both organize the cues in their social environment and attend to those cues.

----

[10] In this connection, it is revealing to compare the conceptions of the socialization process held by Freud and Harry Stack Sullivan. Freud saw the superego as the internalized source of moral life-directions, built in the image of the awesome parents, and transferred thereafter to parent-surrogates such as God, the Leader, Fate. Sullivan does not deny this happens but puts more emphasis on the role of the peer-group—the chum and group of chums who take such a decisive hand in the socialization of the American child. Sullivan's very insistence on the importance of interpersonal relations—which led him to believe, much more than Freud, in the adaptability of men and the possibilities of social peace and harmony—may itself be viewed as a symptom of the shift toward other-direction.

Thus, if a predominantly other-directed individual were placed in an environment without peers, he might fall back on other patterns of direction. Similarly, it is clear that no individual, and assuredly no society, ever exists without a heavy reliance on tradition, much as this may appear to be overlaid by swings of fashion.

It is important to emphasize these overlappings of the several types in part because of the value judgments that readers are likely to attach to each type in isolation. Since most of us value independence we are likely to prefer the inner-directed type and overlook two things. First, the gyroscopic mechanism allows the inner-directed person to appear far more independent than he really is: he is no less a conformist to others than the other-directed person, but the voices to which he listens are more distant, of an older generation, their cues internalized in his childhood. Second, as just indicated, this type of conformity is only one, though the predominant, mechanism of the inner-directed type: the latter is not characteristically insensitive to what his peers think of him, and may even be opportunistic in the highest degree. Thus, he need not always react to other people as if they were merely stand-ins for his parents. Rather, the point is that he is somewhat less concerned than the other-directed person with continuously obtaining from contemporaries (or their stand-ins: the mass media) a flow of guidance, expectation, and approbation.

Let me repeat: the types of character and society dealt with in this book are types: they do not exist in reality, but are a construction, based on a selection of certain historical problems for investigation. By employing more types, or subtypes, one could take account of more facts (or mayhap, the same facts with less violence!), but my collaborators and I have preferred to work with a minimum of scaffolding; throughout, in seeking to describe by one interrelated set of characteristics both a society and its typical individuals, we have looked for features that connect the two and ignored those aspects of behavior—often striking—which did not seem relevant to our task.

II. The Characterological Struggle

We can picture the last few hundred years of western history in terms of a gradual succession to dominance of each of the later two types. The tradition-directed type gives way to the inner-directed, and the inner-directed gives way to the other-directed. Shifts in type of society and type of character do not, of course, occur all at once. Just as within a given culture one may find groups representing all phases of the population curve, so, too, we may find a variety of characterological adaptations to each particular phase. This mixture is made even more various by the migration of peoples, by imperialism, and by other historical developments that constantly throw together people of different character structures, people who "date," metaphorically, from different points on the population curve.

These character types, like geological or archaeological strata, pile one on top of the other, with outcroppings of submerged types here and there. A cross section of society at any given time reveals the earlier as well as the later character types, the earlier changed through the pressure of being submerged by the later. Tradition-direction seems to be dominant in Latin America, agricultural southern Europe, in Asia and Africa. Inner-directed types seem to be dominant in rural and small-town United States and Canada, in northwestern Europe, and to a degree in Central Europe. One notices an energetic campaign to introduce the inner-directed pattern in eastern Europe, in Turkey, and in parts of Asia. And one notices the beginnings of dominance by other-directed types in the metropolitan centers of the United States and, more doubtfully, their emergence in the big cities of northwestern Europe. This last and newest type is spreading outward into areas where inner-direction still prevails, just as the latter is spreading into unconquered areas where tradition-directed types still hang on.

Such a view may help us to understand American character structures. In America it is still possible to find southern rural groups, Negro and poor white, in the phase of high growth potential—and it is here that we look for the remnants of tradition-directed types. Similarly, immigrants to America who came from rural and small-town areas in Europe carried their fertility rates and character patterns with them to our major cities as well as to the countryside. In some cases these people were and are forced to make, in one lifetime, the jump from a society in which tradition-direction was the dominant mode of insuring conformity to one in which other-direction is the dominant mode. More frequently the jump is made in two generations: the peasant is converted to inner-directed ways; his children then make the jump to other-direction.

The mixing of people of different character types, as of different races and religions, as a result of industrialization and colonization, is to be found everywhere in the world. Character types that would have been well adapted to their situation find themselves under pressure from newer, better-adapted types. They may resign themselves to a subordinate position. Or they may be tempted by the new goals which enter their view and may even seek these goals without reference to the culturally prescribed means of attaining them.

Inner-directed types, for instance, in the urban American environment may be forced into resentment or rebellion. They may be unable to adapt because they lack the proper receiving equipment for the radar signals that increasingly direct attitude and behavior in the phase of incipient population decline. They may refuse to adapt because of moral disapproval of what the signals convey. Or they may be discouraged by the fact that the signals, though inviting enough, do not seem meant for them. This is true, for instance, of minority groups whose facial type or coloring is not approved of for managerial or professional positions, or in the value hierarchy portrayed in the mass media of communication. The same thing holds for those whose ancestry is adequate but whose "personality" in subtle ways lacks the pliability and sensitivity to others that is required.

Studies of American Indians provide analogies for some of the things that may happen when an older character type is under pressure from a newer one. Among Sioux reservation children, as described by Erik H. Erikson, there seem to be two reactions to white culture: one is resentful resistance, the other is what might be termed "compliant resistance." The behavior of the former seems, to the white educator, incorrigible; of the latter, almost too ingratiating, too angelic. In both cases, because he has at least the tacit approval of his parents and other Sioux adults, the child preserves something of the Sioux character and tradition whether or not he yields overtly to the whites. The conflict, however, drains the child of emotional energy; often he appears to be lazy. Both the resistant and the seemingly compliant are apathetic toward the white culture and white politics.

I think that there are millions of inner-directed Americans who reject in similar fashion the values that emanate from the growing dominance of other-directed types. Their resentment may be conscious and vocal. As with the Sioux, this resentment is culturally supported both by the old-timers and by the long historical past which is present to all in rural and small-town areas. This past is carried in the tales of the old men and the editorials of the rural press, not yet blotted out by urban sights and sounds. Hence, the resentment can express itself and win local victories over the representatives of other-directed types. Nevertheless, the "moralizers," as we will later term them, do not feel secure—the weight of the urban world outside is against them—and their resentment hardens until these residual inner-directed persons are scarcely more than caricatures of their characterological ancestors in the days of their dominance.

A second locus of resistance and resentment is to be found among the vanishing tradition-directed migrants to America—migrants both from America's colonies: Puerto Rico, the deep South, and previously the Philippines, and from Mexico, Italy, and the Orient. Here it is more difficult to find cultural support for one's resistance to the enforced change of signals called "Americanization." The southern poor white or the poor Negro who moves North does not have to learn a new language, but he is usually about as deracinated as are the migrants from abroad. The costume and manners of the zoot-suiter were a pathetic example of the effort to combine smooth urban ways with a resentful refusal to be completely overwhelmed by the inner-directed norms that are still the official culture of the city public schools.

A similar style of resentment is to be found among miners, lumberjacks, ranch hands, and some urban factory workers. As in many other societies, the active dislike of these workers for the dominant culture is coupled with a feeling of manly contempt for smooth or soft city ways. These men have their own cocky legends as the Sioux have stories of the cowboy as well as of their own belligerent past. We must ask to what extent all these groups may be dying out, like their Sioux counterparts, as other-direction spreads down the class ladder and beyond the metropolitan areas. In the absence of a home base, a reservation, these people have their choice, if indeed there be a choice, between homelessness and rapid acculturation to other-directed values.

The "characterological struggle" does not go on only within a single country and among the groups within that country who stand at different points on the curve of character and population. Whole countries in the phase of incipient decline also feel threatened by the pressure of population and expansion from other countries that are in the phase of transitional growth, and even more by the huge oriental countries still in the phase of high growth potential. These international tensions, acting in a vicious circle, help to preserve, in countries of incipient decline, the inner-directed character types and their scarcity psychology, appropriate in the earlier era of transitional growth. Thus the slate of character types befitting a society of abundance—a society of which men have dreamed for centuries—is held in historical abeyance, and the gap between character structure and the potentialities of the economic structure remains.

It is possible to take various attitudes toward this gap. One would be that, because another world war—this time between the two highly polarized world powers—is possible or even probable, it makes little sense to talk about the age of abundance, its character types, and its anticipated problems. Or, the same conclusion might be reached by a different route, arguing that in effect it is immoral, if not politically impractical, to discuss abundance *in America* when famine and misery remain the lot of most of the world's agriculturists and many of its city dwellers. These are real issues. But I would like to point out as to the first— the imminence and immanence of war—that to a slight degree nations, like neurotics, bring on themselves the dangers by which they are obsessed, the dangers that, in place of true vitality and growth, help structure their lives; though obviously the decision, war or not, does not rest with the United States alone. As to the second issue, it seems to me that to use world misery as an argument against speculation about possible abundance is actually to help prolong the very scarcity psychology that, originating in misery, perpetuates it. Pushed to its absurd extreme, the argument would prevent leadership in human affairs except by those who are worst off. On the other hand, those who are best off may fail as models not only out of surfeit but out of despair. Contrary to the situation prevailing in the nineteenth century, pessimism has become an opiate, and the small chance that the dangers so obviously menacing the world can be avoided is rendered even smaller by our use of these menaces in order to rationalize our resignation and asceticism.

Fundamentally, I think the "unrealistic" Godwin was correct who, in contrast to his great opponent Malthus, thought that we would someday be able to grow food for the world in a flowerpot. Technologically, we virtually have the flowerpots.

II

FROM MORALITY TO MORALE:
CHANGES IN THE AGENTS OF
CHARACTER FORMATION

*Q. Do you think the teachers should punish the children
for using make-up?*

*A. Yes, I think they should punish them, but under-
stand, I'm a modern mother and while I'm strict with my
daughters, I am still modern. You know you can't punish
your children too much or they begin to think you are
mean and other children tell them you are mean.*

From an interview

POPULATION curves and economic structures are only
a part of the ecology of character formation. Interposed
between them and the resultant social character are the
human agents of character formation: the parents, the
teachers, the members of the peer-group, and the storytellers. These are the transmitters of the social heritage,
and they wield great influence over the lives of children
and hence on the whole society. For children live at the
wave front of the successive population phases and are the
partially plastic receivers of the social character of the
future. In this chapter we consider the changing role of
parents and teachers in socializing the young in each of
the three population phases. Chapter III considers the
socializing function of the peer-group. Chapter IV treats
of the changes in the role of the storytellers, or, as they
are now called, the mass media of communication.

We shall concentrate here on the shift from inner-
direction to other-direction as the principal mode of insuring conformity in the urban American middle class. Per-

spective, however, requires a glance at societies in which tradition-direction is the principal mode of insuring conformity; and since the tradition-directed types have played a very minor role in America, we will take examples from primitive and medieval society. As we compare methods of socialization we shall see what is new about the newer types—and particularly what is new about other-direction.

I. Changes in the Role of the Parents

There has been a tendency in current social research, influenced as it is by psychoanalysis, to overemphasize and overgeneralize the importance of very early childhood in character formation. Even within this early period an almost technological attention has sometimes been focused on what might be called the tricks of the child-rearing trade: feeding and toilet-training schedules. The view implicit in this emphasis happens to be both a counsel of optimism and of despair. It is an optimistic view because it seems to say that facile mechanical changes in what the parent does will profoundly alter the character of the progeny. It is pessimistic because it assumes that once the child has reached, say, the weaning stage its character structure is so formed that, barring intensive psychiatric intervention, not much that happens afterward will do more than bring out tendencies already set.

Increasingly it is recognized, however, that character may change greatly after this early period and that cultural agents other than the parents may play important roles. Cultures differ widely not only in their timing of the various steps in character formation but also in the agents they rely on at each step. Each new historical phase on the curve of population is marked by an increase in the length of life and in the period of socialization—that is, the period before full entry into one's adult social and economic role. At the same time there is an increase in the responsibility placed on character-forming agents outside the home, the clan, or the village.

PARENTAL ROLE IN THE STAGE OF TRADITION-DIRECTION

In societies depending on tradition-direction children can be "finished off" at an early point to assume an adult role. Adult roles are almost unchanging from generation to generation, and apart from training toward technical and manual skill, which may often be intensive, grown-up life demands little in the way of complex and literate instruction. Children begin very early to learn how to act like adults simply by watching adults around them. In the population phase of high growth potential there are many children to imitate a comparatively small number of adult models. The children live, ordinarily, in a large family setting. What the adults do is simple enough for children to grasp, so simple that children can often understand and imitate it before they have the physical skills to take a full part. Social maturity waits on biological maturity. Yet the biological roles of adult life are, in many cases, not themselves remote, for since there is little inhibition of childhood play and curiosity, children know what there is to know about sex and other adult functions —even though certain ceremonial mysteries may remain to testify to adult power and child helplessness.

Physical living patterns are an important factor in this setting. Houses consist typically of one room, without walls to separate the age groups and their varied functions. The households are often also economic units; the man does not go off to office or factory—and he does not go far. People are not yet so worried about saving time that they feel children are a nuisance; indeed, they may not feel themselves to be so very different from children anyway.

Furthermore, societies in the phase of high growth potential are characterized by a very low degree of social mobility. The parents train the child to succeed *them*, rather than to "succeed" by rising in the social system. Within any given social class society is age ranked, so that a person rises as a cork does in water: it is simply a matter of time, and little *in him* needs to change.

The upper social groups in such a society mature almost as quickly as the lower ones; the roles to be learned by children in both ranks of society differ only slightly in complexity. Even so, it is likely that a greater degree of individualization occurs at an earlier historical point in the upper strata than in the lower—as seems to have been the case in the Middle Ages when nobles, wandering artists, and priests were often closer to inner-direction than to the peasant's type of tradition-direction. Yet while the training of the leaders is of course somewhat more prolonged and their characters are more individuated, the young at all social levels take their places quickly in work, ceremony, and sexual role.

In summary: the major agency of character formation in societies dependent on tradition-direction is the extended family and its environing clan or group. Models for imitation are apt to be generalized in terms of the adult group as a whole rather than confined to the parents. What is imitated is behavior and specific traits such as bravery or cunning. The growing child does not confront problems of choice very different from those he watched his elders face; and his growth is conceived as a process of becoming an older, and therefore wiser, interpreter of tradition.

PARENTAL ROLE IN THE STAGE OF INNER-DIRECTION

Character and social mobility. With the onset of the transitional-growth phase of the population curve, opportunities open for a good deal of social and geographical mobility. People begin to pioneer on new frontiers: frontiers of production, of colonization, of intellectual discovery. Although this affects only a few directly, society as mediated by the primary group no longer proclaims unequivocally what one must do in order to conform. Rather, the growing child soon becomes aware of competing sets of customs—competing paths of life—from among which he is, in principle, free to choose. And while parentage and social origins are still all but determinative for most people, the wider horizon of possibilities and of wants requires a character which can adhere to rather generalized and more abstractly defined goals. Such a character must produce under its own motive power the appropriate specific means to gain these general ends.

To be sure, the goals and ideals that are held up to children and exemplified for them by their parents' own goals and ideals differ between, on the one hand, the confident, secular man of the Renaissance, glorying in his individuality and freedom from old restraints, and, on the other hand, the God-fearing puritan, driven by conscience and anxious about his salvation.[1] Yet both types are very much individuals, both are internally driven, and both are capable of pioneering. Finally, a society in which many people are internally driven—and are driven toward values, such as wealth and power, which are by their nature limited—contains in itself a dynamic of change by the very competitive forces it sets up. Even those who do not care to compete for higher places must do so in order not to descend in the social system, which has become a more open and less age-graded and birth-graded one.

All these tendencies are reinforced when roles become more complicated as the division of labor progresses. The acceleration of the division of labor means that increasing numbers of children can no longer take their parents' roles as models. This is especially true on the male side; characterological change in the west seems to occur first with men. Mothers and grandmothers could until very recent times train daughters for the feminine role on the basis of tradition alone. Thus in the recent movie, *House of*

---

[1] Margaret Mead, whose contribution to this whole field has been tremendously stimulating, has pointed out how the Protestant parent passed on to the child the legacy of his own unfulfilled strivings to live up to an ideal and how this drive spurred progress and change even though the statement of the ideal as such did not change. See, e.g., "Social Change and Cultural Surrogates," *Journal of Educational Sociology*, 14 (1940), 92; reprinted in *Personality in Nature, Society, and Culture*, ed. Kluckhohn and Murray, p. 511, and especially pp. 520–521.

Strangers, the Italian-born banker who, like Giannini or Ponzi, rises out of an immigrant setting and departs from his own father's pattern, sets for himself ambitious goals of power and money such as he believes to be characteristic of a true-born American, while his wife is a stereotype of the woman who clings to the tradition-directed ways of her early background.

Yet, while parents in the stage of transitional growth of population cannot be sure of what the adult working role and mode of life of their children will be, neither can conformity to that role be left to chance and behavioral opportunism. To possess the drive that is required to fulfill demanding and ever more demanding roles calls for greater attention to formal character training. Especially in the Protestant countries character training becomes an important part of education, though of course this does not mean that most parents consciously undertake to produce children to meet new social specifications.

The new situation created by increased social mobility implies that children must frequently be socialized in such a way as to be unfitted for their parents' roles, while being fitted for roles not as yet fully determined. Homing pigeons can be taught to fly home, but the inner-directed child must be taught to fly a straight course away from home, with destination unknown; naturally many meet the fate of Icarus. Nevertheless, the drive instilled in the child is to *live up to ideals* and to test his ability to be on his own by continuous experiments in self-mastery—instead of by following tradition.

Character training as a conscious parental task. In a society depending on tradition-direction to insure conformity, much of the parent's effort is directed toward keeping the child from being a nuisance to the adult world; and this task is regularly delegated to older brothers or sisters or to other adults. The child soon learns that behavioral conformity is the price of peace, and he learns to propitiate—or at least not to annoy—those around him. The inner-directed parent, on the other hand, asks more of his child, just as he asks more of himself. He can do this because, with the passing of the extended kinship family, the parent has his children much more under his own undivided and intensive scrutiny and control. Not satisfied with mere behavioral conformity, such a parent demands conformity of a more subtle sort, conformity as evidence of characterological fitness and self-discipline. The Puritan, especially, relentlessly scrutinizes his children as well as himself for the signs of election, that is, of salvation by the predestining God. And with secularization these signs are translated into signs predicting social mobility—signs that indicate a future facility in "passing," not from hell to heaven, but in the status hierarchy. On the one hand the parent looks for signs of potential failure—this search arises in part from guilty and anxious preoccupation about himself. On the other hand he looks for signs of talent—this must not be wasted.

In this way begins the process we see in extravagant form in the forced-draft childhood of John Stuart Mill, who studied the classics and wrote long essays under the zealous eye of his father before he was ten. Even when parents are less self-consciously pedagogical than James Mill, they may unconsciously impose their demands on children merely by being forceful, tense, and highly charged themselves. Indeed, the inner-directed man is frequently quite incapable of casual relationships. For one thing, he is preoccupied with his own concerns and therefore worried about wasting time; conversely, by not wasting time he avoids anxious self-preoccupation. For another thing, his relation to people, his children included, is mediated by his continuing, character-conditioned need to test and discipline himself.

This process, in the Renaissance-Reformation character which we term inner-directed, is less tense in the Latin countries than in the Protestant or Jansenist north, and in the north less tense in Lutheran or Anglican communicants than in the Calvinistic and Pietistic sects. Wherever inner-direction has attained relatively undisputed sway in a significantly large middle class, however, the production of the character structures of the coming generation becomes increasingly rationalized, just as is production in the non-household economy. In both cases the responsibility for production is no longer left to an external group sanction or situational pressure but is installed as a drive in the individual, and tremendous energies are unleashed toward the alteration of the material, social, and intellectual environment and toward the alteration of the self.

The social and spatial arrangements of middle-class life make it hard for the child to see through, let alone evade, the pressures put upon him to become inner-directed. As compared with the one-room house of the peasant or the "long house" of many primitive tribes, he grows up within walls that are physical symbols of the privacy of parental dominance. Walls separate parents from children, office from home, and make it hard if not impossible for the children to criticize the parents' injunctions by an "undress" view of the parents or of other parents. What the parents say becomes more real in many cases than what they do—significant training for a society in which words become increasingly important as a means of exchange, direction, and control. The conversation between parents and children, interrupted by the social distance that separates them, is continued by the child with himself in private.

The very pressure applied to the process of socialization by strict child rearing prolongs, as compared with the earlier era, the period in which socialization takes place. Freud has described this situation wonderfully in his concept of the watchful superego as a socializing agency incorporated into the child and accompanying him throughout life with ever renewed injunctions. This concept, while less fruitful in application to other societies, does seem to fit the middle class during the heyday of inner-direction in the west. One might even say that the character structure of the inner-directed person consists of the tension between superego, ego, and id. In a current cliché children are "brought up" rather than, as some would have it, "loved up"; and even when they have left home they continue to bring themselves up. They tend to feel throughout life that their characters are something to be worked on. The diary-keeping that is so significant a symptom of the new type of character may be viewed as a kind of inner time-and-motion study by which the individual records and judges his output day by day. It is evidence of the separation between the behaving and the scrutinizing self.

Passage from home. As the growing child takes over from his parents the duty of self-observation and character training, he becomes prepared to face and meet situations that are novel. Indeed, if he rises in the occupational hierarchy that becomes increasingly elaborated in the phase of transitional growth or if he moves toward the various opening frontiers, he finds that he can flexibly adapt his behavior precisely because he need not change his character. He can separate the two by virtue of the fact that he is an *individual* with a historically new level of self-awareness.

This awareness of the self is cause and consequence of the fact that choice is no longer automatically provided—or, rather, excluded—by the social setting of the primary group. Under the new conditions the individual must decide what to do—and therefore what to do with himself. This feeling of personal responsibility, this feeling that he matters as an individual, apart from his family or clan, makes him sensitive to the signals emanating from his internalized ideal. If the ideal, as in the puritan, is to be "good" or, as in the child of the Renaissance, to be "great," what must he do to fulfill the injunction? And how does he know that he has fulfilled these difficult self-demands? As Max Weber and R. H. Tawney saw very clearly in their portraits of the puritan, little rest is available to those who ask themselves such questions.

The relative uncomfortableness of the more powerfully inner-directed homes—the lack of indulgence and casualness in dealing with children—prepares the child for the loneliness and psychic uncomfortableness of such questions and of the social situations that he may confront.

Or, more exactly, the child's character is such that he feels comfortable in an environment which, like his home, is demanding and which he struggles to master.

We may say, then, that parents who are themselves inner-directed install a psychological gyroscope in their child and set it going; it is built to their own and other authoritative specifications; if the child has good luck, the governor will spin neither too fast, with the danger of hysteric outcomes, nor too slow, with the danger of social failure.

PARENTAL ROLE IN THE STAGE OF OTHER-DIRECTION

Character and social mobility. In the phase of incipient population decline, the conditions for advancement alter significantly.

The inner-directed person is able to see industrial and commercial possibilities and to work with the zeal and ruthlessness required by expanding frontiers in the phase of transitional growth of population. Societies in the phase of incipient population decline, on the other hand, need neither such zeal nor such independence. Business, government, the professions, become heavily bureaucratized, as we see most strikingly, for instance, in France. Such societies increasingly turn to the remaining refractory components of the industrial process: the men who run the machines. Social mobility under these conditions continues to exist. But it depends less on what one is and what one does than on what others think of one—and how competent one is in manipulating others and being oneself manipulated. To look at it from another point of view, when the basic physical plant of a society is felt to be built, or rather when the building can be routinized by management planning, there begins to be room at the top for the other-directed person who can see the subtle opportunities given in the human setting.[2] Though material

---

[2] Of course there is no law that societies in the stage of incipient population decline have to become top-heavy and

abundance becomes technologically possible, people continue to work—and do make-work—at a pace more in keeping with the earlier era of transitional growth: mobility drives are still imbedded in their character. *But the product now in demand is neither a staple nor a machine; it is a personality.*

To bring the other-directed personality type and his typical economic framework together it might be observed that there exists in the production of personality the same sort of "product differentiation" that is characteristic of monopolistic competition generally. The economists apply the term "product differentiation" to a firm's effort to distinguish products not by price but by small differences, sufficient, however, in connection with advertising, to take the product out of direct price competition with otherwise similar competing products. Thus one cigarette is made slightly longer, another nearly oval, while still another is given a cork tip or a green box. *Time* and *Newsweek* engage in product differentiation. So do the makers of automobiles, streamliners, and toothpastes, and the operators of hotels and universities. So, too, people who are competing for jobs in the hierarchies of business, government, and professional life try to differentiate their personalities (as contrasted with their actual technical skills)—without getting as far out of line, let us say, as a 1934 prematurely streamlined Chrysler. In this study, the social aspect of this competitive procedure, since it will be extended to cover persons and services as well as commodities, will be termed "marginal differentiation," and thus distinguished from the related concept used by the economists.

Freud coined the phrase "narcissism with respect to minor differences" for the pride which individuals, groups,

---

bureaucratic. It is conceivable that even more mobility could be opened up by shifting population and other resources rapidly into tertiary services, by greatly expanding leisure and the industries catering to leisure. We shall return to these matters in Part III.

and nations manifest about small insignia which distinguish them from other individuals, groups, and nations. Marginal differentiation sometimes does have this quality of pride or of what Veblen called "invidious distinction." But the phenomenon I have in mind is one of anxiety rather than pride, of veiled competition rather than openly rivalrous display; the narcissism is muted or, as we shall see, alloyed with other, stronger elements.

In these circumstances parents who try, in inner-directed fashion, to compel the internalization of disciplined pursuit of clear goals run the risk of having their children styled clear out of the personality market. Gyroscopic direction is just not flexible enough for the rapid adaptations of personality that are required, precisely because there will be other competitors who do not have gyroscopes. Inhibited from presenting their children with sharply silhouetted images of self and society, parents in our era can only equip the child to do his best, whatever that may turn out to be. What is best is not in their control but in the hands of the school and peer-group that will help locate the child eventually in the hierarchy. But even these authorities speak vaguely; the clear principles of selection that once guided people of inner-directed character no longer apply. For example, social climbing itself may be called into public question at the same time that it is no longer so unequivocally desirable in terms of private wish. As some *Fortune* surveys indicate, a safe and secure job may be preferred to a risky one involving high stakes. What is more, it is no longer clear which way *is* up even if one wants to rise, for with the growth of the new middle class the older, hierarchical patterns disintegrate, and it is not easy to compare ranks among the several sets of hierarchies that do exist. Does an army colonel "rank" the head of an international union? A physics professor, a bank vice-president? A commentator, the head of an oil company?

Increasingly in doubt as to how to bring up their children, parents turn to other contemporaries for advice; they also look to the mass media; and like the mother quoted at the outset of this chapter they turn, in effect, to the children themselves. They may, nevertheless, fasten on some inflexible scheme of child rearing and follow that. Yet they cannot help but show their children, by their own anxiety, how little they depend on themselves and how much on others. Whatever they may seem to be teaching the child in terms of content, they are passing on to him their own contagious, highly diffuse anxiety. They reinforce this teaching by giving the child approval—and approving themselves because of the child—when he makes good.

To be sure, inner-directed parents also often were able to "love" only those children who made good in the outer world. But at least the canons of success were reasonably clear. The other-directed child, however, faces not only the requirement that he make good but also the problem of defining what making good means. He finds that both the definition and the evaluation of himself depend on the company he keeps: first, on his schoolmates and teachers; later, on peers and superiors. But perhaps the company one keeps is itself at fault? One can then shop for other preferred companies in the mass circulation media.

Approval itself, irrespective of content, becomes almost the only unequivocal good in this situation: one makes good when one is approved of. Thus all power, not merely some power, is in the hands of the actual or imaginary approving group, and the child learns from his parents' reactions to him that nothing in his character, no possession he owns, no inheritance of name or talent, no work he has done is valued for itself but only for its effect on others. Making good becomes almost equivalent to making friends, or at any rate the right kind of friends. "To him that hath approval, shall be given more approval."

From bringing up children to "Bringing up Father." The typical other-directed child grows up in a small family, in close urban quarters, or in a suburb. Even more than in the earlier epoch the father leaves home to go to work, and he goes too far to return for lunch. Home, moreover, is no longer an area of solid privacy. As the size and living space of the family diminish and as the pattern of living with older relatives declines, the child must directly face the emotional tensions of his parents. There is a heightening of awareness of the self in relation to others under these conditions, especially since the parents, too, are increasingly self-conscious.

Under the new social and economic conditions, the position of children rises. They are not subjected to a period of deprivation and hardship which leads to compensatory dreams of a life of ease and pleasure. Girls are not, as they were in some earlier societies, drudges at home until, at puberty, they were suddenly given the only "capital" they were ever likely to find—that of their bodies—to live on as income, or exhaust as principal. Even boys from comfortable homes were expected until recently to hit the sunrise trail with paper routes or other economically profitable and "character-building" chores.

The parents lack not only the self-assurance that successful inner-direction brings but also the strategy of withdrawal available to many unsuccessful inner-directed types. The loss of old certainties in the spheres of work and social relations is accompanied by doubt as to how to bring up children. Moreover, the parents no longer feel themselves superior to the children. While children no longer have immediate economic value, they are less numerous, "scarcer" in relation to the number of adults: the effort is made, and it is objectively possible, to want all children who are conceived and to raise very nearly all children who are born. More is staked on every single child than in the earlier epoch when many children were not raised to maturity. In addition, apart from the fact that the children may be better Americans than the parents, in ethnic or social terms—as Jiggs's daughter is more up to date than he—there are undoubtedly other solid reasons (which I shall not go into) for the general emphasis on youth which runs through all forms of popular culture.[3]

Historical changes in the lives of adolescents can be seen most clearly, perhaps, if one looks back to those *Bildungs-romane* of the nineteenth century that described the misunderstood youth who struggled against the harsh or hypocritical tyranny of his parents, particularly if one compares one of the best of such novels, Samuel Butler's *The Way of All Flesh*, with one of the best of our contemporary examples, for instance Lionel Trilling's short story, "The Other Margaret."[4] In Trilling's story we have a picture of a precocious young girl in the intellectual, urban, upper middle class. Margaret, who goes to a progressive school, believes that Negroes are exploited, and she resents the inferior position in the home of "the other Margaret," a Negro domestic. It is the daughter Margaret who is self-righteous, not the parents.

In the face of her criticism, buttressed as it is by the authority of the school, the parents, themselves progressive, are on the defensive. They are tense and very much concerned with what their daughter thinks—and thinks of them. Eventually, all three adults manage to destroy Margaret's illusion of the virtues of the other Margaret—the parents by reasoning; the other Margaret by bad behavior. But in the end the parents are anxious about their victory, lest it harm their sensitive child. They possess little of the certainty and security of Theobald's parents in *The Way of All Flesh*.

In this change of parental attitude the mass media of communication play a dual role. From the mass media— radio, movies, comics—as well as from their own peers, children can easily learn what the norm of parental behavior is, and hold it over their parents' heads. Thus a kind of realism is restored to the child which was his property much more

---

[3]This, too, is a development whose importance Margaret Mead has stressed. See *And Keep Your Powder Dry* (New York, William Morrow, 1942).

[4]*Partisan Review*, XII (1945), 381.

simply in the societies depending on tradition-direction: the other-directed child is often more knowing than his parents—like the proverbial Harvard man, there is little they can tell *him*.[5]

As already noted, the parents also have their sources of direction in the mass media. For in their uneasiness as to how to bring up children they turn increasingly to books, magazines, government pamphlets, and radio programs. These tell the already anxious mother to accept her children. She learns that there are no problem children, only problem parents; and she learns to look into her own psyche whenever she is moved to deny the children anything, including an uninterrupted flow of affection. If the children are cross then the mother must be withholding something. And while these tutors also tell the mother to "relax" and

---

[5] Yet the knowingness, particularly in the middle class, has limits that were less important in the tradition-directed family. There the child, knowledgeable for example about sex, could see reflections of it in the daily adult life around him. He would know that if his uncle was particularly gay or particularly cross at work this was connected with what happened in the village the night before. As against this, the other-directed child knows about sex only, so to speak, in the abstract. He cannot reasonably connect the night life he knows exists with the seriousness of the adult world that faces him at school, at the store, or at home. While he has doffed the myths of sex that Freud found among the young of his day, he still finds passion playing a greater role in the comics and the movies than in the life he is able to observe—the latter being a life in which people are trained to hide their passions and to act generally in a disembodied way. Perhaps this is one reason why sex often remains an exciting mystery for the other-directed adult—as we shall see in Chap. VII—despite all his learning, all his disenchantment, and even all his experience of it. And, in general, the other-directed child's realism about the adult world is hampered not so much by Victorian inhibitions as by the far subtler partitions of adult life itself, such as the shadowy partitions between work and play to be discussed later.

to "enjoy her children," even this becomes an additional injunction to be anxiously followed.

It may be that children today do not gain the strength that adults—no longer inner-directed—have lost. To be sure, this was often a factitious strength, as Samuel Butler saw; but it was usually sufficient both to crush the child's spontaneity and anesthetize his diffuse anxiety. "Shades of the prison-house begin to close upon the growing boy"— and the prisoner might feel oppressed, even guilty, but not too anxious behind his bars. In contrast, what the other-directed child does "learn" from his parents is anxiety—the emotional tuning appropriate to his other-directed adjustment.

The rule of "reason." Despite the diminution of their authority, the parents still try to control matters; but with the loss of self-assurance their techniques change. They can neither hold themselves up as exemplars—when both they and the child know better—nor resort, in good conscience, to severe corporal punishment and deprivations. At most there are token spankings, with open physical warfare confined to the lower classes.

The parents' recourse, especially in the upper middle class, is to "personnel" methods—to manipulation in the form of reasoning, or, more accurately, of rationalizing. The child responds in the same manner. One might summarize the historical sequence by saying that the tradition-directed child propitiates his parents; the inner-directed child fights or succumbs to them; the other-directed child manipulates them and is in turn manipulated.

A movie of several years ago, *The Curse of the Cat People,* while it testified to American preoccupation with certain child-rearing themes which do not directly concern us here, also provides an interesting example of these manipulative relations between parent and child. A little girl lives in a suburban, middle-class home with its typical neatness, garden, and Negro servant. As in "The Other Margaret," there is a terrific pressure of adult emotion focused around this one child from the parents and servant. The child is supposed to invite the other children in the neighborhood for her birthday party; but believing her father's joke that the big tree in the yard is a mailbox, she puts the invitations there and they never go out. When her birthday arrives, the other children whom she had said she would invite tease her and refuse to play with her. Her father scolds her for taking him seriously, and she is also in difficulties for not getting along better with the other children. But the parents (plus servant) decide to go ahead with the party anyway, "as if." There follows a "party" which tries to persuade the child that there has been no tragedy, that this party is just as good as the one which failed.

The parents insist that the child somehow know, without a formal etiquette, when things are supposed to be "real" and when "pretend." The tree as the mailbox is pretend; the party real. Feeling misunderstood and alone, the little girl discovers a real friend in a strange woman who lives almost as a recluse in a great house. The parents frown upon this "friend" and her gift of a ring to the child. The little girl then discovers an imaginary friend at the bottom of the yard, a beautiful older woman with whom she talks. The father cannot see, that is to say "see," this latter friend and punishes the child for lying.

Notice this fictional family's lack of privacy for the child. The discovery of the gift of the ring seems to be typical of the fact that few of her excitements escape parental scrutiny. Moreover, the very fact that the father suggests to the daughter the secret about the make-believe "mailbox tree" is symbolic of the intrusion of his knowledge: the daughter is not allowed her own make-believe but must share it with him, subject to his determination of when it applies. That the daughter and father finally come into open conflict over the little girl's fantasy friend is only to be expected; the girl cannot put a lock on the door of her room or the door of her mind. (In a lower-class home there would be, spatially at least, even less privacy; but there might be more psychic privacy because the parents would often be less interested in the child.)

Notice, in the second place, the "reasonable" but subtly manipulative tone of parent-child relations. This is evidenced by the parental planning of the party for the daughter and her peers and by the parental irritation when the plan miscarries. Still more significant is the way in which the family meets the crisis of blocked peer-group communication symbolized by the nonoperative mailbox—a failure that is itself occasioned by a blockage of understanding about the real and the unreal between daughter and parents.

The fiasco is, obviously enough, a matter that requires immediate corrective action; parents in this pass, it seems, should *do* something. The parents of the child in this movie do nothing; they prefer to talk away the situation, to manipulate the child into the acceptance of a formal illusion of party making. The result is to produce a sort of exaggeration and burlesque of the way in which other-directed persons, in parent-child as in all other relations, constantly resort to manipulation and countermanipulation.

As contrasted with all this, the inner-directed parent is not particularly worried by his child's resentment or hostility. Nor is he as apt to be as aware of it. He and the child are both protected by the gap that separates them. The other-directed parent, however, has to win not only his child's good behavior but also his child's good will. Therefore, he is tempted to use his superior dialectic skill to "reason" with the child. And when the child learns—this is part of his sensitive radar equipment—how to argue too, the parent is torn between giving in and falling uneasily back on the sterner methods of his inner-directed parents. The father in *The Curse of the Cat People*, after trying to reason away the little girl's belief in her fantasy friend, finally spanks her. But such scenes are always succeeded by parental efforts at reconciliation, turning the spanking itself into a step in the manipulative chain.

Finally, we must observe the change in the content of the issues at stake between parent and child. The more driving and tense inner-directed parents compel their children to work, to save, to clean house, sometimes to study, and sometimes to pray. Other less puritanical types of inner-directed parent want their boys to be manly, their girls to be feminine and chaste. Such demands make either economic or ideological sense in the population phase of transitional growth. The large home could absorb enormous amounts of labor; even today those who putter in small house and small garden can still find lots to do. The parents themselves often set the example, in which they are supported by the school, of work and study: these are believed to be the paths of upward mobility both in this world and in the next.

In the other-directed home, on the other hand, the issues between parent and child concern the nonwork side of life. For in the phase of incipient population decline—most markedly, of course, in America but elsewhere too—there is no work for children to do inside the urban home, and little outside. They need not brush and clean (except themselves)—they are less efficient than a vacuum cleaner. Nor is there an array of younger brothers and sisters to be taken care of. The American mother, educated, healthy, and efficient, has high standards for care of the apartment or small home and would, where she is not working, often feel quite out of a job if the children took over the housework. Fortunately released from the quandary of the old woman who lived in a shoe, she faces—just, as we shall see, as her husband does—the problem of leisure; care for the house and children is frequently her self-justification and escape.

So parents and children debate over eating and sleeping time as later they will debate over use of the family car. And they argue tensely, as in *The Curse of the Cat People*, about the contacts of the child with the "others" and about the emotional hue of the argument itself. But by the nature of these discussions the parents have a less easy victory. In the population phase of transitional growth they can point to self-evident tasks that need doing—self-evident at least according to accepted standards that have survived from the still earlier epoch. In the phase of incipient decline, however, the consumption or leisure issues are no longer self-evident; to decide them, if they are to be decided, one has to resort to models outside the particular home—in search of the ever changing norms of the group in which the parents happen to live. And indeed the radio and print bring the models into the home, like a trial record from which the child and parent legalists prepare briefs.[6]

To sum up: parents in the groups depending on other-direction install in their children something like a psychological radar set—a device not tuned to control movement in any particular direction while guiding and steadying the person from within but rather tuned to detect the action, and especially the symbolic action, of others. Thereafter, the parents influence the children's character only insofar as (a) their own signals mingle with others over the radar, (b) they can locate children in a certain social environment in order to alter to a very limited degree what signals they will receive, (c) they take the risks of a very partial and precarious censorship of incoming messages. Thus the parental role diminishes in importance as compared with the same role among the inner-directed.

II. Changes in the Role of the Teacher

Much could be said about the changing configuration of adult authorities, other than the parents, as society moves from dependence on inner-direction to dependence on other-direction. Largely for economic reasons the governess, mammy, or hired tutor, for instance, virtually disappears from middle- and upper middle-class homes. One significant

[6]Morris Janowitz has suggested that if one wanted to get a very rough index of homes in which other-direction was being transmitted, as against those in which inner-direction prevailed, one might separate the homes which took only such magazines as Life, Look, the comics, or movie journals from those which took such periodicals as the Saturday Evening Post or Collier's. The former group is for the whole family, interpreted as easily or more easily by children than by adults. The latter group is mainly for the grownups and not shared with the children.

consequence is that children are no longer raised by people who hold up to them the standard of a family or class. Such a standard is good training in inner-direction—in the acquisition of generalized goals; it is at the same time a partial buffer against the indiscriminate influence of the peer-group. But there is another more subtle consequence. The child who has been raised by a governess and educated by a tutor gains a very keen sense for the disparities of power in the home and in the society. When he goes off to boarding school or college he is likely to remain unimpressed by his teachers—like the upper-class mother who told the school headmaster: "I don't see why the masters can't get along with Johnny; all the other servants do." Such a child is not going to be interested in allowing his teachers to counsel him in his peer-group relations or emotional life.

Furthermore, the presence of these adults in the home—somewhat like the extended family in earlier eras—helps reduce the emotional intensity of parent-child relations. Though the child knows who is boss in the home, he can still play these other "officials" off against parental authority. And, indeed, the inner-directed parents, frequently not overeager for warmth from the child, are quite willing to have the child's experience of affection associated with persons of lower status. The inner-directed young man raised under these conditions learns to find emotional release with prostitutes and others of low status. He becomes capable of impersonal relations with people and sometimes incapable of any other kind. This is one of the prices he pays for his relative impermeability to the needs and wishes of his peers, and helps account for his ability, when in pursuit of some end he values, to steel himself against their indifference or hostility.

Grandmothers as authorities are almost as obsolete as governesses. There is no room for them in the modern apartment, nor can they, any more than the children themselves, find a useful economic role. Nevertheless they endure, concomitant with the increased longevity of the later population phases. The increased personalization of relationships that other-direction brings means that "strangers" in the home are less and less endurable: the in-law problem, a standard joke in many cultures over many centuries, takes on new meaning where sensitive, highly individuated people live without characterological defenses against each other.

The elimination of the grandmother from a central role in the home is, moreover, symbolic of the rapidity of the changes we are discussing. She is two generations removed from current practices on the "frontier of consumption." While the parents try to keep up with their children, both as a means of staying young and as a means of staying influential, this is seldom possible for the grandparents. Hence their role in the formation of the other-directed character is negligible. Far from presenting the child with a relatively consistent "family portrait," standing in back of the parents and strengthening them, grandparents stand as emblems of how little one can learn from one's elders about the things that matter.

A parallel development removes another set of parent surrogates who played an important role in earlier periods: the older brothers or sisters who, like sophomores, hazed the younger in subjecting them to the family pattern of discipline. Today the older children—if there are any—are frequently more willing to earn cash as baby sitters than to supervise the training of their own younger brothers and sisters. The lure of a job may get children to work outside their homes; that still makes sense to them. But within their own home they are the privileged guests in a rather second-rate hotel, a hotel whose harassed but smiling managers they put under constant pressure for renovation.

THE TEACHER'S ROLE IN THE STAGE OF INNER-DIRECTION

One important authority, however, remains: a proxy parent whose power has probably increased as a consequence of the shift to other-direction. This is the schoolteacher, and we turn now to a fuller exploration of the change in her role.

In the period when inner-direction insures middle-class conformity, school starts relatively late—there are few nursery schools. The teacher's task is largely to train the children in decorum and in intellectual matters. The decorum may be the minimum of discipline needed to keep order in the classroom or the maximum of polish needed to decorate girls of the upper social strata. As schools become more plentiful and more readily accessible and "democratic," the obligation to train the child in middle-class speech and manners—that he may be aided in his rise above his parents' rank—falls upon the teacher. But the teacher does not work close to the child's emotional level. And the teacher regards her job as a limited one, sharply demarcated from the equally rigorous task of the home.

The physical setting in school reflects this situation. Seating is formal—all face front—and often alphabetical. The walls are decorated with the ruins of Pompeii and the bust of Caesar. For all but the few exceptional children who can transcend the dead forms of their classical education and make the ancient world come alive, these etchings and statues signify the irrelevance of the school to the emotional problems of the child.

The teacher herself has neither understanding of nor time for these emotional problems, and the child's relation to other children enters her purview only in disciplinary cases. Often she has simply no authority: she is a common scold with too large a brood. Or she manages to maintain discipline by strictures and punishments. But these absorb the emotional attention of the children, often uniting them in opposition to authority.

In the recent Swedish movie *Torment* we see this pattern still at work in the near-contemporary scene. Teachers and parents share the task of instilling inner-directed values. The villain is a harsh and overbearing, neurotic prep-school teacher. All the boys hate him; some fear him; no self-respecting boy would dream—despite the teacher's groping efforts—of being his friend. The hero is a boy who rebels, not so much because he wants to but rather because he is forced to by his teacher. He and his friends suffer, but their parents and teachers do not invade their lives, and they have privacy with each other and with girls, so long as no serious breach of decorum is evident. This rebellion itself—its success is not the issue—is part of the process of developing an inner-directed character.

An equally moving portrait is Antonia White's novel of a girl's convent school, *Frost in May*. Though the nuns at the school go quite far in "molding character" and viciously cut down signs of spontaneity and open-mindedness in the gifted heroine, they have back of them only the old-fashioned sanctions of penance and salvation. Their charges break or bend or run away or join the church—they do not open up to the nuns as friends. The universal uniforms, as in a military school, symbolize the barriers of rank and restraint that separate the authorities from the children.

We may sum all this up by saying that the school of this period is concerned largely with impersonal matters. The sexes are segregated. The focus is on an intellectual content that for most children has little emotional bite. Elocution, like female accomplishment, is impersonal, too; the child is not asked to "be himself"—nor does the school aim to be like "real life." Teachers, whether spinsterly or motherly types, do not know enough, even if they had the time and energy, to take an active hand in the socialization of tastes or of peer-group relations. While parents may permit the teachers to enforce certain rules of morality directly related to school, such as modesty of dress and honesty in examinations, and to inculcate certain rules of manners directly related to social ascent, they hardly allow interference with play groups, even in the interests of enforcing ethnic or economic democracy. The teacher is supposed to see that the children learn a curriculum, not that they enjoy it or learn group cooperation. The present practice of progressive grammar schools which decide whether or not to take a child by putting him in his putative group and seeing how he fits in would hardly have been conceivable.

Nevertheless, despite the social distance between teacher and child, the school's unquestioning emphasis on intellectual ability is profoundly important in shaping the inner-directed character. It affirms to the child that what matters is what he can *accomplish*, not how nice is his smile or how cooperative his attitude. And while the objectivity of the criteria for judging these skills and competences is rightfully called into question today—when we can see very clearly, for instance, the class bias in intelligence tests and written examinations—the inner-directed school is not aware of such biases, and hence its standards can appear unequivocal and unalterable. For this reason these standards can be internalized both by those who succeed and by those who fail. They are felt as real and given, not as somebody's whim. Thus the school reinforces the home in setting for the child goals that are clear to all and that give direction and meaning to life thereafter.

Whatever the security children gain from knowing where they stand—a security they no longer have in the other-directed progressive school—we must not forget how harshly this system bears on those who cannot make the grade: they are often broken; there is little mercy for them on psychological grounds. Brains, status, perhaps also docility, win the teacher, rather than "personality" or "problems." Some of the failures rebel. But these, too, are hammered into shape by the school—bad shape. Occasionally the frontier and other opportunities for mobility provide an exit for the academically outclassed; and, still more occasionally, the rebel returns, like a mythical hero, having lived his troubles down, to alleviate the guilt of other misfits and give them hope for their own future. By and large, however, the very unequivocality of the school's standards that gives the children a certain security also means that the standards will be internalized even by those who fail. They will carry with them the aftereffects of emotional shock whose violence lies beyond criticism—sometimes even beyond recall.

THE TEACHER'S ROLE IN THE STAGE OF OTHER-DIRECTION

Progressive education began as a movement to liberate children from the crushing of talent and breaking of will that was the fate of many, even of those whose inner-direction might have seemed to them and to the observer stable and sound enough. Its aim, and to a very considerable degree, its achievement, was to develop the individuality of the child; and its method was to focus the teacher's attention on more facets of the child than his intellectual abilities. Today, however, progressive education is often no longer progressive; as people have become more other-directed, educational methods that were once liberating may even tend to thwart individuality rather than advance and protect it. The story can be quickly told.

Progressive schools have helped lower the age of school entry; the two- to five-year-old groups learn to associate school not with forbidding adults and dreary subjects but with play and understanding adults. The latter are, increasingly, young college graduates who have been taught to be more concerned with the child's social and psychological adjustment than with his academic progress—indeed, to scan the intellectual performance for signs of social maladjustment. These new teachers are more specialized. They don't claim to "understand children" but to have studied Gesell on the "fives" or the "nines"; and this greater knowledge not only prevents the children from uniting in a wall of distrust or conspiracy against the school but also permits the teacher to take a greater hand in the socialization of spheres—consumption, friendship, fantasy—which the older-type teacher, whatever her personal desires, could not touch. Our wealthier society can afford this amount of individuation and "unnecessary" schooling.

Physical arrangements, too—in seating, age-grading, decoration—symbolize the changes in the teacher's function. The sexes are mixed. Seating is arranged "informally." That is, *alphabetic* forms disappear, often to be replaced by *sociometric* forms that bring together compeers. This often means that where to sit becomes problematical—a clue to one's location on the friendship chart. Gesell grading is as severe as intellectual grading was in the earlier era; whatever their intellectual gifts, children stay with their presumed social peers.[7] The desks change their form, too; they are more apt to be movable tables with open shelves than places where one may hide things. The teacher no longer sits on a dais or struts before a blackboard but joins the family circle.

Above all, the walls change their look. The walls of the modern grade school are decorated with the paintings of the children or their montages from the class in social studies. Thus the competitive and contemporary problems

---

[7] Howard C. Becker ("Role and Career Problems of the Chicago Public School Teacher," unpublished Ph.D. dissertation, University of Chicago, 1951) has been observing the classroom consequences of the decline of the practice both of skipping grades and of holding children back who must repeat the grade. The teachers, faced with a group of identical age but vastly different capacities and willingnesses, meet the situation by dividing the class into two or three like-minded groups. Mobility between groups is discouraged, and children are encouraged to imitate their groupmates. The teacher herself, in the public schools, is probably inner-directed, but she is forced by her situation to promote other-direction among her charges.

The following quotation from Mr. Becker's interviews is a poignant example of how a teacher will promote other-direction in her efforts to get the children to have more interesting weekends: "Every class I have I start out the year by making a survey. I have each child get up and tell what he did over the weekend. These last few years I've noticed that more and more children get up and say, 'Saturday I went to the show, Sunday I went to the show' . . . I've been teaching twenty-five years, and it never used to be like that. Children used to do more interesting things, they would go places instead of 'Saturday I went to the show, Sunday I went to the show' . . . What I do is to give a talk on all the interesting things that could be done—like going to museums and things like that. And also things like playing baseball and going on bike rides. By the end of the term a child is ashamed if he has to get up and say, 'Saturday I went to the show, Sunday I went to the show.' All the rest of the children laugh at him. So they really try to do some interesting things."

of the children look down on them from walls which, like the teacher herself, are no longer impersonal. This looks progressive, looks like a salute to creativeness and individuality; but again we meet paradox. While the school de-emphasizes grades and report cards, the displays seem almost to ask the children: "Mirror, mirror on the wall, who is fairest of us all?"[8]

While the children's paintings and montages show considerable imaginative gift in the pre-adolescent period, the school itself is nevertheless still one of the agencies for the destruction of fantasy, as it was in the preceding era. Imagination withers in most of the children by adolescence. What survives is neither artistic craft nor artistic fantasy but the socialization of taste and interest that can already be seen in process in the stylization of perception in the children's paintings and stories. The stories of the later progressive grades are apt to be characterized by "realism." This realism is subtly influenced by the ideals of the progressive movement. Caesar and Pompeii are replaced by visits to stores and dairies, by maps from *Life*, and by *The Weekly Reader*; and fairy tales are replaced by stories about trains, telephones, and grocery stores, and, later, by material on race relations or the United Nations or "our Latin American neighbors."

These changes in arrangement and topic assist the breakdown of walls between teacher and pupil; and this in turn helps to break down walls between student and student, permitting that rapid circulation of tastes which is a prelude

[8]Still more paradoxically, it often happens that those schools that insist most strongly that the child be original and creative by this very demand make it difficult for him to be so. He dare not imitate an established master nor, in some cases, even imitate his own earlier work. Though the introduction of the arts into the school opens up the whole art world to many children, who would have no time or stimulation outside, other children are forced to socialize performances that would earlier have gone unnoticed by peers and adults.

to other-directed socialization. Whereas the inner-directed school child might well have hidden his stories and paintings under his bed—like the adult who, as we saw, often kept a diary—the other-directed child reads his stories to the group and puts his paintings on the wall. Play, which in the earlier epoch is often an extracurricular and private hobby, shared at most with a small group, now becomes part of the school enterprise itself, serving a "realistic" purpose.

The teacher's role in this situation is often that of opinion leader. She is the one who spreads the messages concerning taste that come from the progressive urban centers. She conveys to the children that what matters is not their industry or learning as such but their adjustment in the group, their cooperation, their (carefully stylized and limited) initiative and leadership.

Especially important is the fact that the cooperation and leadership that are inculcated in and expected of the children are frequently contentless. In nursery school it is not important whether Johnny plays with a truck or in the sandbox, but it matters very much whether he involves himself with Bill—via any object at all. To be sure, there are a few, a very few, truly progressive schools where the children operating on the Dalton plan and similar plans exercise genuine choice of their program, move at their own pace, and use the teacher as a friendly reference library; here cooperation is necessary and meaningful in actual work on serious projects. Far more frequently, however, the teacher continues to hold the reins of authority in her hands, hiding her authority, like her compeer, the other-directed parent, under the cloak of "reasoning" and manipulation. She determines the program and its pace—indeed, often holding the children back because she fails to realize that children, left to themselves, are capable of curiosity about highly abstract matters. She may delay them by making arithmetic "realistic" and languages fun—as well as by substituting social studies for history. In extreme forms of this situation there is nothing on which the children have to cooperate in order to get it done. The teacher will do it for them anyway. Hence when she asks that they be cooperative she is really asking simply that they be nice.

However, though the request seems simple, it is not casually made: the teacher is very tense about it. Deprived of older methods of discipline, she is, if anything, even more helpless than the parents who can always fall back on those methods in a pinch, though guiltily and rather ineffectively. The teacher neither dares to nor cares to; she has been taught that bad behavior on the children's part implies poor management on her part. Moreover, she herself is not interested in the intellectual content of what is taught, nor is this content apt to come up in a staff meeting or PTA discussion. These adult groups are often concerned with teaching tolerance, both ethnic and economic; and the emphasis on social studies that results means that intellectual content and skill become still more attenuated. Consequently, the teacher's emotional energies are channeled into the area of group relations. Her social skills develop; she may be sensitive to cliques based on "mere friendship" and seek to break them up lest any be left out. Correspondingly, her love for certain specific children may be trained out of her. All the more, she needs the general cooperation of all the children to assure herself that she is doing her job. Her surface amiability and friendliness, coupled with this underlying anxiety concerning the children's response, must be very confusing to the children who will probably conclude that to be uncooperative is about the worst thing one can be.

Of course the teacher will see to it that the children practice cooperation in small matters: in deciding whether to study the Peruvians or the Colombians, in nominating class officers for early practice in the great contemporary rituals of electioneering and parliamenteering, and in organizing contributions for the Red Cross or a Tag Day. Thus the children are supposed to learn democracy by underplaying the skills of intellect and overplaying the skills of gregariousness and amiability—skill democracy, in fact, based on respect for ability to do something, tends to survive only in athletics.

There is, therefore, a curious resemblance between the role of the teacher in the small-class modern school—a role that has spread from the progressive private schools to a good number of the public schools—and the role of the industrial relations department in a modern factory. The latter is also increasingly concerned with cooperation between men and men and between men and management, as technical skill becomes less and less of a major concern. In a few of the more advanced plants there is even a pattern of democratic decision on moot matters—occasionally important because it affects piecework rates and seniority rules, but usually as trivial as the similar decisions of grammar-school government. Thus the other-directed child is taught at school to take his place in a society where the concern of the group is less with what it produces than with its internal group relations, its morale.

III

A JURY OF THEIR PEERS: CHANGES IN THE AGENTS OF CHARACTER FORMATION (Continued)

Individualism is a stage of transition between two types of social organization.

W. I. Thomas, THE UNADJUSTED GIRL

I. THE PEER-GROUP IN THE STAGE OF INNER-DIRECTION

WITH the decline of the extended kinship family (the type of tradition-directed family that may include uncles, aunts, cousins, and other relatives), the child is often confronted in the inner-directed home with the close oppressiveness of idealized parents. He may compete with his brothers and sisters for the parents' favors, or to ward off their disapprobation. In theory the children in a family can unite against tyrannical parents, but, judging from the novels, it is more likely that parents divide and rule. Children in a family cannot react as a peer-group because of the age differentials among them. Consequently any given child at any single moment faces obviously unique problems and is alone with them—barring the luck of a sympathetic maid or aunt.

This is the price the inner-directed child pays for a situation in which his maturity is not delayed by having to wait for his age-graded peer-group. His parents do not hold him down because, according to "authorities," he is not ready for something. In Lord Chesterfield's letters to his son we find the assumption that pervades much literature of the earliest industrial period, that the child is simply a young, somewhat inexperienced adult. Lord Chesterfield writes as though his fifteen-year-old son had gained full sexual and intellectual maturity and needed only to ripen in wisdom and to acquire influence in his commerce with adults. The problems of training children to play with other children outside the home or to cooperate amicably with them do not present themselves to the inner-directed adult as part of his parental responsibility.

As a result the child, surrounded by inner-directed adults, often faces demands that are quite unreasonable. He is not held back but neither is he given a break. The growing child may respond to these demands by guilt and desperate effort to live up to the model or by rebellion in solitude against it; he does not respond, as in the other-directed environment, by using the peer-group as a club to bring anxious adults into line if they have unreasonable or even unusual expectations of him. Indeed, in this era, it is sometimes possible to bring up the child in relative isolation from the peer-group, even though he has formal contact with other children at school. The images of the poor little rich boy and poor little rich girl are creations of this epoch, when children are often the social prisoners of parents and governesses.

In fact, the location of the home tends to have entirely different meanings in each of the three phases of the population curve. In the phase of high growth potential the home, except among the hunting and nomadic peoples, is fixed. As the locus of most activities in the socialization process, it symbolizes the extended family's overwhelming importance in that process. In the phase of transitional growth the young adult must navigate the passage from home and found a new home somewhere else. He goes to an undeveloped frontier or an undeveloped city; there he marries and settles down. This new home plays a part of decisive significance in the socialization of his children, though the school and other specialized agencies outside the home also play an increasing part.

In the phase of incipient population decline people still move around, but in search of frontiers of consumption as well as of production. That is, they look for nice neighborhoods in which their children will meet nice people. Although much of the moving about in America today, within and between cities, is in search of better jobs, it is also increasingly in search of better neighborhoods and the better schools that go with them. Since many others, too, will also be shopping for better neighborhoods, this pressure, combined with the rapid shift of residential values and fashions characteristic of American cities, means that no one can ever settle down assuredly for the rest of life. And when the children have grown up and made homes of their own, the parents will feel inclined to move again, perhaps in search of such consumption values as sunlight for themselves. Thus by their very location the other-directed parents show how much store they put on their children's contacts. And, of course, living in a small space with one child or two, the urban and suburban family needs to use space—physical and emotional space—outside the confined home for the activities of the growing children. (During the same period the working-class family has obtained access to much greater living space than during the earlier stages of industrialization; but it is the history of the middle-class family only that we are discusing here.)

Returning now to the situation of the inner-directed child, we see that he finds his playmates either among his own brothers and sisters or in an equally wide age range outside the home. This pattern still exists in country districts, where the gang at the swimming hole or ball field will be widely ranged in age; there are no partitioned playgrounds. However, after an age of "social discretion" is reached, the inner-directed child is expected to confine his friendships to those of approximately his own social class. Class has to be a conscious barrier because neighborhoods are somewhat less carefully restricted along class and ethnic lines than many suburbs are today—just as the southern whites and Negroes still frequently live in close physical proximity. Between five and fifteen, sex is also a barrier for the inner-directed child, since coeducation is infrequent and even where it formally exists little more effort is made to mix the sexes than to mix the social classes: proms for sixth and seventh graders are not yet known. The inner-directed child, limited in his friendship choices and limiting himself by a clear recognition of his status and the status to which he aspires, would seem "choosy" to many other-directed children of today.

Within the limits permitted by geography and taboo, then, the inner-directed child approaching his teens seeks out a chum or two. He may find in an older relative or friend someone to imitate and admire. But in many cases he will choose a chum on the basis of an interest in similar games and hobbies—hobbies that tend to be highly idiosyncratic and that are often continued into adult life. One can still observe this pattern at an English boys' school, where almost everyone has a hobby. Some hobbyists are quite satisfied to be by themselves—their hobby is company enough. Or one will find fast friendships among bird lovers, motorcycle fans, mineral collectors, poetry fanciers.

As we shall see in Chapter XV, a hobby or craft is not of itself a clear sign of inner-direction: hobbies may be pursued also by children who are other-directed. Even, to a degree, the hobbies of both types may nominally coincide. But the meaning and social context of the hobbies are quite different for the two types of children. The inner-directed child will seldom share his hobby with a large peer-group— though stamp collecting may be an exception—and when hobbyists of this sort meet it is to swap technical details and enthusiasms, as two dairy farmers might swap accounts of their respective favorite breeds. There is nothing anxious about such a meeting: no problem of maintaining marginal differentiation (difference, that is, but not too much) in taste such as we find in other-directed hobbyists. The child is not shaken in his own hobby by the fact that others have a different hobby; rather, he is confirmed in the idiosyncrasy which, within wide limits, is respected.

Let me warn the reader, however, not to view all this too nostalgically with, say Penrod or Huckleberry Finn or even perhaps his own idealized childhood, in mind. In sports and studies the peer-group can become fiercely competitive, aided and abetted by coaches, teachers, and other adults. Many boys and girls who win honors in grade school are crushed when they do not surmount the tougher competition of high school. Much is at stake—and still more seems to be at stake—in such contests; and the inner-directed child cannot easily, sour-grapes fashion, change the instilled goals when they loom unattainable. Moreover, parents and teachers in their psychological naïveté may hold up as models the detestable young who work hard, dress neatly, and are polite.

Beyond all that, the fate of many inner-directed children is loneliness in and outside the home. Home, school, and way-stations between may be places for hazing, persecution, misunderstanding. No adult intervenes on behalf of the lonely or hazed child to proffer sympathy, ask questions, or give advice. Adults do not think children's play is very important anyway; they will criticize children who seem too much concerned with play and too little with work. No sociometrically inclined teacher will try to break up friendship cliques in school to see that no one is left out. How savagely snobbish boys and girls can be is typified by the story, in the Lynds' *Middletown*, of the daughter who quit high school because her mother could not afford to give her silk stockings. Often the children, unaware that they have rights to friendship, understanding, or agreeable play—unaware, indeed, that the adults could be greatly interested in such matters—suffer in silence and submit to the intolerable.

Only with the perspective of today can we see the advantages of these disadvantages. We can see that in a society which values inner-direction loneliness and even persecution are not thought of as the worst of fates. Parents, sometimes even teachers, may have crushing moral authority, but the peer-group has less moral weight, glamorous or menacing though it may be. While adults seldom intervene to guide and help the child, neither do they tell him that he should be part of a crowd and *must* have fun.

II. The Peer-group in the Stage of Other-direction

The parents in the era dominated by other-direction lose their once undisputed role; the old man is no longer "the governor"—and the installer of governors. Other adult authorities such as the governess and grandmother either almost disappear or, like the teacher, take on the new role of peer-group facilitator and mediator—a role not too different perhaps from that of many clergymen who, in the adult congregation, move from morality to morale.

As already indicated, moreover, the city in which the other-directed child grows up is large enough and stratified enough—taking into account its ring of suburbs—to create an age- and class-graded group for him. It will be possible to put him into school and playground, and camp in the summer, with other children of virtually the same age and social position. If the adults are the judge, these peers are the jury. And, as in America the judge is hemmed in by rules which give the jury a power it has in no other common-law land, so the American peer-group, too, cannot be matched for power throughout the middle-class world.

The Trial. While the inner-directed parent frequently forced the pace of the child in its home "duties," as, for example, in cleanliness and toilet-training habits, the other-directed parent, more apt to be permissive in such matters, forces the pace, with like impatience, in the child's social life, though often hardly aware of doing so. Parents today are the stage managers for the meetings of three- and four-year-olds, just as, in earlier eras, the adults managed marriages. Hence, while "self-demand" feeding schedules are gaining ground for infants, self-demand is not observed when it comes to socialization outside the home. The daily schedule is an effort, with mother as chauffeur and booking agent, to cultivate all the currently essential talents, especially the gregarious ones. It is inconceivable to some supervising adults that a child might prefer his own company or that of just one other child.

The child is thus confronted by what we have termed his sociometric peers and is not surrounded by those who are his peers in less visible matters, such as temperament and taste. Yet since there are no *visible* differences he is hard put to it to justify, even to be aware of, these *invisible* differences. On the overt level the situation is highly standardized: any given child faces the culture of the fives or the sixes at a particular moment of the fashion cycle in child-training and child-amusement practices. Indeed it is this very standardization which, as we saw, weakens the power of the parents, whose deviation from the standards is felt by them and by the child to demonstrate their inexperience and inadequacy. In this setting the adults are anxious that the child succeed in the peer-group and therefore are concerned with his "adjustment." They, too, tend to ignore and even suppress invisible differences between their child and the children of others. Such differences might cast doubt on their own adjustment, their own correct tuning to the signals concerning child rearing.

The majority of children learn very fast under these conditions; the same adult authorities who patronize children's intellects (and therefore slow them down) are perhaps not sufficiently impressed with how poised in many social situations modern other-directed children are. These children are not shy, either with adults or with the opposite sex whom they have accompanied to proms and parties and seen daily in and out of school. This adaptability, moreover, prepares the child for a type of social mobility somewhat different from the social-climbing experiences of the parvenu in an inner-directed environment. The latter only rarely acquired the intellectual and social graces of his new associates —or he ridiculously accentuated them. He either kept his rough and lowly manners or painfully tried to learn new ones as he moved up; in either case the standard, limited code of conduct expected of him was unequivocal. In contrast with this the other-directed child is able to move among new associates with an almost automatic adjustment to the subtlest insignia of status.

Bearing in mind these positive achievements of other-directed sociability, let us turn our attention from what the peer-group teaches and evokes to what it represses. Today six-year-olds and up have a phrase—"he [or she] thinks he's *big*" (or "he thinks he's *something*"—which symbolizes the role of the peer-group in the creation of other-directed types. The effort is to cut everyone down to size who stands up or stands out in any direction. Beginning with the very young and going on from there, overt vanity is treated as one of the worst offenses, as perhaps dishonesty would have been in an earlier day. Being high-hat is forbidden.

Temper, manifest jealousy, moodiness—these, too, are offenses in the code of the peer-group. All "knobby" or idiosyncratic qualities and vices are more or less eliminated or repressed. And judgments of others by peer-group members are so clearly matters of taste that their expression has to resort to the vaguest phrases, constantly changed: cute, lousy, square, darling, good guy, honey, swell, bitch (without precise meaning), etc. Sociometry reflects this situation when it asks children about such things as whom they like to sit next to or not to sit next to, to have for a friend, a leader, and so on. The judgments can be meaningfully scaled because, and only because, they are all based on uncomplicated continua of *taste*, on which the children are constantly ranking each other.

But to say that judgments of peer-groupers are matters of taste, not of morality or even opportunism, is not to say that any particular child can afford to ignore these judgments. On the contrary he is, as never before, at their mercy. If the peer-group were—and we continue to deal here with the urban middle classes only—a wild, torturing, obviously vicious group, the individual child might still feel moral indignation as a defense against its commands. But like adult authorities in the other-directed socialization process, the peer-group is friendly and tolerant. It stresses fair play. Its conditions for entry seem reasonable and well meaning. But even where this is not so, moral indignation is out of fashion. The child is therefore exposed to trial by jury without any defenses either from the side of its own morality or from the adults. All the morality is the group's. Indeed, even the fact that it is a morality is concealed by the confusing notion that the function of the group is to have fun, to play; the deadly seriousness of the business, which might justify the child in making an issue of it, is therefore hidden.

"The Talk of the Town": The Socialization of Preferences. In the eyes of the jury of peers one may be a good guy one day, a stinker the next. Toleration, let alone leadership, depends on having a highly sensitive response to swings of fashion. This ability is sought in several ways. One way is to surrender any claim to independence of judgment and taste—a kind of plea of nolo contendere. Another is to build a plea for special consideration by acquiring unusual facility in one's duties as a consumer—in performance, that is, of the leisure arts. With good luck one may even become a taste and opinion leader, with great influence over the jury.

Each particular peer-group has its group fandoms and lingoes. Safety consists not in mastering a difficult craft but in mastering a battery of taste preferences and the mode of their expression. The preferences are for articles or "heroes" of consumption and for members of the group itself. The proper mode of expression requires feeling out with skill and sensitivity the probable tastes of the others and then swapping mutual likes and dislikes to maneuver intimacy.

Now some of this is familiar even in the period depending on inner-direction; it is important, therefore, to realize the degree to which training in consumer taste has replaced training in etiquette. Formal etiquette may be thought of as a means of handling relations with people with whom one does not seek intimacy. It is particularly useful when adults and young, men and women, upper classes and lower classes, are sharply separated and when a code is necessary to mediate exchanges across these lines. Thus etiquette can be at the same time a means of approaching people and of staying clear of them. For some, etiquette may be a matter of little emotional weight—an easy behavioral cloak; for others the ordering of human relations through etiquette can become highly charged emotionally—an evidence of characterological compulsiveness. But in either case etiquette is concerned not with encounters between indi-

viduals as such but with encounters between them as representatives of their carefully graded social roles.

In comparison with this, training in consumer taste, which
tends to replace etiquette among the other-directed, is
useful not so much across age and social class lines as within
the jury room of one's age and class peers. As in some
groups—children as well as adults—discussion turns to the
marginal differentiation between Cadillacs and Lincolns, so
in other groups discussion centers on Fords and Chevrolets.
What matters in either case is an ability at continual testing out of others' tastes, often a far more intrusive process
than the exchange of courtesies and pleasantries required
by etiquette. Not, of course, that the child always gets close
to the "others" with whom he is exchanging consumption
preferences—these exchanges are often mere gossip about
goods. Yet a certain emotional energy, even excitement,
permeates the transaction. For one thing, the other-directed
person acquires an intense interest in the ephemeral tastes
of the "others"—an interest inconceivable to the tradition-
directed or inner-directed child whose tastes have under-
gone a less differentiated socialization. For another thing,
the other-directed child is concerned with learning from
these interchanges whether his radar equipment is in proper
order.

It has always been true in social classes dominated by
fashion that to escape being left behind by a swing of fashion requires the ability to adopt new fashions rapidly; to
escape the danger of a conviction for being different from
the "others" requires that one can be different—in look
and talk and manner—from oneself as one was yesterday.
Here, also, it is necessary to see precisely what has changed.
In general the processes of fashion are expanded in class
terms and speeded in time terms. In the leisure economy of
incipient population decline the distributive machinery of
society improves, in terms of both income distribution and
goods distribution. It becomes possible to accelerate swings
of fashion as well as to differentiate goods by very minute
gradients. For, in its late stages, mass production and mass

distribution permit and require a vast increase not only in quantity but in qualitative differences among products—not only as a consequence of monopolistic efforts at marginal differentiation but also because the machinery and organization are present for rapidly designing, producing, and distributing a wide variety of goods.

This means that the consumer trainee has a lot more to learn than in the early days of industrialization. To take one example, the foreigner who visits America is likely to think that salesgirls, society ladies, and movie actresses all dress alike, as compared with the clear status differences of Europe. But the American knows—has to know if he is to get along in life and love—that this is simply an error: that one must look for small qualitative differences that signify style and status, to observe for instance the strained casualness sometimes found in upper-class dress as against the strained formality of working-class dress. In the days of etiquette the differences were far more sharp.

One must listen to quite young children discussing television models, automobile styling, or the merits of various streamliners to see how gifted they are as consumers long before they have a decisive say themselves—though their influence in family councils must not be underestimated. Children join in this exchange of verdicts even if their parents cannot afford the gadgets under discussion; indeed, the economy would slow down if only those were trained as consumers who at any given moment had the wherewithal.

The wider ambit of taste socialization today is shown in still another decisive change from the era depending on inner-direction. Then, by the rules of etiquette and class, certain spheres of life were regarded as private: it was a breach of etiquette to intrude or permit intrusion on them. Today, however, one must be prepared to open up on cross-examination almost any sphere in which the peer-group may become interested. It may become fashionable, as some articles in the "Profile of Youth" series in the *Ladies' Home Journal* have shown, for young girls to discuss their rivals' necking techniques with their particular partner.[1] While the game of post office is old, the break-down of privacy for reasonably serious love-making is new. Dating at twelve and thirteen, the child is early made aware of the fact that his taste in emotions as well as in consumer goods must be socialized and available for small talk. Whereas etiquette built barriers between people, socialized exchange of consumer taste requires that privacy either be given up, or be kept, like a liberal theologian's God, in some interstices of one's nature. Before the peer-group jury there is no privilege against self-incrimination.

The same forces that consolidate the socialization of tastes also make for more socialized standards of performance. The other-directed child, learning to play the piano, is in daily competition with studio stars. He cannot remember a period when either his peers or their adult guides were not engaged in comparing his performance with these models. Whatever he attempts—an artistic accomplishment, a manner of speaking, a sleight-of-hand trick—the peer-group is on hand to identify it in some way and to pass judgment on it with the connoisseurship typical of the mass-media audience. Soon enough this process becomes internalized, and the child feels himself in competition with Eddie Duchin or Horowitz even if no one else is around. Hence it is difficult for the other-directed child to cultivate a highly personalized gift: the standards are too high, and there is little private time for maturation.

The newer pattern of popularity depends less on ability to play an instrument than on ability to express the proper musical preferences. In the fall of 1947 I conducted some interviews among teen-agers in Chicago concerning their

[1] A student has written me: "In male bull sessions one can no longer play the gentleman and keep quiet about sexual adventures. He has to furnish names, dates, and all the exact details of the conquest. Where fellows get into trouble is when they have a sincere feeling for a girl and yet are forced to tell. The measure of the peer-group's strength and their other-directedness is that they can be forced to tell."

tastes in popular music and also consulted professional musicians, juke-box listings, and other sources to round out my impressions. My interest was principally in seeing how these young people used their musical interests in the process of peer-group adjustment. Like the "trading cards" which symbolize competitive consumption for the eight- to eleven-year-olds, the collection of records seemed to be one way of establishing one's relatedness to the group, just as the ability to hum current tunes was part of the popularity kit. The requirements were stiffer among girls than boys, though the latter were not exempt. Tunes meant people: roads to people, remembrances of them. At the same time the teen-agers showed great anxiety about having the "right" preferences. When I had the occasion to interview a group its individual members looked around to see what the others thought before committing themselves—at least as to specific songs or records, if not as to a general type of music, such as symphonic or hillbilly, where they might be certain as to their group's reactions. Readers who have not themselves observed the extent of this fear of nonconformity may be inclined to dismiss it by remarking that young people have always been conformists in their groups. True; yet it seems to me that the point is one of degree and that the need for musical conformity is today much more specialized and demanding than it was in an earlier era, when some children could be, or were forced by their parents to be, musical, and others could leave music alone.

Even among those interviewed who took piano lessons musical interest as such seemed virtually nonexistent. One boy of fourteen did appear to have genuine musical interests, playing "classics" on the piano. His mother told the interviewer, however, that she was not letting him practice too much lest he get out of step with the other boys, and was insisting that he excel in sports. "I hope to keep him a normal boy," she said. These research experiences seem to hint that preferences in the consumption field are not viewed as a development of the human ability to relate oneself discriminatingly to cultural objects. For the objects are hardly given meaning in private and personal values when they are so heavily used as counters in a preferential method of relating oneself to others. The cultural objects, whatever their nature, are mementos that somehow remain unhumanized by the force of a genuinely fetishistic attachment.

Moving somewhere beyond mere taste-exchanging are those opinion leaders[2] who try to influence verdicts as well as to repeat them—a dangerous game indeed. The risks are minimized, however, by playing within the limits imposed by marginal differentiation. Thus my interviews showed that each age group within a limited region and class had its own musical taste; the younger ones, for instance, liked "sweet" stuff that was "corn" to those slightly older. Within this general trend a girl might decide that she could not stand Vaughn Monroe or that Perry Como was tops. If she expressed herself so forcibly in detail, the chances were that she was, or wanted to be, an opinion leader. For many of the young people did not express any strong likes or specific dislikes—though they might share a strong revulsion against a whole taste range, like hot jazz or hillbilly. These latter were the opinion followers, scarcely capable even of marginal differentiation.

---

[2]The concept of the opinion leader and empirical methods for spotting him in a community have been developed particularly by Paul Lazarsfeld, Robert K. Merton, C. Wright Mills of the Bureau of Applied Social Research of Columbia University, and Bernard Berelson of the University of Chicago. The concept is an important one for our purposes, since the spread of other-directed patterns beyond the metropolitan centers is often due to the influence of opinion leaders who have learned these patterns while away at high school, at college, or on a job and who continue to keep in touch with the newer values through the mass media, which in turn support their efforts with their local "constituency." The Columbia group has observed this process in the spread of attitudes and preferences; to see how these in turn shape character is a more complex and as yet unaccomplished task. Walter Bagehot has some interesting speculations on the problem. *Physics and Politics*, ed. Barzun (New York, Alfred A. Knopf, 1948), pp. 91 *et seq.*

The other-directed person's tremendous outpouring of energy is channeled into the ever expanding frontiers of consumption, as the inner-directed person's energy was channeled relentlessly into production. Inner-directed patterns often discouraged consumption for adults as well as children. But at other times, and especially in the higher social strata less affected by Puritan asceticism, the inner-directed person consumed—with time out, so to speak, for saving and for good behavior—as relentlessly as he (or his progenitors) produced. Most clearly in the case of upper-class conspicuous consumption, he lusted for possessions and display, once the old tradition-directed restraints had worn away. He pursued clear acquisition and consumption goals with a fierce individualism. To be sure, his goals were socially determined, but less by a contemporary union of consumers than by inherited patterns of desire, hardly less stable than the desire for money itself. Goals such as fine houses, fine horses, fine women, fine objets d'art—these could be investments because their value scarcely changed in the scale of consumption preference.

These relatively stable and individualistic pursuits are today being replaced by the fluctuating tastes which the other-directed person accepts from his peer-group. Moreover, many of the desires that drove men to work and to madness in societies depending on inner-direction are now satisfied relatively easily; they are incorporated into the standard of living taken for granted by millions. But the craving remains. It is a craving for the satisfactions others appear to attain, an *objectless* craving. The consumer today has most of his potential individuality trained out of him by his membership in the consumers' union. He is kept within his consumption limits not by goal-directed but by other-directed guidance, kept from splurging too much by fear of others' envy, and from consuming too little by his own envy of the others.

Today there is no fast line that separates these consumption patterns of the adult world from those of the child, except the consumption objects themselves. The child may consume comics or toys while the adult consumes editorials and cars; more and more both consume in the same way. In the consumers' union of the peer-group the child's discipline as a consumer begins today very early in life—and lasts late. The inner-directed child was supposed to be job-minded even if the job itself was not clear in his mind. Today the future occupation of all moppets is to be skilled consumers.

This is visible early in children's play-at-consumption, facilitated by a noticeable increase in the range of children's toys. Added to boys' toys, for example production-imitating equipment like trucks and steam shovels or toy soldiers and miniature war matériel, is a whole new range of objects modeled after the service trades: laundry trucks, toy telephones, service stations, and so forth. Added to girls' toys, the doll and her wardrobe, are juvenile make-up outfits and voice recorders.

These props of the child's playtime hours, however, are not so striking as the increasing rationalization of children's preferences in everything they consume. In the period of inner-direction children accepted trade-marked cereals largely because that was what was set for them at table. Today they eat Wheaties, or some other breakfast food, to the tune of some specific reason that all can talk about: "Wheaties makes champions." And comics, children will say if pressed, "relax champions." In this way the other-directed child rapidly learns that there always is and always must be a reason for consuming anything. One "reason" is that the commodity he is consuming is the "best" in its line. As the child develops as a consumer trainee, advertising no longer is given all the credit for answering the question of what is the best in its line. The product approved by most of the others, or by a suitable testimonial from a peer consumer, becomes the "best." The most popular products, by this formula, are the products that happen to be used by the most popular. And to be sure, these pace setters themselves have a "reason," often enough picked out from the mass media, if not from the advertising pages; thus the hunt for the reason goes on in an endless regress. Blake wrote: "The child's toys and the old man's reasons/Are the fruits of the two seasons." In the consumers' union, toys and reasons become amalgamated and, as already stated, the line between childhood and age tends to become an amorphous one.

These patterns place extra burdens on girls, partly because women are the accepted consumption leaders in our society, partly because women, much more than men, feel pressure to play any role they are accepted in by the men. At every social level boys are permitted a greater amount of aggression than girls; they are also permitted a wider range of preferences and can get by with a good deal of aggressive resistance to the taste-exchanging process.

Finally, the child consumer trainee becomes a consumer tutor in the home circle, "bringing up" mother as well as father. *Life* magazine once ran a leading article on "Teen-age Fun," showing the etiquettes and pastimes prevailing in certain American cities; these pastimes were news even to some recent high-school graduates. Teen-agers must initiate adults rather than vice versa; typical is the case, also cited in *Life*, where teachers at a Denver high school imitated the idiomatic greeting style of the "most popular" boy.

THE ANTAGONISTIC COOPERATORS OF THE PEER-GROUP

It is, possibly, no accident that it was his *greeting style* on which this boy exercised his gifts for opinion leadership and marginal differentiation. For indeed, over and beyond the socialization of consumption preferences and the exchange of consumption shoptalk by the consumers' union, the membership is engaged in *consuming itself.* That is, people and friendships are viewed as the greatest of all consumables; the peer-group is itself a main object of consumption, its own main competition in taste. The "sociometric" exchange of peer-group ratings is ceaseless and is carried on, as a conversation with the self, in "private" also; who is my best friend, my next best, and so on, down to the most disliked. The more thoroughly other-directed the individual is, the more unhesitatingly able he is to classify his preferences and to compare them with those of others. In fact, as compared with their inner-directed predecessors, other-directed children are extraordinarily knowledgeable about popularity ratings. Physical prowess probably remains a chief road, though declining, to status among working-class boys. However, popularity among upper middle-class boys and girls seems to hinge on much more vague criteria, frequently impenetrable to the adult observer but, while they last, crystal clear to the peer-group itself.

The tremendous competitive energies which the inner-directed person had available for the sphere of production and, secondarily, for consumption seem now to flow into competition for the much more amorphous security of the peer-group's approval. But just because it is approval for which one is competing one must repress one's overt competitiveness. Here the phrase "antagonistic cooperation," borrowed from other contexts, is apt.

This transformation is so important that we devote several sections to it in Chapter VI, but now we need only note a few reference points. The parents, harking back as they do in their character structures to an earlier era, are themselves competitive—more overtly so than the children. Much of our ideology—free enterprise, individualism, and all the rest—remains competitive and is handed down by parents, teachers, and the mass media. At the same time there has been an enormous ideological shift favoring submission to the group, a shift whose decisiveness is concealed by the persistence of the older ideological patterns. The peer-group becomes the measure of all things; the individual has few defenses the group cannot batter down. In this situation the competitive drives for achievement sponsored in children by the remnants of inner-direction in their parents come into conflict with the cooperative demands sponsored by the peer-group. The child therefore is forced to rechannel the competitive drive for achievement, as demanded by the parents, into his drive for approval from the peers. Neither parent, child, nor the peer-group itself is particularly conscious of this process. As a result all three participants in the process may remain unaware of the degree to which the force of an older individualistic ideology provides the energies for filling out the forms of a newer, group-oriented characterology.

IV

STORYTELLERS AS TUTORS IN TECHNIQUE: CHANGES IN THE AGENTS OF CHARACTER FORMATION

(Continued)

A. I like Superman better than the others because they can't do everything Superman can do. Batman can't fly and that is very important.

Q. Would you like to be able to fly?

A. I would like to be able to fly if everybody else did, but otherwise it would be kind of conspicuous.

From an interview with a twelve-year-old girl.[1]

LANGUAGE, as we noted in the previous chapter, becomes a refined and powerful peer-group tool. For the insiders language becomes a chief key to the taste and mood currents that are prevalent in this group at any moment. For the outsiders, including adult observers, language becomes a mysterious opacity, constantly carrying peer-group messages which are full of precise meanings that remain untranslatable.

When we look more closely at the use of language in the young peer-groups we see how various its aspects are. Language itself becomes a sort of consumption product. It is used neither to direct the work economy, nor to relate the self to others in any really intimate way, nor to recall the past, nor yet as sheer word play. Rather it is used in the peer-groups today much as popular tunes seem to be used:

---

[1] Katherine M. Wolfe and Marjorie Fiske, "The Children Talk About Comics," *Communications Research 1948–1949*, ed. Paul F. Lazarsfeld and Frank Stanton (New York, Harper, 1949), pp. 26–27.

as a set of counters by which one establishes that one is "in" and by which one participates in the peer-group's arduously self-socializing "work." And the peer-groups, while they exercise power more than ever before through the use of words, are more than ever before the victims of words. While they learn to cling desperately to words—most signals are given in words—at the same time they learn to distrust them. As we have seen, verdicts in the peer-group are often quite ambiguous. Some of the older words, such as "bastard" and "skunk," remain, but their meaning is vaguer—they may even be said with a smile! Whole new glossaries crop up every few years.

The peer-group stands midway between the individual and the messages which flow from the mass media. The mass media are the wholesalers; the peer-groups, the retailers of the communications industry. But the flow is not all one way. Not only do the peers decide, to a large extent, which tastes, skills, and words, appearing for the first time within their circle, shall be given approval, but they also select some for wider publicity through contiguous groups and eventually back to the mass media for still wider distribution. If we look at this process we see that the individual who develops, say, a particular style of expression, is either ignored by the peers or accepted by them. If he and his style are accepted, his style is taken over by the group, and in at least this sense it is no longer *his*. But the same thing can happen to a given peer-group in its turn, as in the case of the boy with the individual greeting style we spoke of at the end of the last chapter. The mass media play the chief role in thus reducing to impersonality and distributing over a wide area the personal styles developed by individuals and groups.

In this chapter, however, our focus will be less on the media themselves and their patterns of operation and control than on the effects of imagery and storytelling on the child audience. And of course these effects cannot be considered in isolation from the constellation of parents, teachers, and peer-groupers who operate on the assembly line of character. If we find, for instance, a child who seems more affected by print than by people, it may be because people are so overwhelming for him that he must take refuge in print. Furthermore, cultures differ very much in the perceptions they stress in teaching the child to differentiate among images and to differentiate among people. But in general it seems fair to say that the storytellers are indispensable agents of socialization. They picture the world for the child and thus give both form and limits to his memory and imagination.[2]

In exploring this topic we must not confuse the genres of literature with the problem of social-psychological effects. I am going to use "story" broadly in this chapter to include not only poetry and fiction but any fabulous and embroidered account: a "true" newsreel might by this definition be a story.

Societies in the phase of incipient population decline can afford, can technically provide, and have both the time and the need to receive a bounteous flow of imagery from urban centers of distribution. Industrialism and mass literacy seem to go together. These same societies, moreover, rely more heavily than their predecessors on character-forming agencies outside the home. Hence, as we would expect, the storytellers of the mass media play a considerable role among other-directed children. We can see what has changed in recent generations only by contrasting today's experience with that of children in societies depending on tradition-direction and inner-direction.

I. SONG AND STORY IN THE STAGE OF TRADITION-DIRECTION

Chimney-corner media. Almost by definition, a society depending on tradition-direction makes use of oral traditions, myths, legends, and songs as one of its mechanisms

---

[2]See the remarkable discussion by Ernest Schachtel, "On Memory and Childhood Amnesia," *Psychiatry*, X (1947), 1; see also Evelyn T. Riesman, "Childhood Memory in the Painting of Joan Miró," *ETC*, VI (1949), 160.

for conveying the relative unity of its values. Ambiguity is not absent from these forms. But since the story is told children by a family member or a person closely connected with the family, it can be modulated for them and indeed, since they can criticize, question, and elaborate, put into a manageable context by them. Storytelling, that is, remains a handicraft industry, carried on in the home and in connection with the other processes of socialization that go on there.

Under these circumstances, it is not surprising that songs and stories rendered in face-to-face performance among relatives and friends are often baldly cautionary tales; they tell what happens to those who disobey the community or the supernatural authorities. Or they illustrate by reference to the illustrious what kind of person one ought to be in the culture in terms of such traits as bravery and endurance. A surprising number of tales, however, in many cultures depending on tradition-direction are not cautionary in this direct sense. As in the Bible, some tales recount rebellions, successful or tragic, against the powers that be—though in many cases the theme of rebellion is disguised.

Tales of Norm and "Abnorm." The rebellious note struck in these tales indicates that even in a society depending on tradition-direction there still remain strivings which are not completely socialized. While people accept the harness of their culture, and can hardly conceive of another, they are not unaware of constraint: their stories, as frequently their dreams, are the refuge and succor of this awareness and help to make it possible to go on with daily life. The communal load of shame and guilt is reduced by the common "confession," the common release which the myth permits. There is in these myths, then, a good deal of "realism" about stubborn, unsocialized human nature—this is one reason they appeal to us across the centuries and across the cultural boundaries. They show people to be more fierce, more jealous, more rebellious than appears on the surface.

Why is this so? It appears that if people were only "adjusted"—if they never had even a thought which transcended the cultural prohibitions—life would have so little savor as to endanger the culture itself. Cultures depending upon tradition-direction usually manage to institutionalize a degree of rebellion not only for their deviants but for everybody. Sometimes this is done on a life-cycle basis. Thus some cultures permit, even encourage, sauciness from children only to clamp down on the adult; others allow the older women a bawdiness denied the younger ones. Sometimes there are special days—feast days—when bars are down.

To the degree that the aperture for rebellion lies in the realm of culturally approved fantasy, the socializing function of the tales and stories which are the predecessors of the mass media is a dual one. The elders use the stories to tell the young: you must be like so-and-so if you are to be admired and to live up to the noble traditions of the group. But the young are also told—sometimes in the very same message—that there have been people like so-and-so who broke the rules, who did many worse things than you ever did, and perhaps ever dreamed of, and whether he lived to tell the tale or not, he *did live* and we speak of him. This very ambivalence of the stories helps the young to integrate their forbidden impulses by recognizing them as part of their legacy as human beings, making it possible to form an underground connection, via myth, between repressed sectors of the adults and sectors of the young. Finally, these stories make it possible to hold the young to both more and less than what they see around them, either of approved behavior or of behavior which, while disapproved, is still done; in other words, they provide models for behavior not to be found completely in any given face-to-face group.

And yet it is more complicated than that. Indeed, we may suppose that the change to inner-direction occurs first in circles which, through literacy or otherwise, acquire access to many multiplying ambiguities of direction. As in the mathematical theory of communications all channels mix what is technically called noise with what is technically called information and thus limit the freedom of the sender, so also messages intended or believed to socialize the young cannot help but contain noises which may have diverse effects, effects which may oversocialize or undersocialize them.

II. The Socializing Functions of Print in the Stage of Inner-direction

When societies enter the phase of transitional growth of population, formal schooling increases, in part to train people for the new, more specialized tasks of industry and agriculture, in part to absorb the young who are no longer needed on farms and whose schooling can be supported by the greater productivity of the society. Of course, these young people learn to read. But old as well as young are affected by the excitement and novelty of literacy: there is a widespread hunger for the press and for books—a hunger that the technology and distributive facilities arouse but do not entirely satisfy. This excitement, this hunger, is a sign of the characterological revolution which is accompanying the industrial one.

In the United States, as in other countries of incipient population decline, this hunger has abated; indeed, it has been succeeded for many by a kind of satiety with serious print, coupled with insatiability for the amusements and agenda of popular culture. To remind ourselves of the older pattern we can look at countries such as Mexico and Russia, now undergoing industrialization, where the old are avid for print and the young admired for learning. Some of this we can still see among the largely self-educated Negroes of the deep South who live among our surviving stratum of white and black illiterates.

How this development aided the shift from tradition-direction to inner-direction can be vividly traced in Thomas and Znaniecki's *Polish Peasant*.[3] These writers describe the

[3] W. I. Thomas and Florian Znaniecki, *The Polish Peasant in Europe and America* (New York, Knopf, 1927), II, 1367–1396.

way in which the Polish rural press helped to restructure attitudes and values among the peasantry at the turn of the last century. They show that an individual peasant who learned to read at that time did not merely acquire a skill with little impact on his character; rather he made a decisive break with the primary group, with tradition-direction. The press picked him up at this turning point and supported his uncertain steps away from the primary group by criticizing the values of that group and by giving him a sense of having allies, albeit anonymous ones, in this move.

In this way the press helped link the newly individuated person to the newly forming society. The Polish press also supported very specific "character-building" measures, such as temperance and thrift, and fostered scientific farming as the American agricultural extension services have done; science was viewed as a kind of inner-directed morality as against the superstition of the remaining, tradition-directed peasantry. These attitudes, expounded in newspaper non-fiction, were reinforced in the same media by highly moralistic fiction.

Thus the reader could escape into print from the criticisms of his neighbors and could test his inner-direction against the models given in the press. And by writing for the press himself, as he occasionally might do as local correspondent, he could bring his performance up for approval before an audience which believed in the magic attached to print itself—much like the Americans who, in the last century, contributed poetry to the local press. By this public performance, no longer for a face-to-face audience, the former peasant confirmed himself on his inner-directed course.

THE WHIP OF THE WORD

The tradition-directed person had not only a traditional standard of living but a traditional standard of how hard and long he should work; and print served, along with other agencies of socialization, to destroy both of these standards. The inner-directed man, open to "reason" via print, often develops a character structure which drives him to work longer hours and to live on lower budgets of leisure and laxity than would have been deemed possible before. He can be driven because he is ready to drive himself.

Words not only affect us temporarily; they change us, they socialize or unsocialize us. Doubtless the printing press alone cannot completely assure any particular form of social coercion—and of course not all children, even in the inner-directed middle class, were readers. But print can powerfully rationalize the models which tell people what they ought to be like. Reaching children directly as well as through their parents and teachers, it can take the process of socialization out of the communal chimney corner of the era depending on tradition-direction and penetrate into the private bedrooms and libraries of the rising middle class: the child is allowed to gird himself for the battle of life in the small circle of light cast by his reading lamp or candle.

To understand this more fully we must realize that the rise of literacy affects not only the content and style of the literary and journalistic genres but also their audience reception. The increased quantitative flow of content brings about an enormous increase in each child's power to select, as compared with the era of tradition-direction. As a result, more and more of the readers begin to see messages not meant for them. And they read them in situations no longer controlled and structured by the teller—or by their own participation. This increase in the number, variety, and "scatter" of the messages, along with the general impersonalization in print which induces these specific effects, becomes one of the powerful factors in social change. The classic instance in western history, of course, is the translation of the Vulgate into the spoken languages, a translation which allowed the people to read a book which only the priests could read before.

Some of the difficulties of discussing the shift from the era depending on tradition-direction to that of inner-direction arise from the teleological drift of the language we are likely to use. For example, we are prone to overlook the unintended audience because it is always easier to assume that a given medium was deliberately aimed at the audience it actually succeeded in reaching. Yet there is no proof that the media have ever been so accurate in aim. The very impersonality of the situation in which print is absorbed helps to increase the chances of under-reception or over-reception. Thus the aristocrats were often displeased by what they considered the over-reception to mobility themes in many they would have liked to keep "in their place."

The over-effects I have most in mind, however, are those in individuals whose characterological guilts and tensions were increased by the pressure of print. Their character structure simply could not handle the demand put upon them in a society depending on inner-direction. Their gyroscopes spun wildly and erratically. Not finding justification in print—not finding, as many modern readers do, a "union of sinners," the "One Big Union" of mankind extending back through the past—they experienced print simply as an intensified proof of their maladjustment. A colonial divine armed with print could get his readers to cast themselves into hell-fire on weekdays, even if he could only address them in person on Sundays.

Thus, while the myths and symbolism of the societies depending on tradition-direction support the tradition by integrating the rebellious tendencies of the listener into a pattern of the culture, the word-in-print may disorient as well as orient its audience. This is evident in the cry for censorship which goes up as soon as literacy becomes widespread. And not only formal censorship. In America the increasing piety of print, if we compare, for instance, today's press with that of the early republic, may be in part explained by the sheer weight of the informal pressure put by near-universal literacy on editors who take their responsibility seriously. As the editor of a metropolitan paper used to say if his staff verged on bawdry: "Don't forget, gentlemen, that this paper goes into the *homes*." Or as the *New York Times* puts it: "All the news that's fit to print."

While it is beyond my ability to measure precisely to what degree the media of the early capitalist period might have been "dysfunctional," by reaching unintended audiences in unintended ways, it seems reasonable to suppose that print contains more noise along its channels than does oral, face-to-face transmission.

MODELS IN PRINT

One main purpose of print in the period dependent on inner-direction is to teach the child something about the variety of adult roles he may enter upon and to permit him to "try on" these roles in fantasy. Life during the period of transitional population growth differs from earlier epochs in that the adult frequently engages in activities which the growing child no longer observes or understands. He needs not only the rich vicariousness of print but also a mode of internal direction other than tradition to guide him in unaccustomed places and situations. Both the printed media and other forms of popular culture meet this need by adding their own spurs to the parents' admonitions on behalf of ambition as well as by offering more specific guidance about the variety of new paths to success.

These new paths, in both northern and southern lands after the Renaissance, are conceived and described in adult terms. For in the earlier stages of population growth adult life is not long, on the average; the age difference—and perhaps the difference in maturity—between the literate child and the full-grown adult is less than in the period of incipient decline of population. Moreover, while the distribution of imagery and print becomes wider and cheaper than ever before, there are still many people excluded by poverty from the storyteller's market; some of these are also the overworked young. In such a society the adult stories and adult styles of narrative are often made to do for children. Even when the trick, later so prevalent, of using the child's own language, gets started, the storyteller works on the notion that he can more successfully instill *adult* ideas if he uses the language of children.

Among the earliest signposts erected on the printed path to success, aside from the indirect guides of catechism and religious teaching, were the great authorities on etiquette.

A volume like Castiglione's *The Courtier*, for example, was meant for adults; but there was nothing else on the subject for the near-adult to read. At the same time people were willing to assume, as Lord Chesterfield did, that the young man was ready in his teens to operate successfully in situations requiring etiquette. In the Protestant lands and classes however, after 1600 or so, the purpose of print is concerned more and more directly with how to succeed not in love or diplomacy but in business. Then follows the commercial inspirational literature that reached a sort of climax in Victorian England with the success biographies written by Samuel Smiles—and in the United States with the Horatio Alger books, which come closer to being slanted for the teen-age market.

Franklin's *Poor Richard's Almanack*, the text selected by Max Weber as a typical self-inspirational document of the period of the Protestant ethic, was preceded by books such as *Pilgrim's Progress* or *Robinson Crusoe* which, while not explicitly concerned with proper conduct for would-be enterprisers, nevertheless purvey many similar exhortations. Thus, in *Pilgrim's Progress* we can trace the motive of social election and salvation which can so easily become secularized, while in *Robinson Crusoe* the motive of economic self-sufficiency is expressed in its classical paradigm. Both works aim to fire the ambition and élan, spiritual and adventurous, of inner-directed youth. Thus, with an expanding bourgeois market, marked changes occur in the style of myth, as contrasted with the pre-industrial era dependent on tradition-direction. In the Middle Ages, for example, the individual learns about human nature from accounts no less realistic because couched in symbolic language—whether Christian, classical, or folk. Often, as is well known, they are not in verbal form at all, like the superabundance of messages in the glass and stone of a cathedral. The child is trained to understand—or, better, he is not trained away from understanding—symbolic meanings. As against this, the rising middle class dependent on inner-direction establishes for itself a new style of realism from which any direct use of symbolism is rigorously excluded.

This documentary style is one literary index of an era increasingly dependent on inner-direction. There is leisure in such an era for fiction—but little for fantasy. Defoe may be taken as archetypical. He used a variety of techniques, such as first-person narration, elaborate descriptions of food, clothing, and shelter, diary-like accounts of money transactions, and collaborative witnesses, to provide a realistic setting for his wildly adventurous tales. In this respect he is certainly the ancestor of the comic book, which excels in exploiting realism of detail as a distraction to hide improbability of situation. Such handling of literary material is connected in subtle ways with the handling of life experiences generally for the inner-directed middle-class Protestant. For him life is lived in its detailed externals; symbolic meanings must be filtered through the strenuously concrete.

Gradually, the early naturalism of Defoe gives way, both in England and on the continent, to a more detailed handling of the complex interpersonal relations of town life that arise in the era of transitional growth of population when people are pouring into the cities. With the growth of social classes in the modern sense, the novel begins to concern itself with subtle class differences between individuals: rises, falls, and collisions of status are perhaps its prime preoccupation. The child is instructed in an ambiguous social world, into which he will later move, by learning to recognize the subtly individualizing traits that bespeak class position and class morality.[4] Thus fiction as well as almanac and manual provide vocational (and status-oriented avocational) guidance.

To us today many of the individuals in the early Victorian novels, or in American Victorian melodrama like *East Lynne* or *Intolerance*—or even in some of Balzac's novels—appear as stereotypes. To their earliest audiences, however, these studies of personality and class in a society of shifting possibilities—a society of more people, and more

---

[4] Compare the brilliant discussion by Lionel Trilling in "Art and Fortune," *Partisan Review*, XV (1948), 1271.

people moving around—were perhaps not clichés which hindered understanding but explorations of a confusing world, helping to make sense of that world for the young. One can still attend a modern rural high school production of *Aaron Slick of Punkin Crick* and see to what extent an unsophisticated inner-directed audience will respond to the characterological "realism" of the play in terms of the older stereotypes of class, ambition, and virtue.

Biography as well as fiction allows children, in a society dependent on inner-direction, to move in imagination away from home and into a rationalized world—cooperating in this way with the parental installation of internal, self-piloting processes. In the George Washington myth, for instance, little boys learn that they may grow up to be president and are given scales by which to measure and discipline themselves for the job during boyhood: If they do not tell lies, if they work hard, and so on—if, that is, they act in their boyhoods as the legendary Washington acted in his—then they may succeed to his adult role. The role, moreover, by its very nature, is a continuing one; somebody is always president; thus its heroes do not have the once-for-all quality of those in the myths and legends of the earlier era. In fantasy the little boy not only identifies with young Washington in the French and Indian wars but also with the adult role of president—either role will take him far from home, socially and geographically.

What the story of George Washington could be for a white child the story of Booker T. Washington could be for a black one. Booker T. Washington's whole career could be described as an effort to turn the Negro away from dependence on tradition-direction toward dependence on inner-direction. One of his books addressed to Negroes was called *Character Building*; and *The Negro Worker*, a journal published at Tuskegee, with its strong emphasis on thrift, diligence, and manners, is one of the laggard remnants (of course, under violent attack from northern urban Negroes) of a vast literature concerned not with improving "personality" but with improving "character."

THE OVERSTEERED CHILD

There is, however, a danger for the child in such pious biographical portraits of exemplary persons and roles because of the very fact that he can read in isolation, without the intervention either of adults or peers; he can be "oversteered," that is, find himself set on a course he cannot realistically follow. The inner-directed child, trying to shape his character according to the ideals presented in print, does not see these models, any more than he sees his parents, in a state of undress. There is none of the familiarity with the hero, even the gods in the guise of heroes, to be found in the orally-mediated myths of the society depending on tradition-direction. Thus, Washington or Cromwell, Garibaldi or Bismarck, Edison or Ford, take on some of the awesomeness of the Calvinist God. The result for many is a dreadful insecurity as to whether they live up to their exalted models. This insecurity not even the parents (when they do not themselves make matters worse by trying to be such models) can easily assuage.

Nevertheless, this unmitigated pressure for inner-directed activity in pursuit of goodness and fame succeeded, as we know, in producing in many cases an "adjusted" person because social conditions rewarded inhibitions and solaced insecurities. In other cases, however, the gap between the demand for inner-direction and the capacity for it became too great and the individual broke down—the revival meeting both released and renewed, at one class level, some of the emotional pressures of such a conflict.

I want to emphasize here the dangers of putting some of the task of socializing the child onto other than the face-to-face adults. Just as the whipping Kachinas of the Hopi Indians can tailor their punishing or initiatory blows to a particularly sensitive child, so the adults in the era of tradition-direction can see to it that the bite of the story is not too grim for any in the audience. The child in the inner-directed era, however, leaves home both to go to school and to go to books and other mass-media products; and here such mediation is no longer possible.

Moreover, the child in a period of rising literacy is much more likely than his parents to be able to read. Thus, while some children learn from books and plays how to act in a career which will be different from that of their parents— or indeed that it is possible to have such a career—other children, less able to conform in the characterologically prescribed ways, less self-disciplined and systematic, for instance, learn from precisely the same media how lost they are. They learn this particularly if their parents are lacking in the proper ethos and have not been able to give them the proper early training in inner-direction. Others may find that print reinforces their feelings of inadequacy vis-à-vis their parents if they are characterological black sheep unable to live up to steep demands of the home.

While the stream of print has many dangers, it is seldom without some alleviating tendencies, even in the theocratic regimes. Almost always there is an underground of a more picaresque sort in which the growing boy, if not his sister, can take some refuge. To be sure, the power of the parents in an era dependent on inner-direction may keep out such literature, just as the pastors in puritan countries might also keep it out of the community. But they can hardly destroy the refuge of print itself—and we must not forget that the great reading-hour storehouse of the era depending on inner-direction is the Bible and that the Bible is not one book but many, with an inexhaustible variety of messages.

Such a refuge may encourage and permit the child to free himself from his family and primary group; and he may learn to criticize what he leaves behind, as did the self-emancipating readers of the Polish peasant press. It opens up to him a whole range of models—the "five-foot wardrobe" from which he can try on new roles. The Renaissance is itself testimony to this potency of the written word. Individualistic strivings find support as well as oversupport in the variety of paths of life described in print and drama. To be alone with a book is to be alone in a new way.

III. The Mass Media in the Stage of Other-direction

THE CHILD MARKET

As we have already seen, in the era of incipient decline of population children begin their training as consumers at an increasingly young age. In America middle-class children have allowances of their own at four or five; they have, as opinion leaders in the home, some say in the family budget. The allowances are expected to be spent, whereas in the earlier era they were often used as cudgels of thrift. Moreover, the monopolistic competition characteristic of this era can afford, and is interested in, building up in the child habits of consumption he will employ as an adult. For he will live long, and so will the monopoly. Monopoly is, in fact, distinguished by this very ability to plan ahead, because it can afford specialists to do the planning as well as resources saved from profits to pay for it and its later implementation.

For all these reasons, then, it has become worth while for professional storytellers to concentrate on the child market; and as the mass media can afford specialists and market research on the particular age cultures and class cultures involved, the children are more heavily cultivated in their own terms than ever before. But while the educator in earlier eras might use the child's language to put across an adult message, today the child's language may be used to put across the advertiser's and storyteller's idea of what children are like. No longer is it thought to be the child's job to understand the adult world as the adult sees it; for one thing, the world as the adult sees it today is perhaps a more complicated one.[5] Instead, the mass media ask the child to see the world as "the" child—that is, the *other* child—sees it. This is partly the result of the technical ad-

---

[5] Certainly the adult literature is more complicated and/or more salacious on its top levels, as compared with the earlier era when both child and adult could read Mark Twain even at his most bitter, Dickens even at his most crude, H. G. Wells even at his most involved.

vances that make it possible for the movies to create the child world of Margaret O'Brien and her compeers, for the radio to have its array of Hardys, Aldriches, and other juveniles, and for advertising and cover art to make use of professional child models. The media have created a picture of what boyhood and girlhood are like (as during the war they created the picture of the GI, again using the considerably edited language of the soldier) and they force children either to accept or aggressively to resist this picture of themselves.

The child begins to be bombarded by radio and comics from the moment he can listen and just barely read. The bombardment—which of course inevitably over- and undershoots—hits specifically at very narrow age-grades. For example, there seems to be for many children a regular gradation of comic-reading stages: from the animal stories like *Bugs Bunny* to invincible heroes like *Superman*, and from there to heroes like *Batman* who, human in make-up, are vulnerable, though of course they always win. The study from which the quotation at the head of this chapter is taken finds that the children themselves are aware of the progression, aware of those laggards who still read romper media when they should have graduated to blue jeans.

To be sure, the change from the preceding era of innerdirection in America is not abrupt; such changes never are. Formerly the mass media catered to the child market in at least three fields: school texts or homilies, magazines designed for children, and penny dreadfuls. But when these are compared with the contemporary media we are at once aware of differences. The appraisal of the market by the writers of this earlier literature was amateurish in comparison with market research today. Moreover, they aimed generally to spur work drives and stimulate mobility rather than to effect any socialization of taste. The English boys' weeklies, as Orwell describes them,[6] usually opposed liquor and tobacco—as did the clergyman authors of school and

---

[6] George Orwell, *Dickens, Dali & Others* (New York, Reynal & Hitchcock, 1946), p. 76.

church readers. Such admonitions remind us of the "crime doesn't pay" lesson of the comics, a façade for messages of more importance. The boys' weeklies and their American counterparts were involved with training the young for the frontiers of production (including warfare), and as an incident of that training the embryo athlete might eschew smoke and drink. The comparable media today train the young for the frontiers of consumption—to tell the difference between Pepsi-Cola and Coca-Cola, as later between Old Golds and Chesterfields.

We may mark the change by citing an old nursery rhyme:

> "This little pig went to market;
> This little pig stayed at home.
> This little pig had roast beef;
> This little pig had none.
> This little pig went wee-wee-wee
> All the way home."

The rhyme may be taken as a paradigm of individuation and unsocialized behavior among children of an earlier era. Today, however, all little pigs go to market; none stay home; all have roast beef, if any do; and all say "we-we."

WINNER TAKE ALL?

Yet perhaps the most important change is the shift in the situation in which listening and reading occur. In contrast with the lone reader of the era of inner-direction, we have the group of kids today, lying on the floor, reading and trading comics and preferences among comics, or listening to "The Lone Ranger." When reading and listening are not communal in fact, they are apt to be so in feeling: one is almost always conscious of the brooding omnipresence of the peer-group. Thus the Superman fan quoted at the head of the chapter cannot allow herself to identify with Superman—the others would think her foolish—while they would not think her foolish for believing that flying is very important.

In a society dependent on tradition-direction children are, as we have seen, introduced to stories by adult story-tellers. The latter do not feel themselves to be in critical competition with the young. Hence they can encourage, or at least patronize, children's unsophisticated reactions of alarm or excitement at the tales they are told—and, later on, encourage the youngster's own tall talk and tale embroidery. But the peer-groupers who read or listen together without the protective presence of adults are in no such cozy relation of "listen my children and you shall hear . . ." They cannot afford to let go—to fly.

One correlate is that the comic book differs from the fairy tale in several important respects. In the fairy tale the protagonist is frequently an underdog figure, a younger child, an ugly duckling, a commoner, while the villain is frequently an authority figure, a king, a giant, a stepmother. In the comics the protagonist is apt to be an invulnerable or near-invulnerable adult who is equipped, if not with supernatural powers, at least with two guns and a tall, terrific physique. Magical aid comes to the underdog—who remains a peripheral character—only through the mediation of this figure. Thus, whereas Jack of *Jack and the Beanstalk* gains magical assistance chiefly through his own daring, curiosity, and luck, a comic-book Jack would gain magical assistance chiefly through an all-powerful helper. While vaguely similar themes may be found in the stories of Robin Hood and Sir Galahad, the comics show a quantitative increase in the role of the more or less invulnerable authority-hero.

The relative change in this pattern[7] is not the "fault" of the comics. These merely play into a style of reception that

---

[7] Here, too, the abruptness of the change from inner-direction should not be exaggerated. Eliot Freidson, studying the ability of young children to remember stories, found them much more apt to recall a few traditional fairy tales like *Goldilocks* or *The Three Little Pigs* than either Golden Books or comics or movies. "Myth and the Child: an Aspect of Socialization" (Master's thesis, University of Chicago, 1949).

is fitted to peer-group reading. Indeed, if other-directed child comic fans read or hear stories that are not comics they will read them as if they were comics. They will tend to focus on who won and to miss the internal complexities of the tale, of a moral sort or otherwise. If one asks them, then, how they distinguish the "good guys" from the "bad guys" in the mass media, it usually boils down to the fact that the former always win; they are good guys by definition.

But of course the child wants to anticipate the result and so looks for external clues which will help him pick the winner. In the comics this is seldom a problem: the good guys *look it*, being square-jawed, clear-eyed, tall men; the bad guys also look it, being, for reasons of piety, of no recognizable ethnic group but rather of a generally messy southern European frame—oafish and unshaven or cadaverous and oversmooth. But in movies (and in some comics with slinky beauties in them) this identification is not easy: the very types that are good guys in most comics may turn out to be villains after all. A striking example I have observed is the bafflement of several young comic fans at the movie portrayal of the Countess de Winter (Lana Turner) in *The Three Musketeers*. If she looked so nice, how could she be so mean?

Thus we come to a paradox. The other-directed child is trained to be sensitive to interpersonal relations, and often he understands these with a sophistication few adults had in the era of inner-direction. Yet he can be strikingly insensitive to problems of character as presented by his favorite storytellers; he tends to race through the story for its ending, or to read the ending first, and to miss just those problems of personal development that are not telltale clues to the outcome. It looks as though the situation of group reading, of having to sit on the jury that passes out Hooper ratings, forces the pace for the other-directed child. He cannot afford to linger on "irrelevant" detail or to daydream about the heroes. To trade preferences in reading and listening he need know no more about the heroes than the stamp trader needs to know about the countries the stamps come from.

Fairy tales and the Frank Merriwell books also emphasize winning; hence it is important to see the precise differences introduced by the contemporary media as well as by the changed focus of the readers. One striking difference is that between the older ambition and newer "antagonistic cooperation." Ambition I define as the striving for clear goals characteristic of the period of inner-direction; it may be a striving for fame or for goodness: to get the job, to win the battle, to build the bridge. Competition in the era depending on inner-direction is frequently ruthless, but at the same time people are in no doubt as to their place in the race—and that there is a race. If they feel guilt it is when they fail, not when they succeed. By contrast, "antagonistic cooperation" may be defined as an inculcated striving characteristic of the groups affected by other-direction. Here the goal is less important than the relationship to the "others." In this new-style competition people are often in doubt whether there is a race at all, and if so, what its goals are. Since they are supposed to be cooperative rather than rivalrous, they may well feel guilt about success and even a certain responsibility for others' failure.

Certainly, it is ambition that strikes us as an outstanding trait of the heroes of boys' literature in the era of inner-direction. Moreover, it is an ambition with which the child reader can identify, even if the particular goal—to fight Indians or find the treasure or North Pole or swim icy rivers or detect crime—is at the moment a remote one; that is, the reader could in fantasy emulate the moral qualities of the hero, such as his bravery and his self-control. Thus, while these heroes, like the modern heroes, almost invariably won, the reader was encouraged to be concerned not only with the final victorious outcome but with the inner struggles that preceded it and made it possible.

It is sometimes loosely said that the comic strip merely continues this older set of themes in a new medium, but the fact is that the themes change and the identifications change even more. Where, as often happens, children prefer comics in which the hero is not man but Superman or Plastic Man, possessing obviously unique powers, identification languishes: no amount of willpower, no correspondence course with Lionel Strongfort, will turn one into Superman even in the wildest flight of fantasy. And such flights of fantasy appear to be less available today. Exposed to ever more sophisticated media, the children are too hep for "unrealistic" daydreams; at the movies they soon learn the fine points and will criticize a Western because the hero fired seven shots running from his six-shooter. The media in turn encourage this realism with their color effects and sound effects, which exceed by far the realism of petty detail which Defoe and his successors strove for. The characters in much fiction of the era dependent on inner-direction were props—stereotypes of the sort indicated in the preceding section. In Jules Verne, for instance, it is the adventures, the mechanical details, not the characters, that are sharply delineated; the latter are loose-fitting uniforms into which many boys could fit themselves. The imaginative, tenebrous illustrations of an artist like Howard Pyle also left openings for identification on the part of the reader who wanted to picture himself as the hero.

Little of this looseness of fit remains for the imagination of the modern reader or listener to fill in. Though comic-strip and comic-book characterization is, if anything, less sharp, externals are pinned down conclusively: every detail of costuming and speech is given. This is the more necessary because, with so many mass-media heroes competing for attention, their portrayers must engage in marginal differentiation in search of their trade-mark. Bodies by Milton Caniff must be as instantly recognizable as bodies by Fisher.

There is paradox in the reception of this realism. On the one hand, every additional brush stroke of the comic-strip artist rules out identifications for millions; the small-breasted girl, for example, may find only disapproval for herself in the comics. On the other hand, the same realism is one source of the fear of being conspicuous in our little

Supergirl cited at the chapter head. If she were Superman, she would be instantly recognizable. She would lack the privacy of narcissism permitted the reader of an earlier day who could gloat over the fact that he was M. Vidocq or Sherlock Holmes—only nobody knew it.

These generalizations need not be pushed too far. There are children—at least one has heard of them—who identify with Superman, or, more easily, with Terry or the Saint. Nor is it out of the question to identify, at the same time, on one level of consciousness with the hero and on another level with the person he rescues. And while the heroes of the comics are ageless, having discovered the secret of eternal youth, the growing child can move from one hero to another who better fits his own changing needs and aspirations. These counter-tendencies are encouraged by the gadgetry—Superman cloaks, and so on—that relates children to their radio, movie, and comic-book heroes. But it would be a mistake to assume that each wearer of a Superman cloak identifies with Superman; he may only be a fan, wearing his hero's colors.

Perhaps it is also significant that the comic book compresses into a few minutes' reading time a sequence which, in the earlier era, was dragged out in many pages of print. Think of the Count of Monte Cristo's years in jail, his suffering, his incredible patience, and the industry and study of the abbé's teaching; both his gain and his vengeance are moralized by these prolongations, and he is an old man when, after many chapters, he wins. By contrast, the comic-book or radio-drama hero wins almost effortlessly; the very curtailment of the telling time itself makes this more apparent. To be sure, like his movie counterpart, this hero does frequently get beaten up, but this adds to excitement, not to morality or inner change, and helps justify an even worse beating administered to the "crooks."

Still another aspect of this change is worth looking at. If one does not identify with the winner but is at the very same time preoccupied with the process of winning itself, as the best handle by which one grasps a story, one is prepared for the role of consumer of others' winnings. One is prepared, that is, for the adult role of betting on the right horse, with no interest in the jockey or horse or knowledge of what it takes to be either. The content of the identification is impoverished to the point where virtually the only bond between reader and hero is the fact of the hero's winning. The spectator—the same holds for a quiz game, a sport contest, and, as we shall see, a political contest— wants to become involved with the winner simply in order to make the contest meaningful: this hope of victory makes the event exciting, while the game or contest or story is not appreciated for its own sake.

The victory of the hero, then, is only ostensibly a moral one. To be sure, vestiges of older moralities hang on, often as conventions enforced by censorship or the fear of it. But morality in the sense of a literary character's development, rather than morality in the sense of being on the side of law and right, is not depicted. Consequently, morality tends to become an inference from winning. Just as in a whodunit all appear guilty until they are retroactively cleared by finding the real killer, so the victory of the hero retroactively justifies his deeds and misdeeds. "Winner take all" becomes a tautology.

TOOTLE: A MODERN CAUTIONARY TALE

Parents are sometimes apt to assume that comic books and the radio, as the cheapest and most widespread media, are the principal vehicles of these newer attitudes and values and that, in a home barricaded against Roy Rogers and Steve Canyon, these patterns of audience response would also be excluded. The fact is, however, that many important themes of other-direction are introduced into the socializing and informative books of the non-comic variety which middle- and upper-middle-class children are given— conversely, these "educative" books are probably not without influence on the more socially conscious radio and comic-book artists. A whole range of these media teaches children the lesson given parents and teachers in many recent works on child development. The slant of that lesson is suggested by a passage from a book in use by teachers and PTA groups:

The usual and desirable developmental picture is one of increasing self-control on the part of the individual children, of increasingly smooth social or play technics, and of an emergence at adolescence or early adulthood of higher forms of cooperation. The adolescent should have learned better "to take it" in group activity, should have developed an improved, though not yet perfect, self-control, and should have real insight into the needs and wishes of others.[8]

Tootle the Engine (text by Gertrude Crampton, pictures by Tibor Gergely) is a popular and in many ways charming volume in the "Little Golden Books" series. It is a cautionary tale even though it appears to be simply one of the many books about anthropomorphic vehicles—trucks, fire engines, taxicabs, tugboats, and so on—that are supposed to give a child a picture of real life. Tootle is a young engine who goes to engine school, where two main lessons are taught: stop at a red flag and "always stay on the track no matter what." Diligence in the lessons will result in the young engine's growing up to be a big streamliner. Tootle is obedient for a while and then one day discovers the delight of going off the tracks and finding flowers in the field. This violation of the rules cannot, however, be kept secret; there are telltale traces in the cowcatcher. Nevertheless, Tootle's play becomes more and more of a craving, and despite warnings he continues to go off the tracks and wander in the field. Finally the engine schoolmaster is desperate. He consults the mayor of the little town of Engineville, in which the school is located; the mayor calls a town meeting, and Tootle's failings are discussed—of course Tootle knows nothing of this. The meeting decides on a course of action, and the next time Tootle goes out for a spin alone and goes

---

[8]M. E. Breckenridge and E. L. Vincent, *Child Development* (Philadelphia, W. B. Saunders, 1943), p. 456.

off the track he runs right into a red flag and halts. He turns in another direction only to encounter another red flag; still another—the result is the same. He turns and twists but can find no spot of grass in which a red flag does not spring up, for all the citizens of the town have cooperated in this lesson.

Chastened and bewildered he looks toward the track, where the inviting green flag of his teacher gives him the signal to return. Confused by conditioned reflexes to stop signs, he is only too glad to use the track and tears happily up and down. He promises that he will never leave the track again, and he returns to the roundhouse to be rewarded by the cheers of the teachers and the citizenry and the assurance that he will indeed grow up to be a streamliner.

The story would seem to be an appropriate one for bringing up children in an other-directed mode of conformity. They learn it is bad to go off the tracks and play with flowers and that, in the long run, there is not only success and approval but even freedom to be found in following the green lights.[9] The moral is a very different one from that of *Little Red Riding Hood*. She, too, gets off the track on her trip to the grandmother; she is taught by a wolf about the beauties of nature—a veiled symbol for sex. Then, to be sure, she is eaten—a terrifying fate—but in the end she and grandmother both are taken from the wolf's belly by the handsome woodchopper. The story, though it may be read as a cautionary tale, deals with real human passions, sexual and aggressive; it certainly does not present the rewards of virtue in any unambiguous form or show the adult world in any wholly benevolent light. It is, therefore, essentially realistic, underneath the cover of fantasy, or, more accurately, owing to the quality of the fantasy.

---

[9] It is not made clear in the story what happens to Tootle's schoolmates in engine school. The peer-group relations of Tootle, either to the other engines or the other citizens of Engineville, are entirely amiable, and Tootle's winning can hardly mean that others fail. Who can be sure that Tootle would want to be a streamliner if others were not to be streamliners too?

There is, perhaps, a streak of similar realism in *Tootle*. There the adults play the role we have described earlier: they manipulate the child into conformity with the peer-group and then reward him for the behavior for which they have already set the stage. Moreover, the citizens of Engineville are tolerant of Tootle: they understand and do not get indignant. And while they gang up on him with red flags they do so for his benefit, and they reward him for his obedience as if they had played no hand in bringing it about. Yet with all that, there is something overvarnished in this tale. The adult world (the teachers) is *not* that benevolent, the citizenry (the peer-group) *not* that participative and cooperative, the signals are *not* that clear, nor the rewards of being a streamliner that great or that certain. Nevertheless, the child may be impressed because it is all so nice—there is none of the grimness of Red Riding Hood. There is, therefore, a swindle about the whole thing—a fake like that the citizens put on for Tootle's benefit. At the end Tootle has forgotten that he ever did like flowers anyway—how childish they are in comparison with the great big grown-up world of engines, signals, tracks, and meetings!

AREAS OF FREEDOM

We have discussed the social situation in which the mass media of today are absorbed by their child readers. We have seen the effects of this situation on the process by which the reader identifies with the protagonists and their roles. We have stressed especially the ambiguously competitive nature of these identifications which on the one hand emphasize winning and on the other hand stringently limit all emotional identifications by the code of the peer-group.

If this were all, we would have to conclude that the peer-group, as one of the mediating agencies in child readership and listening, is simply open to manipulation by the professional storytellers. But I want to raise very briefly the alternative possibility: namely, that the peer-group may have a relatively independent set of criteria which helps it maintain not only marginal differentiation but even a certain leeway in relation to the media. It is conceivable that, in those peer-groups which succeed in feeding back styles and values to the mass media, there is some feeling of achievement, of having one's contribution recognized. To be sure, the feeling of having been invaded and chased by popularity or unpopularity off one's island of individuation will also be present, and the total outcome may depend on whether the peer-group feels the mass media to be in pursuit of it or whether the group enjoys playing follow the leader, when it is the leader.

In all probability it is rare enough that a youthful peer-group forces the mass media—and hence other peer-groups —to follow its lead. Far more frequent will be the peer-group's opportunity to establish its own standards of media criticism. Groups of young hot-jazz fans, for instance, have highly elaborate standards for evaluating popular music, standards of almost pedantic precision. We must go further, then, and ask whether there may be areas of privacy which children learn to find inside a superficial adjustment to the peer-group and under the cover of a superficial permeability to the mass media. In other words, we must re-explore the assumption made so far that the other-directed child is almost never alone, that by six or seven he no longer talks to himself, invents songs, or dreams unsupervised dreams.

We are aware that children who have been brought up on the radio can shut out its noise like those automatic devices that are dreamed up to silence commercials. Perhaps such children can also shut out the noise of the peer-group, even while they are contributing to it. Moreover, the comics themselves may be not only a part of peer-group consumption patterns but on occasion a refuge from the peer-group and a defiance against that official adult world which abhors the comics. We shall return in Part III to the question whether the mass media can foster autonomy as well as adjustment, independence from the peer-group as well as conformity to it.

V

THE INNER–DIRECTED ROUND OF LIFE

In
Memory of
Thomas Darling, Esq.
who died Nov. 30, 1789 ———
A Gentleman of strong mental powers,
well improved with science and literature,
——— to the study of philosophy,
habituated to contemplation and reading
——— in moral reasoning.
of deep penetration and sound judgment,
respected for modesty and candor,
benignity and self command
in his intercourse with mankind
honest and benevolent,
amiable in all the relations of social life
and filled a variety of public offices
with fidelity and dignity
eminent abilities as statesman and judge
an early professor of Christianity
its steady friend, ornament, and defender
with a rational and firm faith in his God
and Savior: he knew no other master.
A GRAVESTONE INSCRIPTION IN A NEW HAVEN CEMETERY

THE oldest historical types in America, in terms of the
scheme set forth in this book, are a few still partially tradition-directed people such as some of the French Canadians
of the northeast, the delta Negroes, and the Mexican "wet-
backs" of Texas. These groups survive from societies and
social classes whose modes of conformity were established
in a phase of high population growth potential. The next
oldest type, the inner-directed, survive from the period of

transitional population growth in America and abroad. They are still dominant in many regions and many occupations, even in the cities. They are also probably the most numerous type, if we include among them not only those whose inner-direction is clear and unequivocal but also many working-class people who aspire to be inner-directed but are actually unable to adjust either to inner-directed or to other-directed modes of conformity. Finally, the newest type, the other-directed, are the product of the changes in the agents of character formation discussed in the three preceding chapters—changes most pronounced in the big cities and among the upper income groups.

In this and the following two chapters we shall explore in more detail the way in which the shift of the American population curve into the phase of incipient decline corresponds to a change in the texture of adult work and play. Other-directed character types are produced not only by influences affecting the parents and other early character-forming agents but also by institutions that shape or re-shape the character of adults who grew up in an environment more undilutedly inner-directed. While children are the pioneers of the characterological frontiers of population, it is the adults who, even in a child-centered culture, run the engines, rig the signals, write the books and comics, and play politics and other grown-up games.

An inscription such as the one at the head of this chapter reminds us of one of the ideal types of men who flourished in an era depending on inner-direction. Not all of them, of course, were as good as Mr. Darling is said to have been; we must not equate inner-direction with conscience direction. A scoundrel who knows what he aims for can be as unequivocally inner-directed as a God-fearing puritan. Yet as we turn now to recapture the flavor of an era that is near enough to be thought familiar and not far enough away to be fully understood, it is well to think of a man who knew no other master than his God.

In the first part of this chapter we look at the meaning of work for the inner-directed man of the nineteenth century in America; in the second, we look at the uses he made of leisure. The division is arbitrary because the paths of work and pleasure are deeply intertwined. Moreover, the argument in this and the next two chapters advances in a somewhat dialectic fashion: the inner-directed and other-directed patterns are occasionally stated in their most extreme forms, in order to bring out sharply the contrast between them. Since, however, the problems of the inner-directed are no longer problems many of us face, the reader as well as the writer must be on guard against a tendency to overidealize inner-direction and to be overcritical of other-direction.

I. Men at Work

THE ECONOMIC PROBLEM: THE HARDNESS OF THE MATERIAL

Our task in this and the following chapter is to compare the meaning of work in the epochs depending on inner-direction and other-direction respectively. The change is one of degree, like most historical changes. The inner-directed man tends to think of work in terms of non-human objects, including an objectified social organization, while the other-directed man tends to think of work in terms of people—people seen as something more than the sum of their workmanlike skills and qualities. Thus for the inner-directed man production is seen and experienced in terms of technological and intellectual processes rather than in terms of human cooperation. Human relations in industry, as well as relations among industries and between industry and society as a whole, seem to the inner-directed man to be managed by the anonymous cooperation brought about through the "invisible hand"—Adam Smith's wonderful phrase for economic planning through the free market.

Men were of course aware, in the period most heavily dependent on inner-direction, that the achievement of cooperation in the organization of work was not simply automatic. There was much talk of the need for discipline, sobriety, integrity. Yet it is fair to say that the human mood of the work force was not yet felt to be a major problem. Labor was still too numerous—it spilled over into the factory from the prolific farms and could easily be moved elsewhere in an age before passports. Moreover, labor's work force was disciplined by the new values as well as some kept from the era of tradition-direction; in addition, by evangelistic religion in the advanced industrial countries. The managerial work force, on the other hand, was not felt as a problem either, because the size of the administrative staff was small and because inner-directed types could cooperate with each other on physically and intellectually evident tasks whether or not they liked or approved of each other. Their inner-directed code, rather than their cooperative mood, kept them from constant sabotage.

As a result, even in large and bureaucratized organizations people's attention was focused more on products (whether these were goods, decisions, reports, or discoveries makes little difference) and less on the human element. It was the product itself, moreover, not the use made of it by the consumer, that commanded attention. Despite what Marx called "the fetishism of commodities," the inner-directed man could concern himself with the product without himself being a good consumer: he did not need to look at himself through the customer's eyes. The problem of marketing the product, perhaps even its meaning, receded into the psychological background before the *hardness of the material*—the obduracy of the technical tasks themselves.

The opening frontiers called people to a seeming oversupply of material tasks in industry and trade, geography, and scientific discovery. This is especially clear if we look at the geographical frontier. While the frontiersman cooperated with his sparse neighbors in mutual self-help activities, such as housebuilding or politics, his main preoccupation was with physical, not with human, nature. The American frontiersman, as Tocqueville encountered him in Michigan, was, though hospitable, uninterested in people.

He found physical nature problematical enough: to alter and adapt it required that he become hard and self-reliant.

The same thing was true in other fields of enterprise and pioneering. Missionary zeal, with its determination to carry the gospel to such far distant lands as India, China, and the Pacific isles, reflected the nineteenth-century pioneering spirit fully as much or more than it did any religious impulse of brotherhood. The missionary and his family frequently—as, for example, in Hawaii—became the nucleus of a European element which was finally to gain economic and financial control. So also were the numerous communistic experiments the product of imaginative individualistic thinking. Likewise, intellectual entrepreneurs staked out fields of knowledge and threw themselves with passionate curiosity into discovering the secrets of nature. Though they might be as jealous and competitive as Newton, their contacts with co-workers remained on the whole impersonal; they were in communication with one another through very simple channels of papers and congresses and without much formal organization of team research. Here, too, the invisible hand seemed to rule, and work was felt as a mode of relating oneself to physical objects and to ideas, and only indirectly to people.

It is apparent to us today that, in the economic field at least, the invisible hand was partly a fact, though its historically temporary nature escaped people, and partly a myth.[1] Government did a good deal of planning even after mercantilism waned—planning none the less forceful for being relatively unbureaucratized and none the less systematic for being operated through such time-honored levers as the tariff, the judiciary, and canal and railroad subsidies. Moreover, the impersonality of economic life against which moralists and socialists complained in steady chorus from Sir Thomas More to R. H. Tawney was never quite so great as it seemed. Business was often paternal; as

---

[1] See Karl Polanyi's excellent discussion in *The Great Transformation* (New York, Farrar & Rinehart, 1944).

we can see in such a novel as Thomas Mann's *Buddenbrooks*, it relied heavily on values that survived from feudalism. Tradition-directed tones of personalization survived in many situations, despite the ideology and, to some degree, the existence of free competition. These personalizations undoubtedly ameliorated some of the severities and abuses of inner-directed individualism.

Nevertheless, as compared with today, the economy was quite loose jointed and impersonal and perhaps seemed even more impersonal than it actually was. This encouraged the ambitious labors of men who could attend to society's expanding capital plant, to the bottlenecks in the technology of agriculture, extractive industry, and manufacturing. The capital goods industries were of decisive importance; internally, they were needed to bridge the gap between population and subsistence; externally, they were needed to support war-making and colonization. Indeed, the oversteered men of the period, especially in the regions touched by Puritanism or Jansenism, went far beyond the specifically economic requirements and rewards held out to them. They cut themselves off from family and friends, often from humanity in general, by their assiduity and diligence.

Work, one might add, provided a strategic protection for those who could not live up to all the requirements of the prevailing character ideal. For we have no right to assume that even the successful men of the period were in complete adjustment with the social character imposed on them. Many apparently well-adjusted men of an older time in American life must have been aware that their acceptance of inner-direction involved their own efforts to conform—that their conformity was far from automatic.

The linkage between work and property in an era of private competitive capitalism (as compared with the later capitalism described by Berle and Means in *The Modern Corporation and Private Property*) reinforced the possibilities of isolation from people. Property, for the inner-directed man, became freely transferable; the individual was not attached to it as in the earlier era by sentimental and traditional ties, but he attached it to himself by his choices, by his energetic actions. No longer an affair of the extended family, property became an extended part, a kind of exoskeleton, for the individual self.[2]

Yet private property of this sort, though useful as a safeguard and testing ground for the inner-directed man, was probably not alone a sufficient condition for his rise. On the frontiers of the expanding Russian economy of the early five-year plans, there were entrepreneurs very much like European and American types of many decades earlier: ambitious, energetic, self-reliant men engaged in transforming physical nature, instituting large-scale formal organization, and revolutionizing technology. The inner-directed man—sometimes models of him were imported from America and Germany—made his appearance at Dneprostroi, Magnitogorsk, and the Turk-Sib railroad.

Even today we can watch similar types emerging in India among the leaders of industry and government. It looks as if, in any large and differentiated population, reservoirs of potential inner-direction exist, only awaiting the onset of a western-oriented type of industrialization in order to come to the fore.

AD ASTRA PER ASPERA

The ambitious note in the inner-directed person's attitude toward work in the phase of transitional growth of population was expressed in the schoolbook proverb: *ad astra per aspera*. The stars were far away, but still he aimed for them, in terms of a lifetime of effort. He could afford such a long-term commitment because of the generality of the aim: he wanted money or power or fame or some lasting achievement in the arts or the professions. He wanted to leave a reputation, a memorial, something as tangible

---

[2]Cf. William James's definition of the self in *Principles of Psychology* (New York, Henry Holt, 1896), I, 291–292; and discussion in Erich Fromm, *Man for Himself*, pp. 135–136.

as Mr. Darling's tombstone inscription, still fairly legible after one hundred and fifty years of New England weather.

But there was another, a social, reason why long-term ambition of this sort could be afforded. The beckoning frontier of colonization and industrialization, the beckoning frontier of intellectual discovery, too, required long-term investment. To build a railroad or an Indian civil service or the intellectual system of a Comte, a Clerk Maxwell, or a Marx was not an affair of a few months. Competition was keen. Still, the number of competitors in any single field was small, and if a man was bright and energetic, he could hope that his invention, capital investment, or organizational plan would not be rendered rapidly obsolete by others. For, although the invisible hand of technological and intellectual change moved immeasurably faster than it had done in the still earlier population phase of high growth potential, it moved slowly nonetheless in comparison with today. Change was on the scale of a working lifetime; that is, an individual could hope to keep up with the others, even without paying special notice to them: they were not likely to repeal or revise overnight what he knew or did on his own.

As recently as 1920 an American boy of the middle class was not too worried about the problem of committing himself to a career. If he came of good family, he could count on connections; if not, he could count on the credit of his social—that is, his visibly inner-directed—character. He could dream of long-term goals because the mere problem of career entry and survival was not acute; that he might for long be out of a job did not occur to him. He could orient himself, if he chose a profession, by his daydreaming identification with the stars in his field. A young doctor might think of Osler, a young lawyer of Choate or Elihu Root or Theodore Roosevelt, a young scientist of Agassiz or Pasteur, a young painter or writer of Renoir or Tolstoy. Yet there is often tragedy in store for the inner-directed person who may fail to live up to grandiose dreams and who may have to struggle in vain against both the intractability of the material and the limitations of his own powers. He will be held, and hold himself, to his commitment. Satirists from Cervantes on have commented on this disparity between pursuing the stars and stumbling over the mere earthiness of earth.

II. THE SIDE SHOW OF PLEASURE

The sphere of pleasure and consumption is only a side show in the era of inner-direction, work being of course the main show. This is truer for men than for women. Some men diminish attention to pleasure to the vanishing point, delegating consumption problems to their wives; these are the good providers. Others turn consumption itself into work: the work of acquisition. Still others, perhaps the majority, are able to use the sphere of pleasure as an occasional escape from the sphere of work.

This divergence is characteristic of the shift from tradition-direction to inner-direction. The tradition-directed man does not make a choice whether to work or to play or whether to create a private blend of his own; matters are decided for him by tradition. To some degree play is marked off from work, linguistically and by special costuming and ceremonial. To some degree work and play are blended, for instance in handicraft art applied to articles of daily use or in ceremonials that accompany a socially or economically useful activity. The inner-directed man, however, is freed from the direction of tradition and he is consciously and sharply aware of the difference between work and play. At least where theocratic controls are relaxed, he must decide on his own how much time to allot to play. To be sure, not much room is left for leisure in terms of time: hours are long and work is arduous: the tired businessman is invented. Nevertheless, the width of choice is sufficient to allow us to distinguish between those who work at consumption with the passion of acquisition and those who consume as a more or less licit and occasional escape.

THE ACQUISITIVE CONSUMER

In an era depending on inner-direction men who exhibit the desired arduousness in the sphere of work—as
shown by their productivity—can afford a good deal of independence in their moments spared for consumption.
One result, in the America of the last century, was the crazy
millionaire who, having established his status, save in the
most exalted circles, by satisfying society's requirements
on the productive front, could do as he pleased on the
pleasure front. He could hang the "do not disturb" sign
over his play as well as over his work. Once possessed of
commanding wealth, he could resist or accept as he chose
the ministrations of wives and daughters and even more
specialized advisers on consumption, taste, and connoisseurship.

A period when such men live is, therefore, the heyday
of conspicuous consumption, when energies identical with
those deployed at work are channeled by the rich into their
leisure budget. While the producer dynamically creates
new networks of transportation in order to exploit resources
and distribute the finished and semi-finished product, the
consumer of this period begins to act with equal dynamism
on the market. The producer pushes; the consumer pulls.
The first stage in his consumership is a passionate desire to
make things *his*.

Perhaps he lavishes money and energy on a house, to the
point where it comes to resemble a department store—
recall the wonderful sets and furnishings in the films
Citizen Kane and *The Ghost Goes West*. Perhaps he
gathers the treasures of Europe, including titled sons-in-
law. Perhaps he goes in for steam yachts or diamonds or
libraries or, united with rich cronies in civic spirit, for
theaters, planetariums, and zoos. In most cases the activity
is as self-justifying as the search for the North Pole, pursued with hardly more hesitation or boredom than the tasks
of the production frontier. There is no need to hesitate
because in this period consumption products, like work

commitments, do not become rapidly obsolete but are good for a lifetime.

The type of acquisitive consumer who is less concerned with building up a private hoard or hobby and more concerned with showing his possessions with fashion seems, at first glance, other-directed in his attention. Yet, if we go back to Veblen's classic work, we can see, I think, that the consumers he describes are other-directed in appearance only. The Veblenian conspicuous consumer is seeking to fit into a role demanded of him by his station, or hoped-for station, in life; whereas the other-directed consumer seeks experiences rather than things and yearns to be guided by others rather than to dazzle them with display. The conspicuous consumer possesses a standard allowing him readily to measure what others have, namely cash. This standard can penetrate the opacity of objects, even objects unique in their nature, such as a geographical site (so much a front foot) or a beautiful woman (the best money can buy). This gives the consumption of the inner-directed man its relatively impersonal quality—it is as impersonal as his production, of which it is a residue. Similarly, if he collects old masters, he is taking a standardized step on the consumption gradient for his social class at the same time that he is buying a good investment or at least a good gamble. Moreover, he is, in a way, a "master" himself, a technical man, and he can admire the technique of the Renaissance artist as few other-directed consumers of today, even though they may know a good deal more about art, dare admire the esoteric technique, or seeming lack of it, of a non-representational artist. The conspicuous consumer is engaged, therefore, in an externalized kind of rivalry, as indicated by Veblen's use of such terms as "ostensible," "emulative," "conspicuous," and the rest of his beautifully ironic thesaurus. The other-directed consumer may compete in what looks like the same way, but only to the degree that the peers impel him to. His desire to outshine, as I have already tried to show, is muted.

To be sure, all these changes are changes in degree, and Veblen's emphasis on leisure and consumption—like, in a very different way, Keynes' emphasis on what we might call relentless spending—are indexes of the social changes paving the way for and accompanying the characterological ones.

AWAY FROM IT ALL

The *acquisitive* consumer brings to the sphere of consumption motivations and ideals similar to those he manifests in the sphere of production. The *escaping* consumer seeks, on the contrary, to dramatize an emotional polarity between work and play.

Because the whole concept of escape is a very slippery one, we must always ask: escape from what and to what? The inner-directed individual can afford a certain kind of escape since his character and situation give him a core of sufficient self-reliance to permit dreaming without disintegration. He learns this as a boy when he escapes by himself a good deal of the time—playing hooky from the dreary and demanding tasks of home and school. Unlike Tootle the engine, he is seldom worried by the fear that, if he gathers primroses by the river's brim, he will not make the grade—though he may be punished, since the right to play has not yet been granted school children. Perhaps he will feel guilt when he escapes, but the guilt will lend savor to the adventure, turning escape into escapade. Like the Victorian father, the stability of whose family life often depended on an occasional visit to a prostitute, the inner-directed person can let himself go in "unsocialized" ways because in the ways that count, the ways of work, he has a definitely socialized self to return to.

To be sure, he may often be too inhibited for that. He may be unable to stop timetabling himself by the internalized pocket watch that he has substituted for the chimes of the Middle Ages. He may be unable to shift his one-price, one-role policy even in dealing with status inferiors, though this, in the explicit class structure of the era, is unusual. Above all, he may feel that, with the reining in and observing of the self on all fronts, he cannot afford to undertake unsanctioned experiments in spontaneity. He may feel his character, covert as well as overt, as a kind of capital that might be dissipated in a catastrophic gamble—all the more dangerous in view of the lifetime goals to which he is committed. We see this complex process rationalized by the puritan in terms of "saving himself." The puritan treats himself as if he were a firm and, at the same time, the firm's auditor.

But we speak in this section of those who, despite internal and external inhibitions, are able to escape in some fashion. Escape as we use it here means a shift of pace and attitude from the nearly all-embracing domain of work. Thus, as we shall see below, it may be escape onto a "higher" level than that of business or professional life, or onto a "lower" level.

Onward and upward with the arts. The great events of leisure time "escape upward" are intermittent: Chautauqua, the traveling theater, the Sunday service complete with one antibusiness preacher per year or per city, the itinerant book peddler. To come into contact with them requires some effort, and making the effort is itself a sign of virtue. There is even a change of dress—Sunday-go-to-meeting dress or top hats—to signify the change of role.

There is, moreover, a good deal of amateur performance. Even more perhaps than plumbing, the piano and the cultivation of amateur musical skills mark the boundary of middle-class aspirations to respectability. At the same time, for the mobile youth from the working class there are the mechanics institutes and the many traveling lecturers, from prison reformers to single taxers, who analyze the workings of the system for their eager audiences. We need only recall the tremendous mushrooming of discussion clubs that greeted Bellamy's *Looking Backward*.

Obviously the motives of such participants are not purely escapist. There is the desire, often thinly disguised, to move onward and upward in the social hierarchy. Through religious revivalism and Bible reading the individual may seek to escape not from this world but from the dangers of the next. Daily life is hard and drab; leisure is an occasional essay at refinement.

Aspirations for culture make people want to escape into an image of some past heroic period, as inherited from the pre-nineteenth-century upper class. Thus, the cultivated bourgeois of the nineteenth century looks back in his leisure to an earlier and more heroic quasi-bourgeois epoch, in Periclean Athens or Renaissance Italy. Work driven, chained to routines, he pictures for himself the swagger and versatility of a Benvenuto Cellini or a Leonardo. As the Chautauqua circuit spreads accounts of contemporary travel and discovery, so there exists a semipopular culture about the achievements of the ancient world—note the popularity of *Ben Hur*—and of the Renaissance. Very often the occupational hardness of the era has its obverse side in leisure sentimentality.

Though fashion, of course, plays a role in the vogue of ancient history, of European travel, and of these other escapist pursuits, it is important, I think, for the security of the inner-directed people that these spheres of interest are remote not only from their work but also from their immediate social concerns. Reading about Greece—even visiting Florence—they are not forced to think about their own epoch or themselves in any realistic sense; such identifications with ancient heroes as there are can be fantastic. We must qualify this only when we arrive at the late Victorian or Edwardian stories of Henry James or E. M. Forster, in which travel in Italy may turn out to be much more emotionally problematic than mere escape upward for Anglo-Saxon ladies and gentlemen. These fictional tourists, concerned with whether they are experiencing to the full the cultural contrasts and sensitivities they seek, find foreshadowed the ambiguities of escape that are typical for other-direction.

Feet on the rail. The inner-directed person may escape down as well as up. He finds in dime novels, in cock fighting, in trotting races, in barbershop song, a variant from his working role. While some visit Chartres, others visit the hootchy-kootch on the midway. Despite the efforts of the puritans and women folk to drive out of life these recreations that are reminiscent of medieval pastimes, the middle-class men of the nineteenth century make a firm effort to hang on to them.

Sherwood Anderson's work is an epic of men coming into the house after midnight on stocking feet. How much of this lore survives was made plain a few years ago by Allen Funt, on one of the "Candid Microphone" programs. Funt stood on a street corner at three in the morning and pretended he was afraid to go home. He buttonholed passing men and asked them to come home with him, to explain to the wife why he was overfilled and overdue. All the men were sympathetic. Though none wanted the role of go-between, each suggested the dodge that he himself had found workable in the same spot. One wanted him to telephone first. Another would help him get bandaged up. Still another thought that a present might fix matters. Some suggested stories, others courage. Most of the men, judging from their voices, seemed to be of middle age. Perhaps the major point of all this is that in earlier generations the strictness of the American proper-female regime gave a glamour to sin that obscured its inevitable limitations.

In thinking of the meaning of escape for the inner-directed man we must not, however, put too much emphasis on the merely convention-breaking patterns of Victorian amusement, vice, and sinful fantasy. Even where the conventions were absent or fragile, another issue was involved. This was the issue of competence in the enjoyment and judgment of recreation.

On the one hand, the American inner-directed man was committed in every generation to face increasingly the demand that his escape be upward with the arts. Sometimes he sought out this escape on his own. More usually, perhaps, mobility strivings and feminine influence put pressure on the man to go beyond the sphere where he felt competent: the sleepy businessman dragged to the opera sung in a language he could not understand. But on the other hand, he combated becoming merely a passive consumer by protecting, as a rebel in shirt sleeves, his escape downward to the lower arts of drink mixing and drink holding, poker, fancy women, and fancy mummery. Thus he protected in his minor sphere of play, as in his major sphere of work, his feeling of competence in the living of life. The separateness of the play sphere was dramatized precisely because the personal competence involved in these downward escapes could contribute little, or negatively, to his social status in the world of work and family. Because play competence could not be directly geared to the production economy, the inner-directed man was somewhat less likely than other-directed men today to exploit his recreation by telling himself that he owed it to himself to have fun. If he went to baseball games (one of the few sports where the other-directed man's competence, too, rests considerably on having once played the game), it was not part of an act designed to prove himself "one of the boys."

However, we must not exaggerate these distinctions between inner-directed and other-directed escapes. Many inner-directed men worked painfully hard to maintain their showing of recreational competence. The Reverend Endicott Peabody, later founder of Groton, established himself as the hero of a western frontier town in which he held a pastorate by getting up a baseball team. A similar strategy, with its roots in an era depending on tradition-direction, appears in the modern movie characterization of the Catholic priest, brother, or nun who is a good sport—as in Bing Crosby's Going My Way. Moreover, many inner-directed American business and professional men exploited, and still exploit, their leisure to make contacts. Their golf game was anything but an escape, and their wives' gardening was often harnessed to the same mobility drives. Such men had a great deal at stake economically, even if they had less at stake psychologically than the other-directed.

But there were often psychological stakes, too. The oversteered men of the period, unable either to throw off or accept their inhibitions, were not always able to guard them by withdrawal into privacy. Where there was pressure to prove oneself a good fellow in tavern or brothel, their bodies sometimes betrayed them into nausea or impotence —in the effort to be competent weakness of the flesh gave away unwillingness of the spirit. On the whole, however, the inner-directed man was much less susceptible than men are today to the requirement that he be liked for his recreations and loved for his vices.

III. The Struggle for Self-approval

We may sum up much that is significant about inner-direction by saying that, in a society where it is dominant, its tendency is to protect the individual against the others at the price of leaving him vulnerable to himself.

One bit of evidence for this is in the widespread fear of and attack upon apathy which seems to date from the era of inner-direction. The monastic orders had faced the problem of sloth or *accidie* as psychological dangers to their regimen—dangers of which St. Augustine was acutely aware in his own struggle with himself. When puritanism, as Max Weber put it, turned the world into a monastery, the fear of this inner danger began to plague whole social classes and not merely a few select monks. The puritan inner-directed man was made to feel as if he had constantly to hold on to himself; that without ceaseless vigilance he would let go and drift—on the assumption that one can let go if one wills or, rather, if one stops willing. It is as if his character, despite its seeming stability, did not feel stable and, indeed, the puritan, in a theological projection of this inner feeling, had constantly to fight against doubts concerning his state of grace or election.

Out of his continuing battle against the Demon of Sloth that sometimes turned into a hypochondria about apathy he built up a myth, still very much with us, that the tradition-directed person is completely easy going, lacking "get up and go." This attack against others as apathetic—as today, for instance, in the constant complaints over political and civic apathy—sometimes served as a way of fighting against apathy in oneself. In fact, the inner-directed person testifies to his unconscious awareness that his gyroscope is not *his* but is installed by others through his chronic panic that it will stop spinning, that he is really not a self-starter, that life itself is not a process and renewal but an effortful staving off of psychic death.

Moreover, for easier bookkeeping in the control of apathy, the inner-directed person frequently divides his life into sectors, in each of which he can test his psychic defenses against it. Within himself he remains the child, committed early to goals and ideals that may transcend his powers. If these drives are demanding, no amount of contemporary acclaim can drown the feeling of inadequacy: the acclaim of others may in fact be the by-product of efforts to satisfy the self. Within himself he must find justification not only in what he does but in what he is—not by works but by faith is he saved. And while clever bookkeeping can transmute works into faith, self-criticism is seldom completely silenced. *Mere behavioral conformity cannot meet the characterological ideal.*

These internalized standards of the inner-directed man allow him, on the other hand, a certain freedom to fail in the eyes of the others without being convinced by *them* of his own inadequacy. Like Edison he will try and try again, sustained by his internal judgment of his worth. For while the others cannot protect him against self-criticism, self-criticism can protect him against the others. The inner-directed man can justify his existence not only by what he has done but what he will do. But this holds only up to a point. If repeated failures destroy his hope of future accomplishment, then it is likely that his internal strengths can no longer hold the fort against the external evidence. Overwhelmed with guilt, he will despise himself for his failures and inadequacies. The judgment, though set off by external happenings, is all the more severe for being internalized. Durkheim was right to see comparatively high suicide rates in the advanced industrial countries as symptoms of a psychological malaise uncontrolled by any cultural tradition.

VI

THE OTHER–DIRECTED ROUND OF LIFE:
FROM INVISIBLE HAND
TO GLAD HAND

Since sociability in its pure form has no ulterior end, no content and no result outside itself, it is oriented completely about personalities. . . . But precisely because all is oriented about them, the personalities must not emphasize themselves too individually.

Georg Simmel, THE SOCIOLOGY OF SOCIABILITY

THE inner-directed person is not only chained to the endless demands of the production sphere; he must also spend his entire life in the internal production of his own character. The discomforts of this internal frontier are as inexhaustible as the discomforts of the frontier of work itself. Like the fear of being retired or unemployed in the economic realm, apathy in many sectors of his inner or outer life is felt as underemployment of characterological resources. The inner-directed man has a generalized need to master resource exploitation on all the fronts of which he is conscious. He is job-minded.

The frontiers for the other-directed man are people; he is people-minded. Hence both work and pleasure are felt as activities involving people. Many of the job titles that exist today existed in the earlier era; many recreations likewise. My effort is to see how change of character is connected with change of meaning in the same pursuits as well as with development of new pursuits.

I. THE ECONOMIC PROBLEM: THE HUMAN ELEMENT

As the phase of transitional growth drew to an end in America, the "no help wanted" sign was posted on the frontier in 1890, in imagination if not in actual land-grant practice, and the same sign was hung out on our borders in 1924 with the virtual cutting off of immigration from Europe. With these valedictories a great symbol of hope and movement in the western world was destroyed. The combination of curtailed immigration and a falling birth rate eventually altered the population profile of the country; and, in the ways already hinted at, its characterological profile as well. Today it is the "softness" of men rather than the "hardness" of material that calls on talent and opens new channels of social mobility.

Whereas the production frontier, and even the land frontier, may actually be roomy even in the phase of incipient population decline, it nevertheless feels crowded; and certainly the society is no longer felt as a wilderness or jungle as it often was earlier.

This is particularly true in industry and the professions. Take, for example, the position of the foreman. He no longer stands alone, a straw boss in a clear hierarchy, but is surrounded with people. He is a two-way communication channel between the men under him and a host of experts above and around him: personnel men, safety directors, production engineers, comptroller's representatives, and all the rest of the indirect managerial work force. The plant manager is hardly better off for emotional elbowroom: he is confronted not only with the elaborate intra-plant hierarchy but with the public outside: the trade association group, the unions, consumers, suppliers, the government, and public opinion. Likewise, the professional man feels surrounded by a swarm of competitors, turned out by the vastly expanded educational system of a society whose capital plant is in such good shape that it can afford to devote—in fact, can hardly help devoting—a large share of the national income to the service trades and professions and to education for their proper use.

People, therefore, become the central problem of industry. This does not mean that the older revolutions in tooling, the machine process, and factory organization come to a halt. Rather, advances here are increasingly routinized; the continuing increment in productivity becomes a by-product of institutional forms. However, the newer industrial revolution which has reached its greatest force in America (although it is also beginning to be manifest elsewhere, as in England) is concerned with techniques of communication and control, not of tooling or factory layout. It is symbolized by the telephone, the servomechanism, the IBM machine, the electronic calculator, and modern statistical methods of controlling the quality of products; by the Hawthorne counseling experiment and the general preoccupation with industrial morale. The era of economic abundance and incipient population decline calls for the work of men whose tool is symbolism and whose aim is some observable response from people. These manipulators, of course, are not necessarily other-directed in character. Many inner-directed people are successful manipulators of people; often, their very inner-direction makes them unaware of how much they do manipulate and exploit others. Nevertheless, for manipulating others, there is a somewhat greater compatibility between characterological other-direction and sensitivity to others' subtler wants.

This can be explained more clearly by reference to one of our interviews. The man interviewed is the vice-president for sales and advertising of a large west coast machine-tool company, and he is also head of one of the leading trade associations for his industry. In origin he is the son of a Congregationalist preacher in a small midwestern town. His background, his mobility drive, his initial technical orientation are typical for the inner-directed; but his situation calls for the negotiating skill and interpersonal sensitivity more characteristic of the other-directed. This conflict produces strain. Asked about political issues on which he has recently changed his mind, he says:

. . . I don't think this fits the category you're working on now, but I've become a great deal more tolerant of labor leaders and organizers [then catching himself]—not agitators, necessarily. I've come to appreciate what they're doing. They don't have much choice in taking the particular methods and means sometimes. I need a psychoanalyst.

He also told the interviewer that his principal worry is that he does not get along too well with another top executive of his company. He was troubled when a suggestion of his that was rejected later turned out to be right—and the other chap knew it was right. In such a situation he felt exposed. He cannot eat before going into a board meeting, and wondered to the interviewer whether he might not be better off running his own small company rather than as an official of a large one. For recreation he plays golf, though he does not seem to care for it and, in good inner-directed style, or perhaps simply good American style, does "a little fooling around with tools in the basement."

Material from interviews is, of course, open to a variety of possible interpretations, and I have no great confidence that those here suggested are correct. It would surely be erroneous to conclude that this executive has doubts about himself because he is not fully other-directed or inner-directed (by the very definition of these terms, no one is fully one or the other). The point is rather that the modern executive, regardless of the blend of the two modes of conformity he displays, is put under constant social pressure, in and out of the office. This executive is perhaps better able than most to verbalize the strain this pressure sets up.

FROM CRAFT SKILL TO MANIPULATIVE SKILL

The pressure toward social competence, with its concurrent playing down of technical competence, suggests another aspect of this executive's history which is typical for the emergence of a new pattern in American business and professional life: *if one is successful in one's craft, one is forced to leave it.* The machine-tool man began in the shop; as V.P. for sales and advertising he has become an uneasy manipulator of people and of himself. Likewise, the newspaperman who rises becomes a columnist or deskman, the doctor becomes the head of a clinic or hospital, the professor becomes a dean, president, or foundation official, the factory superintendent becomes a holding company executive. All these men must bury their craft routines and desert their craft companions. They must work less with things and more with people.

To be sure, business was always work with people. But when the size of enterprises was small, the head could remain a colleague among other colleagues; he did not cut connections entirely and enter a new milieu. William Allen White's *Autobiography* shows that he was able to maintain all his life the amiable fiction that he was only a working newspaper man. Similarly, the older generation of college presidents was composed largely of men who continued to think of themselves as scholars. So, too, the older generation of business executives kept their hats on in the office, chewed tobacco, and otherwise tried to retain their connections with the shop. Today, however, the familiar organizational concepts of "staff and line" symbolize the cutting off of direct contact between the executive and the working staffs of both staff and line. To sit at his new big desk—or to get there—he has to learn a new personality-oriented specialty and unlearn or at least soft-pedal his old skill orientation.

To the point is a story of an engineer who is offered the far more lucrative job of sales manager.[1] He loves engineering, but his wife won't let him turn down the promotion. His sponsor in the organization tells him it is now or never: does he want to be wearing a green eyeshade all his life? He reluctantly accepts. That night he has a dream. He has a slide rule in his hands, and he suddenly realizes that he does not know how to use it. He wakes in panic. The dream clearly symbolizes his feeling of impotence in a new job where he is alienated from his craft.

The executive who has moved up from a professional position can hardly help feeling that his work is air con-

---

[1] Professor Everett Hughes of the University of Chicago, who has guided me in the analysis of changing career lines in business and the professions, tells this story.

ditioned: fine only so long as the machinery below runs smoothly. Those colleagues whom he has left behind will not be slow, in their envy, to remind him that he can no longer consider himself a competent craftsman among his fellow craftsmen, that he does not fool them if, as an editor or by-line columnist, he occasionally attends a presidential press conference; or, as a college administrator, an occasional scholarly convention; or, as a sales manager, occasionally makes a mark on a drawing board.

Indeed, a society increasingly dependent on manipulation of people is almost as destructive of the craft-oriented professional and businessman as a society in the earlier stages of industrialization is destructive of the handicraft-oriented peasant and artisan. The professional of the more recent period is pushed upstairs into the managerial class while the artisan of the earlier period was pushed into the proletariat; and this testifies to a profound difference in the two historic situations. Yet in both cases the industrial process advances by building into machines and into smooth-flowing organizations the skills that were once built, by a long characterological and apprenticeship process, into men.

Despite this pattern, there are many positions in business, and in particular in the older professions, that offer comfortable places to inner-directed types. In medicine and law the ideology of free enterprise is strong. The attempt to apply objective criteria in selecting personnel persists, and is strengthened by the otherwise odious emphasis on grades in the educational and licensing system. In a hospital, a law firm, a university, there is room not only for those who can bring people together but for those who can bring together chemicals, citations, or ideas. There are many niches for the work-minded craftsman who does not care to learn, or cannot learn, to move with the crowd.

Even in big industry some such areas can continue to exist because not all technological problems—problems of the hardness of the material—have been solved or put on a routine problem-solving basis. Moreover, there are certain key spots in big business and big government where at times it is precisely an inner-directed rate-buster who is needed—for instance, a man who can say no without going through an elaborate song and dance. At the same time the values characteristic of other-direction may spread at such a rate as to hit certain sectors of the economy before these sectors have solved their technological problems. In the United States the lure of other-directed work and leisure styles cannot be everywhere modulated to the uneven front of economic advance.

FROM FREE TRADE TO FAIR TRADE

Very soon after the Federal Trade Commission Act of 1914 outlawed unfair competition it became clear that what was unfair was to lower the price of goods, though this view was concealed under attacks against cheating or mislabeling of goods. But in the NRA period this covert attitude received government and public sanction, and it became libelous to call someone a price cutter. With the passage of the Robinson-Patman Act and state fair-trade laws, free trade and fair trade became antithetical terms. Prices come to be set by administration and negotiation or, where this is too likely to bring in the Antitrust Division, by "price leadership." Relations that were once handled by the price mechanism or fiat are now handled by negotiation.

Price leadership often looks to the economist simply as the manipulation of devices to avoid price wars and divide the field. But price leadership has other aspects as well. It is a means by which the burden of decision is put onto the "others." The so-called price leaders themselves look to the government for clues, since cost—that mythical will-of-the-wisp—is no longer, if it ever really was, an unequivocal guide. Follow-the-leader is also played in arriving at the price and working conditions of labor; and unions have profited from their ability to play on the wishes of top management to be in stride with the industry leaders, and to be good fellows to boot. As we shall see later, the other-directed pattern of politics tends to resemble the other-directed pattern of business: leadership is in the same amorphous state. Moreover, both in business and in politics, the other-directed executive prefers to stabilize his situation at a level that does not make too heavy demands on him for performance. Hence, at various points in the decision-making process he will vote for an easier life as against the risks of expansion and free-for-all competition.

Such a business life does not turn out to be the "easy" one. For one thing, the other-directed people do not have things all their own way in business any more than they do in politics. Free trade is still a powerful force, despite the incursions of the fair traders. Many observers, judging the degree of monopoly by looking at the percentage of assets controlled by the large, administered-price corporations, overlook the fact that even a small percentage of companies outside the range of the glad hand can have a leverage quite disproportionate to their assets. Rubber may be a monopoly, but will we always need rubber? Movies may be monopolistic, but what about television? In the small and marginal industries, the monopolies not of today but of tomorrow, there is often no need to be a good fellow. What is more, the dynamics of technological change remain challenging; whole departments within industries, as well as whole industries themselves, can become obsolete, despite their ability to negotiate repeated stays of technological death sentence. Even within the great monopolistic industries there are still many technologically oriented folk as well as many technologically oriented departments; no management planning in any one company can completely smooth out and routinize the pressure resulting from their innovations.

To the extent that the businessman is freed by his character and situation from cost considerations, he must face the problem of finding new motives for his entrepreneurship. He must tune in to the others to see what they are saying about what a proper business ought to be. Thus, a psychological sensitivity that begins with fear of being called a price cutter spreads to fear of being unfashionable in other ways. The businessman is as afraid of pursuing goals that may be obsolete as of living a style of life that may not be stylish. Oriented as he is to others, and to the consumption sphere, *he views his own business as a consumer.*

By and large, business firms until World War I needed only three kinds of professional advice: legal, auditing, and engineering. These were relatively impersonal services, even when, in the case of the lawyers, the services included buying—for cash on the barrelhead—a few legislators or judges. Since the number of available specialists was fairly small in comparison with demand, they could be absorbed into either or both of the two types of prevailing nexus: one, the family-status-connection nexus which persisted from earlier times in the smaller communities and does so even today in these communities and in the South; the other, the cash nexus based on performance, or on "character" in the older sense. Today the buyer is, first of all, not sure which of many services to buy: shall he get a lawyer or a public relations man or a market research agency or call in a management consulting firm to decide; second, he is not sure of his choice among the many potential suppliers of each of these services—none of whom must he accept either for family-status-connection reasons or for obviously superior character and performance. Thus choice will turn on a complex of more or less accidental, whimsical factors: a chance contact or conversation, a story in *Business Week* or a "confidential" newsletter, the luck of a salesman.

We can see the shift in many corporate histories. A business that begins as a small family enterprise, whose founders have their eye on the main chance—with a focus on costs and a "show me" attitude about good will and public relations—often alters its aims in the second generation. *Fortune* is put on the table, a trade association is joined, and the aim becomes not so much dollars as the possession of those appurtenances which an up-to-date company is supposed to have. We see a succession of demi-intellectuals added to the staff: industrial relations directors, training directors, safety directors. A house organ is published; consultants are called in on market research, standard operating procedures, and so on; shop and store front have their faces lifted; and in general status is sought, with profits becoming useful as one among many symbols of status and as the reserve for further moves toward a status-dictated expansion.

In many cases this shift is accompanied by a conflict of the older, more inner-directed with the younger, more other-directed generation. The older men have come up through the shop or through a technical school with no pretensions in the field of human relations. The younger ones are imbued with the new ethic. They seem still to be concerned about making money, and to some extent they are, but they are also concerned with turning their company into the model which they learned at business school. Businessmen recognize this new orientation when they speak of themselves, as they frequently do, as trustees for a variety of publics. And while they try to manipulate these publics and to balance between them, they, like the political leaders, are manipulated by the expectations the public has, or is thought to have, of them.

If one had to set a date for the change, one might say that the old epoch ended with the death of Henry Ford. After his death the firm, a last stronghold of older ways, completed the installation of new labor, accounting, and other management techniques and orientations.

The word *fair* in part reflects a carry-over of peer-group values into business life. The peer-grouper is imbued with the idea of fair play; the businessman, of fair trade. Often this means that he must be willing to negotiate matters on which he might stand on his rights. The negotiator, moreover, is expected to bring home not only a specific victory but also friendly feelings toward him and toward his company. Hence, to a degree, the less he knows about the underlying facts, the easier it will be to trade concessions. He is like the street-corner salesman who, reproached for selling for four cents apples that cost him five, said "But think of the turnover!" Here again craft skill, if not an actual drawback, becomes less important than manipulative skill.

Obviously, much of what has been said applies to the trade unions, the professions, and to academic life as well as to the business world. The lawyer, for instance, who moves into top positions inside and outside his profession is no longer necessarily a craftsman who has mastered the intricacies of, let us say, corporate finance, but may be one who has shown himself to be a good contact man. Since contacts need to be made and remade in every generation and cannot be inherited, this creates lucrative opportunities for the mobile other-directed types whose chief ability is smooth negotiation.

FROM THE BANK ACCOUNT TO THE EXPENSE ACCOUNT

In this phrase Professor Paul Lazarsfeld once summed up some recent changes in economic attitudes. The expense account is tied in with today's emphasis on consumption practices as firmly as the bank account in the old days was tied in with production ideals. The expense account gives the glad hand its grip. In doing so it still further breaks down the wall that in the era depending on inner-direction separated the paths of pleasure and of work. The successful other-directed man brings to business the set of attitudes learned in the consumption sphere not only when he appraises his own firm with a customer's eye but also when he is "in conference."

Business is supposed to be fun. As World War II inflation cooled off, the business pages repeatedly carried speeches at conventions on the theme: "Now selling will be fun again!" The inner-directed businessman was not expected to have fun; indeed, it was proper for him to be gloomy and even grim. But the other-directed businessman seems increasingly exposed to the mandate that he enjoy the sociabilities that accompany management. The shortening of hours has had much greater effect on the life of the working class than on that of the middle class:

the executive and professional continues to put in long hours, employing America's giant productivity less to leave for home early than to extend his lunch hours, coffee breaks, conventions, and other forms of combining business with pleasure. Likewise, much time in the office itself is also spent in sociability: exchanging office gossip ("conferences"), making good-will tours ("inspection"), talking to salesmen and joshing secretaries ("morale"). In fact, depleting the expense account can serve as an almost limitless occupational therapy for men who, out of a tradition of hard work, a dislike of their wives, a lingering asceticism, and an anxiety about their antagonistic cooperators, still feel that they must put in a good day's work at the office. But, of course, Simmel would not admit, in his brilliant essay from which I quoted at the head of this chapter, that this kind of sociability, carrying so much workaday freight, was either free or sociable.

For the new type of career there must be a new type of education. This is one factor, of course not the only one, behind the increasing vogue of general education and the introduction of the humanities and social studies into technical high school and university programs. The educators who sponsor these programs urge cultivating the "whole man," speak of training citizens for democracy, and denounce narrow specialisms—all valuable themes. Indeed this book grows in part out of the stimulation of teaching in a general social science program. But while it may be doubtful that engineers and businessmen will become either better citizens or better people for having been exposed to these programs, there is little question that they will be more suave. They may be able to demonstrate their edge on the roughnecks from the "tech" schools by trotting out discourse on human relations. Such eloquence may be as necessary for professional and business success today as a knowledge of the classics was to the English politician and high civil servant of the last century.

Meanwhile, I do not wish to exaggerate the emphasis on human relations even in the bureaucratized sectors of the economy. There is much variety still: some companies, such as Sears Roebuck, seem to be run by glad handers, while others like, let us say, Montgomery Ward, are not; some, like Anaconda, are public relations conscious; others, like Kennecott, are less so. Much current progress in distribution, even in selling, tends to reduce the importance of the salesman. This is clear enough in the Automat. Moreover, the personality aspects of selling can be minimized wherever a technician is needed: for instance, salesmen of specialized equipment which requires a reorientation of the customer's work force. Though IBM salesmen have to be go-getters, they also have to know how to wire a tabulating machine and, still more important, how to rationalize the information flow within a company. Hence, although they are facilitators of the communications revolution, they must be no less craft oriented than the salesmen of the less complex equipment of an earlier era. Within most such industries there is a great need for technically minded people who are, to a considerable degree, protected by their indispensable skills from having to be nice to everybody, with or without an expense account.

II. THE MILKY WAY

In the preceding chapter, I symbolized the ambition of the inner-directed man by referring to a frequent motto of his period: ad astra per aspera. The inner-directed man, socialized with reference to an older model, might choose for emulation a star from the heroes of his field. By contrast, the other-directed person does not so often think of his life in terms of an individualized career. He seeks not fame, which represents limited transcendence of a particular peer-group or a particular culture, but the respect and, more than the respect, the affection, of an amorphous and shifting, though contemporary, jury of peers.

To attain this goal he struggles not with the hardness of the material but with the very antagonistic cooperators who are engaged in the same pursuit and to whom he looks at the same time for values and for judgments of value. Instead of referring himself to the great men of the past and matching himself against his stars, the other-directed person moves in the midst of a veritable Milky Way of almost but not quite indistinguishable contemporaries. This is partly a tribute to the size of the educated middle class in the phase of incipient decline of population.

The uncertainty of life in our day is certainly a factor in the refusal of young people to commit themselves to long-term goals. War, depression, military service, are felt today as obstacles to planning a career far more than in the period prior to World War I. But these changes are not the whole story: the type of man who will not commit himself to long-range goals rationalizes his perspective on the future and his deferral of commitment by pointing to the all too evident uncertainties. We can conceive of people living at a time of equal uncertainty who would, out of ignorance and insensitivity as much as out of strength of character, plow ahead in pursuit of extensive aims. Doubtless, many other factors are also in the air: such as the fact, mentioned in a preceding section, that mobility often depends on leaving one's craft skill behind; and this very fork in the road which separates avenues within a craft from those achievable only by leaving the craft, suggests itself at an early stage of occupational life and complicates the career planning of the mobile youth.

There are certain positive sides to this development. The seemingly sure commitment of many inner-directed youths was based on an unquestioning acceptance of parental orders and parental ranking of occupations. The other-directed youth of today often asks more of a job than that it satisfy conventional status and pecuniary requirements; he is not content with the authoritative rankings of earlier generations. The age of other-direction does open up the possibilities of more individual and satisfying career choice, once society's pressure for an early decision, and the person's feeling of panic if he can make no decision, can be relaxed.

It follows from all this that the heavens of achievement look quite different to the other-directed youth than to his inner-directed predecessor. The latter found security in moving to the periphery of the various frontiers and establishing an isolated and recognizable claim on a new piece of territory—often with quite grandiose and imperialistic trappings. If he founded a firm, this was his lengthened shadow. Today the man is the shadow of the firm. Such long-term aims as exist are built into the firm, the institution; this is also the repository of the imperialist drives that sometimes take shape as the institution harnesses the mild and tractable wills of many other-directed people who are competing for places of marginal differentiation on the Milky Way.

To outdistance these competitors, to shine alone, seems hopeless, and also dangerous. To be sure, one may try to steal a march—to work harder, for instance, than the propaganda about working would permit—but these are petty thefts, not major stick-ups. They do, however, keep the competition for a position on the major streamlined runs of occupational life from being entirely cooperative. Yet even such behavior that may marginally flout the prevailing concepts of fairness looks to the peer-group for its norms of what is to be desired. And since each projects his own tendencies to unfair play onto the others, this, too, requires living in a state of constant alert as to what the others may be up to.

Hence the Milky Way is not an easy way, though its hardships differ from those of the earlier era. Obliged to conciliate or manipulate a variety of people, the other-directed person handles all men as customers who are always right; but he must do this with the uneasy realization that, as Everett Hughes has put it, some are more right than others. This diversity of roles to be taken with a diversity of customers is not institutionalized or clear cut, and the other-directed person tends to become merely his succession of roles and encounters and hence to doubt who he is or where he is going. Just as the firm gives up the one-price policy for an administered price that is set in secrecy and differs with each class of customer depending on the latter's apparent power and "good will" requirements, so the other-directed person gives up the one-face policy of the inner-directed man for a multiface policy that he sets in secrecy and varies with each class of encounters.

United with others, however, he can seek a modicum of social, economic, and political protection. The peer-group can decide that there are certain outcasts, in class or ethnic terms, to whom the glad hand need not be extended, or who can (like the Negro in the South) be forced to personalize without the privilege of demanding a reciprocal response. A class of customers can be politically created who are by definition wrong. Yet no amount of exclusiveness, though it may make life a bit easier for the insiders, can completely guarantee continuance in a place of visibility and approval in the Milky Way.

VII

THE OTHER–DIRECTED ROUND OF LIFE
(Continued): THE NIGHT SHIFT

But it must not be supposed that in the midst of all their toils the people who live in democracies think themselves to be pitied; the contrary is noticed to be the case. No men are fonder of their own condition. Life would have no relish for them if they were delivered from the anxieties which harass them, and they show more attachment to their cares than aristocratic nations to their pleasures.

Tocqueville, DEMOCRACY IN AMERICA

THE only thing that has changed since Tocqueville wrote (no small change, it is true) is that the sphere of pleasures has itself become a sphere of cares. Many of the physical hardships of the older frontiers of production and land use have survived in altered, psychological form on the newer one of consumption. Just as we saw in the previous chapter that the day shift of work-mindedness is invaded by glad-hand attitudes and values that stem in part from the sphere of leisure, so the night shift of leisure-mindedness is haunted by the others with whom one works at having a good time.

First of all, however, with the rise of other-direction, we see the passing both of the acquisitive consumers and of the escapists of the earlier era. The passion for acquisition diminishes when property no longer has its old stability and objective validity; escape diminishes by the very fact that work and pleasure are interlaced. We can see these new tendencies, in what is perhaps their most extreme form, the attitudes toward food and sexual experience prevailing among some upper middle-class groups.

I. Changes in the Symbolic Meaning of Food and Sex

From the Wheat Bowl to the Salad Bowl. Among inner-directed types there is of course great variation as to interest in food. In America—the story is different among the food-loving peoples of the rest of the world—puritans and nonpuritans of the recent past might use food for display, with relatively standardized menus for company and for dining out; what was put on display was a choice cut of meat, an elegant table, and good solid cooking. All this was an affair largely of the women, and in many circles food was not a proper topic for dinner conversation. Having the proper food was something one owed to one's status, one's claim to respectability, and more recently to one's knowledge of hygiene with its calories and vitamins. (This last pattern did not spread to the South, where an older, more gastronomically rugged tradition of ceremonial fondness for food prevailed.) The earlier editions of the *Boston Cooking School Cookbook* breathe this air of solidity, conservatism, and nutrition-mindedness.

The other-directed person of the midtwentieth century in America, on the contrary, puts on display his taste and not directly his wealth, respectability, cubic capacity, or caloric soundness. Indeed we saw in Chapter IV how the radio begins the other-directed person's training in food taste even before the child goes to school and how seriously he takes his lessons. While well-educated upper middle-class parents are becoming hesitant to tell children to eat something because it is good for them—lest they create oral complexes—they join the radio in discussion of what is "good" as a matter of taste. Often, in fact, this merely disguises the emotion focused on the child's eating habits, almost as much emotion as their parents concentrated on the regimen of no-nonsense plate cleaning. The other-directed person is thus prepared for the search for marginal differentiation not only in what he sets before his guests but in how it is talked about with them.

Earlier there existed a small coterie of gourmets; fastidious enjoyment of food was one hobby, among others, that inner-directed people might choose. Today, in wide circles, many people are and many more feel that they must be gourmets. The abundance of America in the phase of incipient population decline is perhaps the most important factor in this development; it has made the good foods available to nearly everybody. The seasonal and geographic limitations that in the earlier period narrowed food variations for all but the very rich have now been largely done away with by the network of distribution and the techniques of food preservation—both being legacies from the phase of transitional population growth. The consumer's choice among foods need therefore no longer be made on the basis either of tradition or of Malthusian limits.

As a result, both the setting of the meal and its content are affected. Informality breaks down the puritan inhibition against talking about food and drink, just as Mexican casseroles and copper kettles replace the white napery and classic decor of the nineteenth-century middle-class table. More important still, the housewife can no longer blame the preferential and limited cuisine offered by a kitchen servant for her failure to personalize her own tastes in food. In the period of incipient population decline servants disappear from the middle-class home, and where they do not, they lack any traditional pattern of prerogatives that allows them, rather than the host and hostess, to control the menu and its stylized serving. No walls of privacy, status, or asceticism remain to protect or prevent one from displaying personalized taste in food and decor as an element in one's competition with others. The diner has the power, unlike Jiggs, to decide that corned beef and cabbage is an amusing dish; he can ransack immigrant cookeries or follow the lead of food columnist Clementine Paddleford toward exoticism. Only at conventional conventions can one still find the uniform menu of steak or chicken, potatoes, and marbled peas. And at home, in place of the staple menu, the hostess today is encouraged to substitute her own specialty, such as lasagna or rüstoffel. Men are involved almost as much as women, and in the kitchen as well as at the back-yard grill.

The most popular cookbook today is said to be *The Joy of Cooking*, and the number of specialized cookbooks—ethnic, chatty, and atmospheric—constantly increases to meet the demand for marginal differentiation. The very change in titles—from the *Boston Cooking School Cook-book* to *How to Cook a Wolf* or *Food is a Four Letter Word*—reveals the changing attitude. For the other-di-rected person cannot lean on such objective standards of success as those which guided the inner-directed person: he may be haunted by a feeling that he misses the joy in food or drink which he is supposed to feel. Mealtime must now be "pleasurable"; the new *Fireside Cookbook* is offered to "people who are not content to regard food just as some-thing one transfers periodically from plate to mouth." And if one still fails to get much joy out of the recipes given there, he may search in books like *Spécialité de la Maison* to see what "others" are eating—to get the "favorite rec-ipes" of such people as Noel Coward and Lucius Beebe. Fred MacMurray and Claudette Colbert testify to the de-lights of new concoctions such as "The Egg and I Julep"; and "There is nothing," writes MacMurray in a little col-lection of his favorite egg recipes, "so appealing as a pair of fried eggs with their limpid golden eyes gazing fondly at you from the center of a breakfast plate, festooned with strips of crisp bacon or little-pig sausage. Or poached, gaily riding a raft of toast." The most popular translation of an old French cookbook, *Tante Marie*, is also extremely chatty, and *The Joy of Cooking* explains its chattiness by saying that originally the recipes were collected and written down for the author's daughter, who in turn thought "other daughters" might like them. (As there is today less teaching of daughters by mothers, the daughter must rely on the instruction of an outsider, if she is to cook at all.) In short, the other-directed person in his approach to food, as in his sexual encounters, is constantly looking for a qual-itative element that may elude him. He suffers from what

Martha Wolfenstein and Nathan Leites call "fun-morality."[1]

Of course, putting matters this way exaggerates the disadvantages of the shift: undeniably, many more people today really enjoy food and enjoy talk about food than was the case when the monotony of the American diet was notorious.

Many people, to be sure, follow the new fashions in food without being other-directed in character, just as many personnel directors in industry are zealous inner-directed believers in the glad hand. Even so, if we wanted to demarcate the boundaries of other-direction in America, we might find the analysis of menus to provide a not too inaccurate index. As tossed salads and garlic, elaborate sauces, dishes en casserole, *Gourmet* magazine, wine and liqueurs, spread west from New York and east from San Francisco, as men take two-hour lunch periods and exhibit their taste in food and wine, as the personalized cookbook tends to replace the Boston Cooking School type—in all these signs of the times we see indications of the new type of character. Recently, Russell Lynes, in his article, "Highbrow, Lowbrow, Middlebrow,"[2] sought to delineate the contemporary urban American social system in terms of similar consumption indexes. Thus, the tossed salad is the sign of the high-brow, who may also be tagged by his taste in cars, clothes, and posture. What we really see emerging is an embryonic social system whose criteria of status are inconsistent with the criteria of the more traditional class system. This has been seen by Lloyd Warner, who actually defines class less in terms of wealth or power and more in terms of sociability habits and consumption styles. These observers, however, are exceptional; as we shall see in Chapter XI, most Americans continue to see their social structure in terms of an older one based on wealth, occupation, and position in the society-page sense. But beneath these older rubrics, I believe that a much more amorphus structure is emerging in

[1] In *Movies* (Glencoe, Illinois, The Free Press, 1950).

[2] *Harper's*, 198 (1949), 19.

which taste leadership is increasingly important, and in which the "brow" hierarchy competes for recognition with the economic and production hierarchies.

Sex: the Last Frontier. In the era depending on inner-direction sex might be inhibited, as in classes and areas affected strongly by the Reformation and Counter Reformation. Or its gratification might be taken for granted among men and within given limits, as in Italy, Spain, and the non-respectable elements, such as the "riverbottom people," in every population. In both cases there was a certain simplification of sex, in the one instance by taboos, in the other by tradition. Economic or power problems, problems of mere existence or of "amounting to something," were uppermost; and sex was relegated to its "proper" time and place: night, the wife or whore, occasional rough speech, and daydreams. Only in the upper classes, precursors of modern other-directed types, did the making of love take precedence over the making of goods (as alleged in France) and reach the status of a daytime agenda. In these circles sex was almost totally separated from production and reproduction.

This separation, when it goes beyond the upper class and spreads over almost the whole society, is a sign that a society, through birth control and all that it implies, has entered the population phase of incipient decline by the route of industrialization. In this phase there is not only a growth of leisure, but work itself becomes both less interesting and less demanding for many; increased supervision and subdivision of tasks routinize the industrial process even beyond what was accomplished in the phase of transitional growth of population. More than before, as job-mindedness declines, sex permeates the daytime as well as the playtime consciousness. It is viewed as a consumption good not only by the old leisure classes but by the modern leisure masses.

The other-directed person, who often suffers from low responsiveness, may pursue what looks like a "cult of effortlessness" in many spheres of life. He may welcome the routinization of his economic role and of his domestic life;

the auto companies may tempt him by self-opening windows and self-shifting gears; he may withdraw all emotion from politics. Yet he cannot handle his sex life in this way. Though there is tremendous insecurity about *how* the game of sex should be played, there is little doubt as to *whether* it should be played or not. Even when we are consciously bored with sex, we must still obey its drive. Sex, therefore, provides a kind of defense against the threat of total apathy. This is one of the reasons why so much excitement is channeled into sex by the other-directed person. He looks to it for reassurance that he is alive. The inner-directed person, driven by his internal gyroscope and oriented toward the production problems of the outer world, did not need this evidence.

While the inner-directed acquisitive consumer could pursue the ever receding frontiers of material acquisition, these frontiers have lost much of their lure for the other-directed person. As we saw in Chapter III, the latter begins as a very young child to know his way around among available consumption goods. He travels widely, to camp or with his family. He knows that the rich man's car is only marginally, if at all, different from his own—a matter at best of a few additional horsepower. He knows anyway that next year's model will be better than this year's. Even if he has not been there, he knows what the night clubs are like; and he has seen television. Whereas the deprived inner-directed person often lusted for possessions as a goal whose glamour a wealthy adulthood could not dim, the other-directed person can scarcely conceive of a consumption good that can maintain for any length of time undisputed dominance over his imagination. Except perhaps sex.

For the consumption of love, despite all the efforts of the mass media, does remain hidden from public view. If someone else has a new Cadillac, the other-directed person knows what that is, and that he can duplicate the experience, more or less. But if someone else has a new lover, he cannot know what that means. Cadillacs have been democratized. So has sexual glamour, to a degree: without the mass production of good-looking, well-groomed youth, the

American pattern of sexual competition could not exist. But there is a difference between Cadillacs and sexual partners in the degree of mystery. And with the loss or submergence of moral shame and inhibitions, but not completely of a certain unconscious innocence, the other-directed person has no defenses against his own envy. He is not ambitious to break the quantitative records of the acquisitive sex consumers like Don Juan, but he does not want to miss, day in day out, the qualities of experience he tells himself the others are having.

In a way this development is paradoxical. For while cookbooks have become more glamorous with the era of other-direction, sex books have become less so. The older marriage manuals, such as that of Van der Velde (still popular, however), breathe an ecstatic tone; they are travelogues of the joy of love. The newer ones, including some high school sex manuals, are matter of fact, toneless, and hygienic—Boston Cooking School style. Nevertheless, much as young people may appear to take sex in stride along with their vitamins, it remains an era of competition and a locus of the search, never completely suppressed, for meaning and emotional response in life. The other-directed person looks to sex not for display but for a test of his or her ability to attract, his or her place in the "rating-dating" scale—and beyond that, in order to experience life and love.

One reason for the change is that women are no longer objects for the acquisitive consumer but are peer-groupers themselves. The relatively unemancipated wife and socially inferior mistresses of the inner-directed man could not seriously challenge the quality of his sexual performance. Today, millions of women, freed by technology from many household tasks, given by technology many "aids to romance," have become pioneers, with men, on the frontier of sex. As they become knowing consumers, the anxiety of men lest they fail to satisfy the women also grows—but at the same time this is another test that attracts men who, in their character, want to be judged by others. The very ability of women to respond in a way that only courtesans were supposed to in an earlier age means, moreover, that qualitative differences of sex experience—the impenetrable mystery—can be sought for night after night, and not only in periodic visits to a mistress or brothel. Whereas the pattern of an earlier era was often to make fun of sex, whether on the level of the music hall or of Balzac's *Droll Stories*, sex today carries too much psychic freight to be really funny for the other-directed person. By a disguised asceticism it becomes at the same time too anxious a business and too sacred an illusion.

This anxious competitiveness in the realm of sex has very little in common with older patterns of social climbing. To be sure, women still use sex as a means to status in spheres controlled by men. But they can do this chiefly in industries that are still competitive in the pre-monopolistic patterns. Thus until recently the theater and the movies were controlled by *novi homines* who remind us of those early nineteenth-century British mill owners who, before the Factory Acts, relied on their mills as a harem.[3] And Warner, Havighurst, and Loeb in *Who Shall Be Educated?*[4] describe how women schoolteachers may still cabin-date their way up the relatively unbureaucratized hierarchies of local school systems. These, however, are exceptional cases; the search for experience on the frontier of sex is, in the other-directed era, generally without ulterior motives.

II. CHANGES IN THE MODE OF CONSUMPTION OF POPULAR CULTURE

ENTERTAINMENT AS ADJUSTMENT TO THE GROUP

In Chapter IV we saw how the inner-directed youth was made ready to leave home and go far both by directly didac-

---

[3] See G. M. Young, *Portrait of an Age* (London, Oxford University Press, 1936), p. 16, n. 1.

[4] W. Lloyd Warner, Robert J. Havighurst, and Martin Loeb, *Who Shall Be Educated?* (New York, Harper, 1944), e.g., p. 103.

tic literature and by novels and biographies that gave him a sense of possible roles on the frontiers of production. In contrast to this, the other-directed person has recourse to a large literature that is intended to orient him in the non-economic side of life. This orientation is needed because, with the virtually complete disappearance of tradition-direction, no possibility remains of learning the art of life in the primary group—a possibility that persisted even in the mobile families of the era dependent on inner-direction. The child must look early to his mass-media tutors for instruction in the techniques of getting life directions as well as for specific tricks of the trade.

We can trace an edifying sequence that runs from the success biography of the Samuel Smiles or the Horatio Alger sort to the contemporary books and periodicals that deal with peace of mind. The earlier books are directly concerned with social and economic advance, dealt with as achievable by the virtues of thrift, hard work, and so on. Then we find in the first years of this century the development in America of the now almost forgotten "New Thought" movement. As described by A. Whitney Griswold, the movement's motto was: "Think Your Way to Wealth."[5] That is, wealth was to be achieved no longer by activity in the real world but by self-manipulation, a kind of economic Couéism. But wealth itself as a goal was unquestioned.

From then on, inspirational literature becomes less and less exclusively concerned with social and economic mobility. Dale Carnegie's *How to Win Friends and Influence People*, written in 1937, recommends self-manipulative exercises for the sake not only of business success but of such vaguer, leisure goals as popularity. Perhaps it is not only the change from depression to full employment that led Carnegie to write *How to Stop Worrying and Start Living* in 1948, in which self-manipulation is no longer oriented to-

---

[5] "The American Cult of Success" (Doctor's thesis, Yale University, 1933); abstracted in *American Journal of Sociology*, XL (1934), 309–318.

ward some social achievement but is used in a solipsistic way to adjust one to one's fate and social state. The same tendencies can be found in a large group of periodicals, with an interlocking directorate of authors and with titles such as *Journal of Living, Your Personality, Your Life,* which testify to the alteration of mobility paths and hopes and the increase of anxiety as a spur to seeking expert help. The *New York Times Book Review* of April 24, 1949, advertises *Calm Yourself* and *How to be Happy While Single;* the latter deals according to the advertisement with such problems as "how to handle the men in your life (heavy dates, office companions, friends, drunks) . . . making conversation . . . liquor, boredom—just about every problem you'll encounter on your own." Certainly, there are many positive sides to a development that substitutes for the older, external, and often pointless goals such as wealth and power, the newer, internal goals of happiness and peace of mind, though of course, one must always ask whether, in changing oneself, one is simply adapting to the world as it is without protest or criticism.

Here, however, I am not evaluating these trends but am interested in showing how popular culture is exploited for group-adjustment purposes not only in the form of manifestly didactic literature and services but also in fictional guise. There is nothing new in the observation that people who would rather not admit their need for help, or who prefer to spice it with fun, look to the movies and other popular media as the sources of enlightenment. In the studies of the movies made under the Payne Fund twenty years ago, much evidence was gathered concerning use of the movies by young people who wanted to learn how to look, dress, and make love.[6] The combination of learning and excitement was clear in these cases, especially among children of lower-class origin suddenly brought face to face with sex and splendor. Today, however, as audiences have

---

[6] See, for example, Herbert Blumer and Philip Hauser, *Movies, Delinquency, and Crime* (New York, Macmillan, 1933), pp. 102 *et seq.*

become more sophisticated, the mixture of messages has become more subtle.

From a sample of a group of women's magazines, *Ladies' Home Journal, American, Good Housekeeping,* and *Mademoiselle,* for October, 1948, I concluded that a good many stories and features and, of course, far less subtly, many ads, dealt largely with modes of manipulating the self in order to manipulate others, primarily for the attainment of intangible assets such as affection. Two stories will illustrate: "The Rebellion of Willy Kepper" by Willard Temple in *Ladies' Home Journal* and "Let's Go Out Tonight" by Lorna Slocombe in the *American* magazine.

Handling the office. "The Rebellion of Willy Kepper" is unusual in that it deals with a work situation rather than a domestic and leisure one. It is the story of a paint salesman, Willy, a shy young man who has worked himself up through the factory. There is a pretty file clerk whom Willy wants to know better but does not know how to approach. At this point the stockholder's son enters the business, gets the promotion Willy hoped for, and makes time with the file clerk. Willy, previously so mild, loses his temper and becomes gruff and rasping with people in the office and shop. This is his "rebellion." This change of mood is of course noticed at once.

Willy, however, has built up an enormous capital of good will by his previous good temper, so that plant people, instead of turning on him, try to find out what the trouble is; it cannot be Willy's fault. They discover that the stockholder's son is to blame, and they set out to hex him—he trips into paint, gets orders mixed up, and rapidly learns how dependent he is on others' liking him if he is to do his job. Willy, in fact, saves him from his worst jam with a customer, and after a few knocks of this sort the son decides to start at the bottom in the factory, in order to earn his own capital of good will. Thus the road to Willy's promotion is reopened. At the end Willy asks the stockholder's son what techniques he used with the file clerk. He tells

Willy to compliment her on her eyes; he does so and succeeds in making a date.

There are some fairly obvious things to be said about this story. In the first place, though it is set in the sphere of production, it deals with the sales end of a factory which is a net of interpersonal relations that will deliver paint to the customer only against a bill of lading marked "good will." The work situation is seen in terms of its human element and its noneconomic incentives. There are no problems about paint, but only about people. In the second place, the stockholder's son was able to date the girl not because of his wealth and position but because of his line, his skill in the leisure arts of language. Language is presented as a free consumers' good; one, moreover, of which the consumer is also a producer; there is no patent or monopoly on lines. Finally, we have a picture of the "antagonistic cooperators" of the same sex—Willy and the son—whose rivalry for job and girl is so muted that they can exchange advice on how to win both; in a way, they are more interested in each other's approval than in victory. In the end Willy has regained his lost good temper and his rival has given up his early arrogance.

Handling the home. "Let's Go Out Tonight" pictures the consumption frontier of a young, college-bred suburban matron. Her husband is a good provider and faithful; her two children are healthy; she has everything—except enough attention from her tired businessman spouse. The latter comes home, reads a paper, goes to bed, and his wife complains to her friend in their morning telephone chat that they never go places and do things any more. She looks back nostalgically on her college days when he was courting her and when life seemed glamorous. Suddenly she decides to go back to her college to see just what the magic was in those days.

When she gets to her old room she realizes that only in retrospect was her college dating effortless. Actually, she recalls, she slaved to arrange parties for her future husband,

to manipulate him into kissing her and finally into propos-
ing. She concludes that she just has been loafing on her job
as a housewife, and returns full of tolerant understanding
for her husband and enthusiasm for new and improved
manipulation. By buying a new dress, arranging with a sit-
ter to have the children taken care of, and similar measures,
she inveigles her husband into a theater date and is able to
report success to her friend on the telephone.

In the era of inner-direction, stories of a similarly orienta-
tional cast often encouraged the reader to aspire to distant
horizons, to play for big stakes; many such stories today
strike us as escapist and sentimental. In contrast, the type
of "realism" in modern magazine fiction is neither uplift-
ing nor escapist. There is an all too sensible refusal, in a
story like "Let's Go Out Tonight," to admit that there can
be decisively better marriages than this one, with its continuous petty deception. The reader of these stories will
by no means always find his ideals and ways of life approved
—it is a mistake to suppose that such magazines as Ladies'
Home Journal are edited by a formula of giving "the public
what it wants"—but he is seldom stimulated to make great
demands on life and on himself. In both of the stories I
have used here as illustration, the assumption is made that
a solution of conflict is available that involves neither risk
nor hardship but only the commodities—interpersonal
effort and tolerance—that the other-directed person is already prepared to furnish.

"Conspiracy" theories of popular culture are quite old,
summed up as they are in the concept of "bread and cir-
cuses." In "The Breadline and the Movies" Thorstein Veblen presented a more sophisticated concept, namely, that
the modern American masses paid the ruling class for the
privilege of the very entertainments that helped to keep
them under laughing gas. Such views assume the culture to
be more of a piece than it is. Group adjustment and orien-
tational influence in contemporary popular culture does
not serve the interest of any particular class. In fact, pressures for other-directed conformity appear strongest in the

better educated strata. The form these pressures take may be illustrated by a few examples.

Heavy harmony. The head of a progressive boarding school in the East recently addressed the parents of its children as follows:

The music department at X School wishes to provide for every child, as rich a musical experience as possible.

We believe that music is a necessary part of life and its influence is felt in every phase of living. Singing and playing together can bring understanding and good-will and it seems to me that this world needs more of this kind of harmony.

At X, we try to provide some kind of music participation for every child and wish to encourage more musical activity, especially that of playing with a group in an orchestra.

This letter does not betray much interest in music as such. It sees music primarily as a way of bringing people together locally and internationally too. Music as a way of escape into one's individual creative life—a private refuge —would strike many such school authorities today as selfish.

A similar theme appears in more refined form in Helen Howe's novel of Harvard academic life, *We Happy Few.*[7] The heroine Dorothea is viewed by Miss Howe as a selfish woman who, during the war, escapes from her social duties by having a love affair and by playing Bach and Mozart to herself on the piano. She is taken in the novel through a series of group-adjustment experiences that deflate what Miss Howe regards as her intellectual snobbery. Becoming a nurse's aid, she meets other nurse's aids socially; they are fine and dull. Traveling to Coeur d'Alene to be near her son in training, she "sees" America: in the stench of the

---

[7] I have dealt with the implications of this book in more detail in "The Ethics of We Happy Few," *University Observer*, I (1947), 19; I draw on this article in what follows.

ladies' room, the sadness of platform partings, the good-heartedness of midwesterners. The townsfolk of Coeur d'Alene are another group-adjusting experience; they, too, are fine and dull. At the end Dorothea returns to Cambridge a sadder and wiser woman: her pride is gone, and she has learned humbly to admire the great open spaces and the open sentiments usually associated with them in song and story.

As a symbol of the learning process, Miss Howe writes that Dorothea, while a nurse's aid staggering through agonizing days at the hospital, learns in her few off hours to enjoy Schumann as well as her beloved Bach and Mozart: "Her aesthetic as well as her human taste was stretching, too—cruder, possibly, but warmer and more inclusive."

This quotation hardly needs comment. Instead of permitting the heroine to escape either up or down from the exasperating human contacts of a nurse's work day, Dorothea must move sideways. She must acquire warmer, group-adjusted musical tastes—she would be forgiven even more, doubtless, if she learned to like Ethelbert Nevin.[8]

Yet granting Dorothea should learn this interpersonal art as a benefit to her work as a nurse's aid—perhaps the sick are a special case and do need warmth of this sort—it is striking that she must bring the identical attitude into her leisure time: no change of roles is permitted. Leisure and work must, like Dorothea herself, be stretched (assuming, falsely, that Schumann's sentimentality is "warmer") until they completely overlap. The theme of both is group adjustment.

---

[8] The reference to warmth is especially significant in the analysis of peer-group preferences in people. In a very interesting set of experiments, Solomon E. Asch has shown that the warm-cold axis is for his student subjects the controlling dimension of personality: people who are said to be warm are positively valued no matter what other traits they have, while people who are cold are distrusted no matter how honorable and brave they may be. See Solomon E. Asch, "A Test for Personality," *Journal of Abnormal and Social Psychology*, 41 (1946), 258–290.

What I have said is not to be understood as a polemic for coldness as against warmth or as a criticism of the genuine elements in the other-directed person's concern for warmth, in himself and in others. Certainly it is an advance from the compulsory emotional constriction, the frightening coldness, of many inner-directed Americans, to open up group sociability to a wider and more outgoing responsiveness.

Lonely successes. In our discussion of the comics, of *Tootle,* and of "Willy Kepper," we saw how modern popular culture stresses the dangers of aloneness and, by contrast, the virtues of group-mindedness. In a thoughtful article, "The Gangster as Tragic Hero," Robert Warshow deals with a number of recent gangster films from this perspective.[9] He notes that, inevitably, the gangster's success spells his undoing. For it cuts him off from the group—not only the law-abiding community but also his own gang. At the peak of success he is therefore miserable and frightened, waiting to be cut down from the heights.

We can interpret this as a cautionary tale about what happens if one goes off on one's own pursuits. Success is fatal. According to the code of the movies one is not permitted to identify with the lonely escapist; his lot is pictured, like that of Dorothea in the novel, as a set of miseries and penances. The movie *Body and Soul* points a similar moral. The hero is a Jewish boy from the East Side who gets to be boxing champion and proceeds to alienate all surrounding groups: his family circle and faithful girl; his unambitious, devoted retinue; the East Side Jews who see him as a hero. He agrees for a large sum to throw his last fight and bets against himself; his losing will complete his alienation from these groups. En route to the fight he is told that the Jews see him as a hero, a champion in the fight against Hitler. Recalled to "himself," he double-crosses his gangster backers by winning the fight; and, poor again, he is restored to the primary group of family, girl, and Jews.

A movie or book occasionally comes along that departs from this formula. *The Fountainhead*, by Ayn Rand, a popular book and movie, pictures its architect hero as standing out, in violent integrity, against the pressure for group adjustment and, in the end, successfully bringing the jury of his peers along with him. He does take all: the heights of fame, his rival's wife, the death of his rival. What is most striking in all this, however, is the unintended caricature, both of group adjustment and of group resistance. The group is made out not tolerant but mean, inartistic, and corrupt. And group resistance is seen in terms of nobility on the part of the sadistic hero, who wants to deny any ties to humanity, any dependency. This superman for adults is the very apotheosis of the lonely success, to be admired perhaps by the reader but too stagey to be imitated.

In all likelihood, moreover, the Ayn Rand audience that applauds fiery denunciations of group-mindedness and submission to others is quite unaware of its own tendencies to submission in the small, undramatic situations of daily life. In that sense *The Fountainhead* is escapist.

GOOD-BYE TO ESCAPE?

So far, in these illustrations, we have seen little that would correspond to the unambiguous escapes of the inner-directed. Rather, we have seen popular culture used, often quite desperately, for training in group adjustment. In the same way, we may find popular culture used as training in consumer orientation, which is hardly a less serious problem (in many ways it is the same problem) for the other-directed person. Despite appearances the other-directed person seems often unable to get away from himself or to waste time with any gestures of abundance or abandon. (Of course, if we compared patterns of alcoholic escape, we might come up with somewhat different results.)

The inner-directed person, if influenced by Protestantism, is of course also unable to waste time. The mobile youth from the lower classes shows his commitment to inner-direction by cutting himself off from hard-drinking, horse-play-indulging pals: he continues the production of an inner-directed character through practicing a kind of mental bookkeeping by which the demons of Waste and Sloth are ruthlessly driven out. Such a person has little leisure, unless he can justify it as self-improving, and a life that has never an idle moment must have many a tense one. On the face of it the other-directed person is no puritan; he seems much less preoccupied with waste; his furnishings, manners, and morals are more casual. But an attenuated puritanism survives in his exploitation of leisure. He may say, when he takes a vacation or stretches a weekend, "I owe it to myself"—but the self in question is viewed like a car or house whose upkeep must be carefully maintained for resale purposes. The other-directed person has no clear core of self to escape from; no clear line between production and consumption; between adjusting to the group and serving private interests; between work and play.

One interesting index of this is the decline of evening dress, especially among men, and conversely, the invasion of the office by sport clothes. This looks like an offshoot of the cult of effortlessness, and of course men say "it's too much trouble" in explaining why they don't change for dinner or the evening. But the explanation lies rather in the fact that most men today simply do not know how to change roles, let alone mark the change by proper costuming. Another reason may be the fear of being thought high-hat; one can wear gaudy shirts but not stiff ones. Thus the sport shirt and casual dress show that one is a good fellow not only on the golf course or on vacation but in the office and at dinner too.

Women are still permitted to dress for the evening, a sign, perhaps, of their laggard response to changing modes. They are more involved than men in the dying patterns of conspicuous consumption. However, they probably make more of an actual shift from housework and babies to dinner party than many men do, who exchange office gossip both at work and play: moreover, they really like the shift, dragging the men, who would just as soon be in the office, along with them. I have observed that women's shop talk of children and domestic matters is often—though certainly not always!—conducted with more skill, interest, and realism than that of men since the change of role refreshes both work and play.

What is it that drives men who have been surrounded with people and their problems on the day shift to seek often exactly the same company (or its reflection in popular culture) on the night shift? Perhaps in part it is the terror of loneliness that the gangster movies symbolize. But certainly it makes for strain. Though popular culture on one level "fills in" between people so as to avoid any demand for conversational or sexual gambits, on another level the popular-culture performance is not simply a way of killing time: in the peer-group situation, it makes a demand that it be appraised. The other-directed girl who goes in company to the movies need not talk to the others during the picture but is sometimes faced with the problem: should she cry at the sad places or not? What is the proper reaction, the sophisticated line about what is going on? Observing movie audiences coming out of a "little" or "art" theater, it is sometimes apparent that people feel they ought to react, but how?

In contrast to this, the inner-directed person, reading a book alone, is less aware of the others looking on; moreover, he has time to return at his own pace from being transported by his reading—to return and put on whatever mask he cares to. The poker game in the back room, with its praise of masks, fits his habituation to social distance, even loneliness. His successor, dreading loneliness, tries to assuage it not only in his crowd but in fantasy pursuits that, like a mirror, only return his own concerns to him.

III. The Two Types Compared

We have completed our direct confrontation of the two types; and it now becomes necessary to redress the balance against other-direction, which, I know, has come off a bad second in these pages. It is hard for us to be quite fair to the other-directed. The term itself suggests shallowness and superficiality as compared to the inner-directed, even though direction in *both* cases comes from outside and is simply internalized at an early point in the life cycle of the inner-directed.

There are factors outside of terminology that may lead readers to conclude that inner-direction is better. Academic and professional people are frequently only too pleased to be told that those horrid businessmen, those glad-handing advertisers, are manipulative. And, as we all know, the businessmen and advertisers themselves flock to plays and movies that tell them what miserable sinners they are. Of course it is especially gratifying to look down one's nose at Hollywood, soap opera, and other mass-culture phenomena.

Inner-directed persons of high status, moreover, are associated with the Anglo-Saxon tradition and with the reverence we pay to those among the aged who are still powerful. Furthermore, since the inner-directed face problems that are not the problems of the other-directed, they seem to be made of sterner and more intrepid stuff. As we already find the Victorians charming, so we can patronize the inner-directed, especially if we did not personally suffer from their limitations, and view the era depending on inner-direction with understandable nostalgia.

Furthermore I do not want to be understood as saying it is wrong to be concerned with the "others," with human relations. That we can afford to be concerned with such problems is one of the important abundances of a high technology society. We must ask anyone who opposes the manipulation of men in modern industry whether he prefers to return to their brutalization, as in the early days of the industrial revolution. In my scheme of values, persuasion, even manipulative persuasion, is to be preferred to force. There is the danger, in fact, when one speaks of the "softness of the personnel," that one will be understood to prefer hardness. On the contrary, one of the main contentions of this book is that the other-directed person, as things are, is already too hard on himself in certain ways and that his anxieties, as child consumer-trainee, as parent, as worker and player, are very great. He is often torn between the illusion that life should be easy, if he could only find his way to the proper group-adjustment practices, and the half-buried feeling that it is not easy for him. Under these conditions it would only complicate his life still further to hold up the opposite illusion of stern inner-direction as an ideal, though this is just what many people propose. In fact, just because he is other-directed he is often overready to take some intransigent and convinced person as a model of what he himself ought to be like; his very sympathy and sensitivity may undo him.

It is easy to score verbal triumphs over American personnel practices and popular culture, for age-old snobberies converge here. Thus, a critique of the glad hand can be made from many points of view, radical or reactionary. The context out of which I have written is, however, somewhat different—it is an effort to develop a view of society which accepts rather than rejects new potentialities for leisure, human sympathy, and abundance. Both the glad hand and the search for adjustment lessons in popular culture are themselves often poignant testimonials to these potentialities. The values of the era of the invisible hand accompanied scarcity, and thus require re-interpretation before they become relevant to an era of abundance. The promising alternative to other-direction, as I shall try to make clear in Part III, is not inner-direction, but autonomy.

PART II: POLITICS

VIII

TRADITION–DIRECTED, INNER–DIRECTED, AND OTHER–DIRECTED POLITICAL STYLES: INDIFFERENTS, MORALIZERS, INSIDE–DOPESTERS

In some countries, the inhabitants seem unwilling to avail themselves of the political privileges which the law gives them; it would seem that they set too high a value upon their time to spend it on the interests of the community . . . But if an American were condemned to confine his activities to his own affairs, he would be robbed of one half of his existence; he would feel an immense void in the life which he is accustomed to lead, and his wretchedness would be unbearable.

Tocqueville, DEMOCRACY IN AMERICA

I TURN in this part of the book to an introductory effort to apply to American politics the theory of character developed in the preceding part. First, however, the problems and limitations of this sort of approach to politics must be pointed out. My general thesis is that the inner-directed character tended and still tends in politics to express himself in the style of the "moralizer," while the other-directed character tends to express himself politically in the style of an "inside-dopester." These styles are also linked with a shift in political mood from "indignation" to "tolerance," and a shift in political decision from dominance by a ruling class to power dispersal among many marginally competing pressure groups. Some of these shifts may be among the causative factors for the rise of other-direction.

Having said this, I must immediately make certain qualifications. Once again, I must call to the reader's attention the limitations of social class and region which bound the picture of character in America I have presented. Furthermore, as I have also said before, real people are blends, more complicated and various—things of shreds and patches—than any scheme can encompass. They may, for example, be on the whole other-directed, but politics may be a sphere in which they are more inner-directed than otherwise. Or, people may manage to be productive in politics—to have a style that is superior to that of the moralizer and that of the inside-dopester—even though in their life as a whole they appear to be "lost": politics may be their most healthy activity; or politics may be a sphere in which, for any number of reasons, they are less adequate than in others.

But these problems of character are not the only factors that forbid us to explain or predict specific political behavior on psychological grounds alone. To take only one instance, the crisis mood of much contemporary politics, its often unimaginative alternatives, may be enough, or virtually enough, to explain the failure of people to develop new political styles—to bring new motivations to politics and new ways of defining what politics is, even though their character may have changed.

My investigation is not directly concerned with the political as defined from the point of view of the state or from the point of view of the groups, parties, and classes into which the state is divided for purposes of formal political analysis, but is concerned instead with the process by which people become related to politics, and the consequent stylizing of political emotions. Obviously, the line between these two spheres cannot be too neatly drawn; the great tradition of modern political science that runs from Machiavelli and Hobbes to Tocqueville and Marx is concerned with both. This is one reason why, in speaking of the political consequences of character, I use the impressionistic term "style."[1] If politics is a ballet on a stage set by history,

---

[1] While the term "style" is used here in a different sense from that employed by Lasswell in his "Style in the Lan-

style tells us neither whence the dancers come nor whither they move but only in what manner they play their parts and how the audience responds.

When I proceed, later on, from the problem of style to the problem of power, the connection between character structure and political structure will become even more tenuous than the word "style" implies. It is obvious, on the one hand, that many people today flee from the realities of power into psychological interpretations of social behavior in order either to avoid the challenge of contemporary political faiths or to restore a wished-for malleability to politics by reliance on a new analytical gadget. Nevertheless, it should be equally obvious that a political realism that ignores the dimension of character, that ignores how people interpret power configurations on the basis of their psychic needs, will only be useful in very short-run interpretations and not always even there.

I. THE INDIFFERENTS

OLD STYLE

Just as the notion that all adult members of a community must be involved in its policy-making is recent, so is the view that political indifference and apathy constitute problems. Thus, in ancient oriental societies where only the dynasty and a small group of advisers and nobles were called into the sphere of participation, the rest of the population could not properly be termed apathetic: it was simply politically asleep. Likewise, in the Greek city-state we can think of apathy as a problem only among the citizens—women, aliens, and slaves were simply excluded from the sphere of political involvement.

---

guage of Politics," in Harold D. Lasswell, Nathan Leites, et al., *Language of Politics* (New York, George W. Stewart, 1949), pp. 20–39, I am indebted to this essay; and my collaborators and I, in trying to relate politics to character, owe much to Lasswell's great body of work in this field which began with *Psychopathology and Politics*.

The few tradition-directed people in America are numbered among political indifferents of this type. Theirs is the classic indifference of the masses of antiquity or the Middle Ages—the people who, throughout history, have accepted, with recurrent cynicism and sporadic revolts, the tyranny of an elite. They have no means of being articulate politically, nor have they any conception of what this would involve. They lack the elementary political tools of literacy, political education, and organizational experience.

In the United States today the number of such tradition-directed indifferents is small. There are few "reservations" where people can avoid being affected by inner-directed or other-directed values or both. However, among some immigrant groups and rural Negroes, the old indifference of tradition-direction remains, at least to a degree. I will take one example from an interview[2] with a middle-aged cleaning woman from the British West Indies, now living in Harlem. Though she has been strongly affected by inner-direction, her political attitudes (allowing for guarded response) do seem representative of certain themes of an indifference resting on tradition-direction.

Q. Do you consider yourself a person who's very interested in politics, not so interested, or hardly interested at all?

A. Nooooo. My husband yes. He's a talker. He can hold debates.

Q. Do you make up your mind about what's going on? Like do you know who you want to win the election?

A. No. I believe the best man wins.

Q. You don't think it makes any difference who wins, then?

A. No difference. The best man wins. They're all alike anyway when they get in. All the same. They do the same

---

[2]The interview was one of a number conducted in 1948 by Dr. Genevieve Knupfer among migrants to Harlem from the deep South, the Caribbean, and Italy. It is published in full in *Faces in the Crowd*, pp. 98–119.

things. A Republican gets in, or a Democrat. They're all the same.

Q. Do you ever hear things on the radio about politics that make you mad?

A. No, I not interested so I no get mad.

Q. Do you hear anything else over the radio that makes you mad—not politics?

A. No.

Q. Do you hear anything that makes you glad?

A. No.

Q. What kind of people do you think are interested in politics?

A. Oh . . . I believe more rich folks. Poor class would be too, but they don't have no chance.

Q. Do you think wars can be avoided?

A. No. The Bible says the Romans will fight. (Something like that—I didn't quite get it.) I believe there will always be wars (said almost with satisfaction, as you'd say "There'll always be an England"). Generation after generation—the Bible tells you that.

Q. Do you think we can do something to avoid depressions?

A. I think you can work and try to have something—but some times will be hard and some times better. And if you have a little something it's better but you can get along somehow. . . .

Q. Do you think the people in Washington know better than other people whether there'll be a war?

A. Only God in Heaven knows. Man don't know. We just hope. . . .

Q. Do you think that on the whole the United States is a democracy?

A. I'll say one thing, she is a blessed country. Out of all the countries of the world, she is blessed.

Characteristic of the tradition-directed indifferent is an attitude that politics is someone else's job; with the interviewee above, politics is for her husband, the rich, and very likely the club of the white man. The depth and tenacity

of these proxy conventions are such that the political indifferent of this type, though excluded from direct political
participation, has no cause to feel at sea. Having no sense
of personal responsibility for the political sphere, such a
person seeks no power over, and therefore seldom feels
frustrated or guilty about, politics. Indeed, beyond the
ministrations of the "wise, the good, and the rich"—to use
Fisher Ames's words—responsibility for the political is not
man's, but God's.

NEW STYLE

So much for the increasingly rare indifferents whose political style is compatible with a tradition-directed character, lowly class position, poverty, and lack of political
education. Much more important are the indifferents who,
no longer tradition-directed, have acquired the elementary
political tools of literacy, a certain amount of organizational
competence, and a certain awareness of the uses that may
be made of political activity. To be sure, when we study the
efforts to bring political education and organization to those
who live either in rural or in urban slum areas, it often appears that the conditions of their life do not train them in
the political motivations or techniques (such simple techniques, for instance, as the easy use of the telephone) that
are taken for granted in some politically conscious and
active sections of the middle class. Yet in the course of the
last century the spread of education, the shortening and
easing of working hours, the rise of unions and other more
or less formal associations, the increase in experience with
government forms and routines, seem to have increased the
ability, if not the desire, of the poorer citizens to maneuver
in the political sphere.

Nevertheless, these people are, in the main, indifferent
to politics, although their indifference is not the classic,
quiescent indifference of the tradition-directed. It is to a
large degree the indifference of people who know enough
about politics to reject it, enough about political information to refuse it, enough about their political responsibilities

as citizens to evade them. Some of these new-style indifferents we may classify as inner-directed or other-directed people who happen not to have adopted a political style more characteristic for their type. Otherwise, they are people who are on the move, characterologically and socially, from one character type and social situation to another: uprooted tradition-directed people not yet acculturated to inner-direction, inner-directed people not yet acculturated to other-direction, and all shades between.

This is speculative, of course. External factors in the present political scene are often sufficient to explain a similar indifference in all classes and all character types. It is clear that an individual may withdraw completely from politics because the scene looks so hopeful that no action seems necessary. One might argue that American life can be sufficiently satisfying, even for many in lower-income ranks, to justify indifference to political efforts at improvement: in this light, as Americans are rich enough and comfortable enough to afford more food, more telephones, more trips than most people, in their security they can afford more political indifference. Contrariwise, a person may withdraw completely from politics because the scene looks so confused that no action seems adequate or so hopeless that no action looks promising; and these too, are the feelings of many Americans. A failure to act politically or to inform oneself, motivated in any of these ways, does not mean that the individual's indifference has anything to do with his character. However, a person's habitual failure over a long period of time to make any overt response to political stimuli may contribute to, or in fact constitute, a withdrawal of affect, and this can spread from politics to other spheres as well as vice versa, with consequences for character formation.

To illustrate the problem, I will draw on a group of interviews conducted (by Martin and Margy Meyerson) in a small county-seat town in Vermont, where the older generation seems to be heavily inner-directed, and the younger generation is becoming increasingly other-directed. The old people in this community express feelings of responsibility for politics. Despite their lack of actual participation, they feel their relatedness to government, though it is often expressed only in grievance and guilt feelings. Thus, they say they ought to take part in politics. In referring to events they use the pronoun "I": "I" think, "I" want, "I" hate, and so on. They talk as if it were up to them to judge what happens in politics and, to the limit of their gifts and available energies, to guide it.

The young people of the town, on the other hand, while they have greater education and the elementary political tools, feels that political doings are no business of theirs. They have less grievance and less guilt. Both kinds of feelings, which might relate them to politics, even though inadequately, have been withdrawn. Instead, they take whatever government gives them, including the draft, with an almost total passivity.[3] Their references to politics are almost devoid of the pronoun "I"; sometimes the reference is to a group "we" and mostly to a group "they." More "socialized," more cooperative than their parents, they do not react as individuals to what happens to them. They have passed from the indignation of their elders to indifference. This, plainly, is not the indifference of the tradition-directed person. Perhaps it is the indifference of those caught between inner-direction and other-direction.

Whether their political style—even their character—will change when they in turn are the elder generation, no one can predict. Very likely, there may be a life cycle of political styles for the individual, in which relatedness is gained as well as lost as one grows older. Nevertheless, I am inclined to think that the new-style indifferents, passive and resigned today, will scarcely alter their political stance as they grow older—provided, of course, that general social conditions do not change appreciably. Their life experiences may

---

[3] I am not saying, of course, that they should resist the draft by becoming conscientious objectors—that requires a rare heroism or fanaticism. It is their subjective attitude of which I speak, not their overt behavior: they have surrendered the privilege to criticize, to respect and express at least their own feelings.

bring them some degree of competence—if, for instance, they get involved with the Farm Bureau or union political leg work, but even their frustrations will be accepted, not resisted. We see here, if these speculations are correct, evidence of a long-range historical change in political style rather than evidence for the existence of a phase in the life cycle in which anyone might be indifferent.

Indifferents, old style and new style, as I define them, probably account for more than a majority of the American population. They are not necessarily equivalent to the nonvoters: these indifferents may perform quite a few political chores, for a price or under pressure. Nor are they devoid of political opinions. Indeed, if we accept the evidence of public opinion polls, it would seem that only some 10 per cent of the population refuses to be polled at all, while another 10 per cent or so gets into the "Don't Know" column. From this, we might conclude that people in all regions and social classes have a sense of direct and easy influence on the forum of opinion and policy and that their willingness to have and state an opinion is a sign of political health. But closer examination of the attitudes that accompany the interviewing and polling process fails to support that judgment. Actually, these political opinions are connected neither with direct political self-interest nor with clear emotional ties to politics. They resemble, rather, the peer-group exchange of consumption preferences, though unlike the latter, the preferences are seldom taken into the political market and translated into purchases of political commodities. For the indifferents do not believe that, by virtue of anything they do, know, or believe, they can buy a political package that will substantially improve their lives. And so, subject to occasional manipulation, they tend to view politics in most of its large-scale forms as if they were spectators.

Since, however, these new-style indifferents have some education and organizational competence and since they are neither morally committed to political principles nor emotionally related to political events, they are rather easily welded into cadres for political action—much as they are capable of being welded into a modern mechanized and specialized army. The old-style tradition-directed indifferents, on the other hand, have no such potential; at best, they are capable of sporadic and more or less spontaneous action. The new-style indifferents, however, are attached neither to their privacy, which would make politics intrusive, nor to their class groupings, which would make politics limited: rather, like the young Vermonters previously described, they are socialized, passive, and cooperative —not only in politics, of course. Their loyalty is at large, ready to be captured by any movement that can undercut their frequent cynicism or exploit it. In all these ways they place hardly any barriers, even those of their own tastes and feelings, between themselves and the politically organized community. The only barrier is their apathy.

This apathy cuts two ways. It deprives them of the capacity for enthusiasm and for genuine political involvement, but it also helps protect them from falling for many of the fairy tales about politics that have mobilized people in the past for political adventures. And while the tradition-directed person can sometimes be roused, in his inexperience, into indignation and is even sometimes hungry for political indoctrination (as for literacy of any sort) the modern indifferent in this country has built up a fairly high and often fairly useful immunity to politics—though not to cynical attacks on "politics."

II. THE MORALIZERS

Sometimes people call me an idealist. Well, that is the way I know I am an American. America is the only idealist nation in the world.

Woodrow Wilson

The typical style of the inner-directed person in nineteenth-century American politics is that of the moralizer. Since the inner-directed man is work driven and work oriented, his profoundest feelings wrapped up in work and the competence with which work is done, when he turns to politics he sees it as a field of work—and judges it accordingly. Presented with a political message, he sees a task in it, and, far from seeking to demonstrate his knowledge of its meaning in terms of personalities, he responds with emotional directness and often naïveté. (Of course not all inner-directed people are responsive to politics and not all who are, are moralizers.)

One variant of the moralizer projects on the political scene his characterological tendency toward self-improvement: he wants to improve all men and institutions. The fringes of the Granger Movement harbored such types in the last quarter of the nineteenth century, and perhaps the Cross of Gold speech marked a peak of enthusiastic moralizing of the "fisc." But by the time the issue arose of American adherence to the League of Nations, Wilson was considered by many to be merely a moralizer, an idealist, unable to get his friends, his enemies, and perhaps himself to understand how aware he was of practical, manipulative problems. Another variant on the type expresses his moralizing capacity less by desire to achieve the possible good than to prevent the perpetual recurrence of evil. This interest in repressing the evil rather than in evoking the good is carried over from his own personal struggle. Evil defines itself for him with ease and clarity: for instance, a lack of seriousness toward work is sloth, a comfortable attitude toward pleasure is debauchery, a skeptical attitude about property is socialism.

The inner-directed man, when he approaches politics, has a tendency to underestimate the values of easygoing looseness of political articulation. He does not look to politics for intellectual orientation in a confusing world, and generally he does not see it as a game to be watched for its human interest. Rather, he turns to politics to protect his vested interests, and whether these are of a "practical" or an "ideal" sort, he feels little ambivalence about them. Thus we might find in the same characterological and even political camp a tariff logroller and a prohibitionist or prison reformer, provided only that the former had some emotional charge behind his political pressure.

As we saw in discussing the characterological struggle in the first chapter, it makes a great deal of difference whether a character type is on the increase or the wane. The moralizer-in-power is representative of a class (the "old" middle class) and of a character type (the inner-directed) dominant in the nineteenth century. The moralizer-in-retreat represents the same class and character in their mid-twentieth-century decline.

THE STYLE OF THE MORALIZER-IN-POWER

Much of what we know of nineteenth-century American politics may be seen in terms of inner-directed self-interest and inner-directed moralizing. While today we tend to think of moralizing and self-interest as contradictory approaches to politics, amalgamated only through hypocrisy, this very outlook says something about our own loss of political simplicities. In the nineteenth century moralizing and self-interested stances were compatible because, in comparison with today, there was little conflict between the clear emotions felt and the clear interests recognized by the inner-directed. The *Federalist Papers* are perhaps the classic example of this. To be sure, with the broadening of the electorate it became increasingly difficult to be as frank as the Founding Fathers—as Nicholas Biddle learned to his sorrow—and one result was an increasing tendency to divorce interest from morality or to cloud their junction in vague, demagogic ideology. Even so, until the Civil War, unconcealed economic interests constantly intruded on the political sphere, shaping up in great arguments over fiscal policy, internal development, taxation, and property interests in slavery or antislavery. Likewise, moralizing interests made themselves felt quite openly in the government of towns, in arguments about manhood suffrage, universal education, and slavery.

The platforms and programs of the pre-Civil War unions and Mechanics' Associations illustrate these nineteenth-century patterns of political relatedness. The self-educated workmen of these organizations were passionately concerned with questions of political, legal, and economic justice and only indirectly interested in wages and working conditions. These workmen were unashamed moralizers, eager to participate in middle-class religious and educational values. Their press and their meetings did not look at everything from the labor angle. (Today such an outlook has all but vanished from the labor press and program, save for a few old-time Socialists or ex-ministers in the CIO. It has not been succeeded by a vision of clear labor interest, but rather by a labor line laid down as an ideology by the union officials to an indifferent mass of nominal union members.)

In general the press in the era depending on inner-direction fortified its readers in their political role playing—reassured them that they had roles, and that politics was responding to their playing of them. Journalism zealously preserved an individualistic slant, personal rather than personalized—as it could more easily do before the days of the AP, mailed boilerplate, and chain newspapers—and its individualism helped foster the feeling of the reader that his individual political decision always mattered for him and usually mattered for the country. Cynicism toward politics as a whole (as against cynicism about democracy or bossism or other specific political form or usage) was virtually unknown. Indeed, a feeling prevailed in many circles that the millennium was near. The defined political problems of the period were felt to be manageable by their customary devotees: a few professionals (the bosses and a small corps of career officials) and the amateurs who worked part time or full time (the statesmen and good government people).

Thus, the limits of the political sphere as well as its meaning were self-evident to the inner-directed man of the nineteenth century. Political activity was no more baffling in terms of motivation than work. So many political tasks needed doing and were obviously obligatory on the basis of one's class position, regional location, and morality, that each active person could find satisfying political employment. This employment was satisfying because many problems were indeed finally overcome by the reformer's zeal: not only was the franchise extended and free education spread, but the prisons and asylums were somewhat ameliorated, factory legislation was introduced, and so on. Perhaps it was only because these were, at least when taken singly, relatively limited goals that reformers were so successful.

In fact, it was characteristic of the moralizers, and perhaps of inner-directed people generally, not to be aware of the narrow limits they imposed on their relation to the political sphere. Each reform movement of the nineteenth century powerfully channeled the energies of its friends and foes, without necessarily producing in either group a larger, more comprehensive and hence more realistic political awareness. If the aim sought was attained, whether it was emancipation or railroad legislation, the moralizer's grip on politics vanished in success. If the aim sought did not succeed, as the women's movement did not succeed in the nineteenth century, its members remained prisoners of a crusade. Even then, however, they felt the political sphere to be malleable: success would come, as it would to their own mobility strivings, if they worked hard enough and were of good character.

In conclusion, when we think of the inner-directed man's political style, we must always think of the interests he brought to the political sphere. He participated not because he felt obliged to further a highly cooperative group life but because he had something specific at stake: a responsibility to himself or to others or both. In general, and despite its partial compartmentalization, the political sphere served to further the interests of his class position, class aspirations, or class antagonisms. Since politics existed to satisfy needs other than amusement and psychic escape, it was felt to react passively to the pressure of those needs; men were masters of their politics. Conversely, politics could not and did not invade a man's privacy, since it could only touch him so far as he felt that it was responding, or refusing to respond, to the pressure of what he was sure were his interests. And this is perhaps one major reason why the political was a comparatively well-defined and indeed often overdefined and constricted sphere in the nineteenth as compared to the twentieth century.

With new developments, the style of the moralizer-in-power is no longer suitable. Politics today refuses to fit into its nineteenth-century compartment. With the mass media behind it, it invades the privacy of the citizen with its noise and claims. This invasion destroys the older, easy transitions from individual to local, local to national, and national to international interests and plunges the individual directly into the complexities of world politics, without any clear-cut notion of where his interests lie.

At the same time politics becomes more difficult to understand in a purely technical sense, partly because it invades previously semi-independent spheres like economics, partly because of the growing scope and interdependence of political decisions. For instance, in modern war people must understand that higher taxes are necessary, not to meet government expenditures or even to redistribute income, but because industrial and private consumers must be kept from spending too much and fueling inflation and because the government needs to buy goods and services that would be scarce if people were left with money to buy them.

The incomprehensibility of politics gains momentum not only from the increase in its objective complexity but from what is in some respects a drop in the general level of skills relevant to understanding what goes on in politics. While formal education has increased, the education provided by the effort to run a farm, an independent business, or a shop, has decreased along with the increase in the number of employees; and while there may be little or no decline in the number of independent entrepreneurs, a larger proportion of the factors leading to success or failure is no longer in the hands of those remaining as entrepreneurs. No longer can one judge the work and competence of the political or government administrator from the confident, often overconfident, base line of one's own work and competence.

THE STYLE OF THE MORALIZER-IN-RETREAT

Many moralizers in the nineteenth century already viewed politics not only in a confused and ethically limited but also in a slightly paranoid and autistic way. These men, precursors of the modern displaced inner-directed, did not so much steer politics as permit themselves to be oversteered by their fears, which they projected onto politics. How else can we explain the emotion generated by the recurrent antiforeign crusades, the campaigns against mysterious secret orders, Catholic, Masonic, Phi Beta Kappa? It was often difficult for some Americans to see the difference between the mumbo-jumbo voluntary association such as the Masons, for example, and a social and class conspiracy. Likewise, the feeling of political conservatives that the world will come to an end if "that man" is elected does not make its appearance for the first time under the second Roosevelt.

Morbid anxiety of this sort is the fruit of an envy and bewilderment that are rooted in character. While the tradition-directed indifferents feel neither helpless about nor invaded by politics, because of the curtain that separates them from the political world, the inner-directed indignants can easily feel helpless and invaded when things do not go well with them. As we saw in Chapter V, the inner-directed man becomes vulnerable to himself when he fails to achieve his internalized goals. Able to forget the invisible hand as long as he is successful, he seeks in his baffled failure to make it visible so that he can smite it. His politics, like his character, becomes curdled when lack of success reveals and renders intolerable his lack of understanding.

It is in part the indignant person's baffled incomprehension that makes him see the city slicker as having a great and disagreeable sureness of grasp compared with his own. He envies this, and overrates it. The urban magnates and lawyers of the nineteenth century were, in their character, almost as clearly inner-directed as their rural and small-town enemies. Yet the communications bridge between them, as between regions and classes, was always on the verge of collapse.

Today it is often assumed that, because the gap in education between city and country has narrowed and because such mass media as the radio attract both urban and rural audiences, it follows that the gap in character structure has also narrowed. Perhaps in some parts of the country this has occurred. But I think it more likely that the gap between other-directed city dwellers and inner-directed rural folk has increased and that the well-meant efforts to bridge the gap have frequently served only to make the latter feel still more envious and unsure.

Envy and the feeling of displacement—sources of a political style of curdled indignation—are of course also to be found among those rural immigrants to town who are city dwellers in name only. As long as such people, urban or rural, have political power, their malaise vis-à-vis the other-directed elements in American life may be muted; they can shape their world and force it to make sense to them. But when even this avenue toward understanding is cut off, the curdled indignant lashes out in helpless rage or subsides into the sort of passive, frustrated resistance that we commented on in Chapter I in connection with Erikson's studies of American Indians.

Another variety of moralizer, those we might term the "enthusiasts," far from resigning themselves to political frustration, hopefully tackle the most intractable tasks. The changing meaning of the word enthusiast says much about the history of political styles. The enthusiasts in the days of Cromwell and the Long Parliament were the men of spirit and vision, the Quakers or Levellers or Diggers. But in eighteenth-century England the word enthusiast had already begun to lose this religious meaning and to become instead a term of ridicule rather than fear or admiration. It is perhaps part of the same development which has added "do-gooder," "world improver," "reformer," and "Boy Scout" to our colloquial vocabulary as terms of contempt or friendly dismissal: to want to "do good" in politics is obviously to be naïve!

The enthusiast resembles the indignant in that his political emotions frequently outweigh his political intelligence; they lead him into half-thought-out crusades. But he differs from the indignant in the quality of these emotions: these are rosy and cheerful as against the darker emotional hue of the indignant.[4] In the nineteenth century the enthusiast was unceasingly active. If challenged, he argued, as he would argue today, that there is always work, and political work, for idle hands to do. Such an argument rests on ascetic feelings of obligation about engaging in or concerning oneself with politics and rests also on the American penchant for activity as such—a penchant outlasting the belief in progress which rationalized ceaseless activity for many of the inner-directed in the nineteenth century.

Wars and technological changes, as well as the shift from inner-direction to other-direction, have brought the moralizing style, in either its indignant or enthusiast versions, into disrepute. The Civil War, itself a complex catharsis of the moral indignation that accompanied the political sphere in the preceding years, initiated a process that has since continued. Probably the few living veterans of the Civil War still retain a fighting faith in the righteousness of their cause. The veterans of World War I are less involved in their cause, though still involved in their experience. The veterans of World War II bring scarcely a trace of moral righteousness into their scant political participation. These men "ain't mad at nobody." It looks as though since the Civil War there has been a decline in the emo-

---

[4] Indignation or hatred of this type is well described in the essay by Svend Ranulf, *Moral Indignation and Middle Class Psychology* (Copenhagen, Levin & Monksgaard, 1938). Though our emphasis throughout is on character, perhaps we cannot avoid here the interjection of temperament factors, such as the ancient distinction between choleric and sanguine types.

tionality of political differences, a decline in the histrionic violence of electoral campaigning, and a decline in the reserves of indignation and enthusiasm available to any side of an easily moralized issue.

Certainly, salient examples of the indignant style remain. The sallies of Mencken in the 20's hit at the social groups in which most of the extreme moralizing was still to be found: the country people, the midwesterners, the small-town Protestants, the southern APAs, the corn-fed shouting sects, the small lodge-joining businessmen. That such groups have been somewhat more cosmopolitan in recent years during which other-direction has spread, does not mean the older patterns have vanished.

Today, however, just as inner-direction in character is partly the result of a moralizing political style, so loss of emotion in politics leads to other-direction in character. In other words, politics itself, as it impinges on the lives of people and shapes their experiences and interpretations of them, becomes one of the agencies of character formation. This complex interplay is one reason why, within our broad scheme of character types linked to the curve of population, we find, and would expect to find, different national variants rooted in different national historical experience. For example, both England and America are countries that have arrived at incipient decline of population as the result of industrialization, urbanization, and the spread of contraceptive substitutes for a Malthusian morality. But both countries encountered these historic crises, as they encountered civil war, at very different periods in their political development. Congreve, living in a postwar reign of tolerance, might have been surprised at the recurrence of moralizing in the Victorian Age, when the combination of evangelical revival and the pace and politics of industrialization upset the older political styles. Likewise, in view of the indeterminacies of history, it would be rash to predict that the moralizing style is doomed and that no revival in America is possible. Indeed, if influential men become moralizers, the other-directed person, because he is other-directed, will try to be a moralizer, too.

III. The Inside-dopesters

For all the Athenians and strangers which were there spent their time in nothing else, but either to tell, or to hear some new thing.

Acts

The spread of other-direction has brought to the political scene the attitude of the inside-dopester, originating not in the sphere of work but of consumption. This attitude is not entirely new, any more than other-direction is entirely new. Here, again, the change is a matter of degree.

The other-directed man possesses a rich store of social skills—skills he needs in order to survive and move about in his social environment; some of these he can deploy in the form of political skills. One of these is his ability to hold his emotional fire, which he tries hard to do because of the cooperative pattern of life to which he is committed. This skill is related to his inescapable awareness, lacking in the inner-directed man, that in any situation people are as important as things.

The inside-dopester may be one who has concluded (with good reason) that since he can do nothing to change politics, he can only understand it. Or he may see all political issues in terms of being able to get some insider on the telephone. That is, some inside-dopesters actually crave to be on the inside, to join an inner circle or invent one; others aim no higher than to *know* the inside, for whatever peer-group satisfactions this can bring them.

The inside-dopester of whatever stripe tends to know a great deal about what other people are doing and thinking in the important or "great-issue" spheres of life; he is politically cosmopolitan rather than parochial. If he cannot change the others who dominate his political attention, his characterological drive leads him to manipulate himself in order not to change the others but to resemble them. He will go to great lengths to keep from looking and feeling like the uninformed outsider. Not all other-directed people are inside-dopesters, but perhaps, for the lack of a more mature model, many of them aspire to be.

The inside-dopester is competent in the way that the school system and the mass media of communication have taught him to be competent. Ideology demands that, living in a politically saturated milieu, he know the political score as he must know the score in other fields of entertainment, such as sports.

The majority of inside-dopesters take no active part in politics, but there are those who do. Thus, we find many government and party officials who handle the political news in the way encouraged by their jobs, in fragments of office gossip. There are political newsmen and broadcasters who, after long training, have succeeded in eliminating all emotional response to politics and who pride themselves on achieving the inside-dopesters' goal: never to be taken in by any person, cause, or event. On the other hand, some feeders on inside dope, particularly those elements influenced by Stalinism, in its various disguises, seem to fall among the political indignants. Frequently, they use their inside knowledge simply as a means of getting themselves worked up about American political abuses: they have a positive tropism to evidences of race discrimination, police brutality, corporate skulduggery, etc. This political stance becomes de rigueur among some groups; in these circles group conformity leads not to tolerance and political consumption but to indignation and political action. This seeming paradox can serve as a reminder that I speak of other-direction in terms of patterns of conformity and response to others, and not in terms of the ideological and behavioral content of that response. Usually, there will be compatibility between the mechanism of conformity and the values and realities to which one tries to conform, but this is only a tendency and there are many cases, such as this one, where successful other-direction leads to behavior which simulates inner-direction (we shall encounter other examples in Chapter XV).

THE BALANCE SHEET OF INSIDE DOPE

In the days of his power, the inner-directed moralizer had great confidence in the continuance of the social structure—the concept of the invisible hand symbolizes this—even when and perhaps especially when he did not understand how it worked. The inside-dopester, on the contrary, knows too much about politics to be so easily comforted, while still knowing too little to appreciate the opportunities for change available to him. For his understanding is cramped by his preoccupation with the highly selective classification of events handed out as the inside story, or made still more alluring by being stamped as classified or confidential information. Concerned with being "right," fearing to be taken in, or to be thought guilty of wishful thinking (which he equates with any introduction of his humaneness into his judgments), the inside-dopester deprives himself of one of the best yardsticks he could use actively to control his experience, namely his own reactions as a sensitive participant in the political life of his time. It is not only that he withdraws emotional allegiance from a political scene which strikes him as too complex and too unmanageable—it strikes him so in part precisely because he has withdrawn.[5]

---

[5] On the face of it this outlook might be thought to resemble that of nineteenth-century political observers who insisted that man was limited and to some extent rendered impotent to effect far-reaching social changes, by his own nature and by the organic nature of society that followed its own laws of development. Edmund Burke and other conservative critics of the French Revolution at the beginning of the century, and the Social Darwinists at its end, represent two strands in this general line of thought. However, these feelings of limitation were not necessarily accompanied by subjective feelings of powerlessness; and, at least in the case of the Social Darwinists and perhaps also in the case of Burke, a positively optimistic view was taken as to the course of society's organic development. If

Furthermore, in order to keep up with the political branch of the consumers' union, the inside-dopester must be prepared for rapid changes of line. In this respect he is like the negotiator whom we discussed earlier, who is better able to bring home the bacon of good will if he is hazy about and has not pressed his legal rights in the matter; the inside-dopester can make an easier opinion shift if he has lost the moralizer's ability to relate political events to himself and his practical interests. That is perhaps why the portrait of the inside-dopester as an official, in *Anna Karenina* (the image of Stepan Arkadyevitch Oblonsky as quoted in Chapter I), of Bilibin in *War and Peace*, and of Ivan Ilyitch in Tolstoy's short story "The Death of Ivan Ilyitch"—why these nineteenth-century Russians, attuned to the class media of the court, seem under their strange names so very contemporary.

There is evidence that in America rapid fluctuation of opinion is to be found primarily in the better educated groups, the groups in which we also expect to find the inside-dopesters. Thus, the very interesting study made at the Harvard Department of Social Relations of attitudes toward Russia provides evidence that middle-class opinion vis-à-vis Russia has swung much more widely than lower-class opinion, which was always hostile and suspicious. For the middle class, Russia became a wartime ally and, for a time, a postwar friend; this has been succeeded by violent

---

the world took care of itself—if reformers would only let it alone—one would not need to feel frustrated and helpless: one merely had to acknowledge this limitation and devote oneself to less than apocalyptic changes.

Contemporary forms of social determinism, on the other hand, tend to assume that our civilization is running down, a view we find in the nineteenth century only in a few observers, like Brooks Adams, who could hardly believe their own prophecies—even the pessimists of the last century could not envisage how terrible politics might become in the twentieth century. But today men feel politically impotent, and their philosophizing reinforces the mood that befits their character and situation.

hostility. Other studies show the same thing with respect
to isolationism and war. On all these matters the middle
classes, being caught up in politics and, on the whole, susceptible to the way the mass media present events, are
capable of attending to a much more rapid change of signals
than the lower classes.

Politics, indeed, serves the inside-dopester chiefly as a
means for group conformity. He must have acceptable
opinions, and where he engages in politics he must do so
in acceptable ways. In the upper class, as among radical
groups, the influence of the moralizing style is still strong,
and many people who set the cultural patterns carry on
with an ideology of political responsibility; they act as if
politics were a meaningful sphere for them. The college student or young professional or businessman of the upper
middle class may take up politics as he takes up golf or
any other acceptable hobby: it is a fulfillment of social
role and in addition it is good fun, good business, and a
way to meet interesting people. It happens, of course, that
people who enter politics, on one or another level, with
inside-dopester motivations, may find themselves becoming emotionally involved, and stay for quite other reasons.
More common, probably, are those inside-dopesters who
use their political experience to justify their emotional
anemia, drawing on their acquaintance with the inside
story to look down on those who get excited.

These inside-dopesters of the upper middle class should
be contrasted with those found in small towns and rural
areas who are in easy contact with their local and even state
officials. In the small towns social distance between the
politically influential and the non-influential is small, and
very little in the machinery of government is opaque—
the telephone party line on which everybody listens may
be thought of as symbolizing this. Though ordinarily these
people can muster quite a bit of indignation over the local
issues, this is not always the case; and we find occasional
small-town and rural people who, bringing to politics the

cosmopolitan style of the other-directed types, give a good imitation of urban inside-dopesters.[6]

Actually, the distinction between the inside-dopester and the indifferent is often hard to draw. This may serve as another illustration of the point made earlier, that there are striking similarities between the tradition-directed and the other-directed. Both groups feel helpless vis-à-vis politics, and both have resorted to varieties of fatalism which the inner-directed moralizer would sternly reject. However, there are important differences. The inside-dopester, unlike the indifferent, is subordinate to a peer-group in which politics is an important consumable and in which the correct—that is, the unemotional—attitude toward one's consumption is equally important. The new-style indifferent can take politics or leave it alone, while the inside-dopester is tied to it by motivations hardly less compelling than those of the moralizer.

The inside-dopester does bring to politics a certain kind of realism that the moralizer often lacked. The notion of transcending the inevitable never arises for the inside-dopester. As spectator, as well as operator, he has a very good idea of what the limits are; he does not set his sights very high. The other-directed man has carried what are essentially political skills into many areas outside of formal political science as defined by the moralizer—for example, into the field of city planning and labor-management relations. Moreover, as against the oversimplifications of many moralizers, the inside-dopesters include a corps of specialists who know much more than the often narrowly partisan indignants and enthusiasts even in the days of their power, let alone in the days of their wane. Many people, not only specialists, have become accustomed to thinking

---

[6] Compare the valuable discussion in Robert K. Merton, "Patterns of Influence: a Study of Interpersonal Influence and of Communications Behavior in a Local Community," *Communications Research 1948–1949*, ed. Lazarsfeld and Stanton, pp. 180–219.

in world-political terms, and cross-cultural terms, such as were hardly to be found amid the ethnocentrisms—or world-brotherhood idealisms—of even a generation ago. Most nineteenth-century press discussions of international politics drew on such parochial slogans as "national honor" —in the case of Mason and Slidell, for instance, or the *Maine*. Today, however, the mass media almost invariably discuss world politics in terms of strategic, including propaganda, considerations. The public is often asked to support a policy because such support, in a kind of self-manipulative balancing act, will influence public opinion; such arguments can only be made because of the heightened understanding, in an era increasingly dependent on other-direction, of psychological forces in politics.

Some may find current talk about our "way of life" reminiscent of discussions of national honor. But the change is not merely one of phrasing. "National honor" could be a hypocritical phrase to cover such clear-cut class interests as led to our invasion of Haiti, or it could be grouped with the various internal xenophobias of the nineteenth century. Yet however vague the content of the phrase, what it demanded of the national enemy was quite specific. "Our way of life," on the other hand, has many more psychological connotations; it is fairly specific in domestic content but highly unspecific in foreign policy demand. "National honor" sometimes strait-jacketed our foreign policy in moralizing beyond our power resources or power readiness. As against this, "our way of life" gives almost no moral guidance to foreign policy, which seems, therefore, to be left to *Realpolitik*. Only seems to be, however. For just as the phrase "national honor" calls to mind a Victorian form of hypocrisy, so the phrase "our way of life" reminds us that the other-directed man conceals from himself as well as from others such morality as he possesses by taking refuge in seemingly expediential considerations. A young veteran interviewed in 1947 by the University of Michigan Survey Research Center, when asked whether he thought the United States had given in or had its own way too much in the United Nations, replied:

This will sound funny, but I think we are getting our own way too much. (Why do you say that? he was questioned.) Because we don't want the other nations to feel that we are trying to take over their countries. They know that Russia wants that and I think that's why there is so much argument. But if they feel we are trying to grab, they won't trust us either and then we won't be able to steer this whole program which is what I think we should do. So when we don't get what we want and the headlines say we have been beaten on something, I think that's really good because it makes the other countries feel that we're just like them and that we are having troubles too. That would make them more sympathetic to us and more friendly.[7]

Psychological understanding such as this represents a real advance. The moralizer would not ordinarily have been capable of such subtleties, or interested in them.

Many important questions remain. Why do so many peer-groups in which the other-directed move continue to put politics on their bill of fare, and why is it that fashion does not, as it has with many intellectuals, substitute something else, for instance, religion? What should surprise us in America is not the number of the indifferents but why their number is not greater still and why people hang on as moralizers and seek to inform themselves as inside-dopesters. I suggest as a partial explanation that the mass media of communication play a complex part in the training and sustaining of people (of appropriate character) in both these latter styles. The media are at the same time continuous bringers of information and tutors in tolerance for would-be inside-dopesters, and tutors and provocateurs in indignation for would-be moralizers.

---

[7] Taken from the pamphlet, *Four Americans Discuss Aid to Europe*, Study No. 18 (Ann Arbor, Michigan, University of Michigan Survey Research Center, 1947), p. 13.

IX

POLITICAL PERSUASIONS:
INDIGNATION AND TOLERANCE

The super market that "offers the shopper the subtle,
psychological values" will have a better chance to build a
profitable customer following than one which depends
solely on low price and good quality merchandise, G. L.
Clements, vice-president and general manager of the Jewel
Food Stores of Chicago, asserted here today . . .

In determining how to provide "psychological values"
attractive to the customer, Mr. Clements said he thought
a business should seek to develop "the same traits that we
like in our friends." He outlined these traits as being cleanliness, up-to-date appearance, generosity, courtesy, honesty,
patience, sincerity, sympathy, and good-naturedness. Each
store operator, he said, should ask himself whether his
store has these traits. . . .

Mr. Clements asserted that in seeking to understand the
psychological forces motivating customers "we might start
out by asking the question: 'Do people really know what
they want?'" The answer to the question indicates that
people do not know what they "want," Mr. Clements
said. But they do know what they "like or do not like," he
asserted. . . .

> From the report of the twelfth annual convention
> of the Super Market Institute, New York Herald
> Tribune, May 10, 1949

THE inner-directed moralizer brings to politics an attitude
derived from the sphere of production. The other-directed
inside-dopester brings to politics an attitude derived from
the sphere of consumption. Politics is to be appraised in
terms of consumption preferences. Politicians are people—

and the more glamorous, the better. Moreover, in imitating consumption patterns, politics becomes a place where the manner and mood of doing things is quite as important as what is done. This corresponds with the other-directed man's tendency to put more emphasis on means than the inner-directed man did, and less emphasis on ends.

The mass media of communication are perhaps the most important channels between the other-directed actors on the stage of politics and their audience. The media criticize the actors and the show generally, and both directly and indirectly train the audience in techniques of political consumership. The direct training media are those which are openly political, such as the modern descendants of the *Springfield Republican* or the *New York Tribune* and a very small number of old-time newspapers, with their inner-directed moralizing editorializers. Much larger and more influential are the media of indirect training: they include the whole range of contemporary popular culture from comic books to television. They dominate the use of leisure in all American classes except at the very top and perhaps also the very bottom; and their influence is very great in creating the styles of response compatible with other-direction.

Although the pattern of this influence is complex it may be summed up in three tentative generalizations.

First, since popular culture is in essence a tutor in consumption, it teaches the other-directed man to consume politics and to regard politics and political information and attitudes as consumption goods. They are products, games, entertainments, recreations; and he is their purchaser, player, spectator, or leisure-time observer.

Second, the media, by their very sensitivity to pressure, have a stake in tolerance. But even where they are moralizers in intention, the mood of the audience of peer-groupers will cause the indignant message to be received in an unindignant way. This audience situation, moreover, leads to an emphasis not on what the media say in terms of content but on the "sincerity" of the presentation. This focus on sincerity, both in popular culture and in politics, leads the audience tolerantly to overlook the incompetence of performance.

Third, while there is a significant residue of inner-directed moralizing in American political news coverage and editorializing, it slows down but does not halt the persuasions exercised by popular culture in favor of other-directed tolerance and passivity.

I. Politics as an Object of Consumption

The other-directed man's inability to know what he wants, while being preoccupied with what he likes—as observed by the retailer quoted at the head of the chapter —applies to politics as well as to other spheres of life. In contrast to this, the inner-directed man, in those spheres of life, such as politics, that he identified with work, knew what he wanted but did not really allow himself to know what he liked.

A striking illustration of this far from verbal point is to be found in a group of interviews conducted in the newly built suburb of Park Forest near Chicago. Park Forest is a development of a federally-aided private concern called American Community Builders; the homes are rented to occupants, and the ACB retains the financial functions of government, in cooperation with a sort of town council of residents. Residents were asked in the interviews how they felt about ACB, and what part, if any, they took in local politics, including griping and gossip. Many had complaints about their living quarters and community arrangements generally. What was noteworthy was that these complaints were frequently put in terms of the allegedly—and, as it appeared, actually—"bad public relations" of ACB. That is, direct criticism, based on the residents' wants and feelings, was muted; rather, "they" were criticized because their public relations were so mishandled as to leave people—presumably, people other than the speaker—critical. In effect, people were complaining not about their direct grievances but because they had not been so manipulated as to "make them like it." Their wants (in concrete living arrangements) took second place to their likes (as to the proper degree of skill deemed suitable for a large organization).[1]

Under these conditions of passive consumership we would expect people to drop out of the league of inside-dopesters into the great mass of the new-style indifferents. Left to themselves, perhaps many would do so. But they are not left to themselves. The mass media act as a kind of barker for the political show. These have discovered one sovereign remedy, glamor, to combat the danger of indifference and apathy. Just as glamor in sex substitutes for both love and the relatively impersonal family ties of the tradition-directed person, and just as glamor in packaging and advertising of products substitutes for price competition, so glamor in politics, whether as charisma—packaging—of the leader or as the hopped-up treatment of events by the mass media, substitutes for the types of self-interest that governed the inner-directed. In general: *wherever we see glamor in the object of attention, we must suspect a basic apathy in the spectator.*

The result of the search for glamor in politics is the effort, not dissimilar to that of the retailer quoted above, "to provide 'psychological values' attractive to the customer." And, as Mr. Clements told the Super Market Institute, the values are "the same traits that we like in our friends," namely "cleanliness, up-to-date appearance, generosity, courtesy, honesty, patience, sincerity, sympathy, and good-naturedness." Many of the maneuverings of politics can be interpreted in these terms. In 1948, Truman was felt to lack the up-to-date appearance; Dewey, the sincerity, sympathy, and good-naturedness. Eisenhower seemed irresistibly attractive on all these scores—he had "everything." People wanted a candidate with both appeals, and the spontaneous elements in the Eisenhower movement were to a large degree a tribute to people's desperate search

---

[1] The Park Forest study is the work of Herbert J. Gans ("Political Participation and Apathy," unpublished Divisional Master's Paper, University of Chicago, 1950).

for glamor. The Eisenhower supporters in the 1948 campaign were saying, in effect, that a candidate who "has everything"—whom one could wholeheartedly *like*—would surely know what one *needed*.

Where likable qualities are less evident than with Eisenhower, people try hard to find a candidate with charm. To be sure, this was true in earlier eras, but I think it likely that this style of political appeal has been growing steadily in the United States in the radio age. For even the hardheaded political bosses in America have learned, enduring their experience of Franklin Roosevelt, to take these appeals into account; the wider the electorate, of course, the more glamor tends to displace issues or old-fashioned patronage considerations. But this is as yet only a tendency; I do not mean to suggest that people now ignore their wants in voting their likes, or that an understanding of the other-directed character will help us predict elections better than an understanding of economic currents, ethnic traditions, and political organization.

II. The Media as Tutors in Tolerance

There are several reasons why the mass media of communication develop an attitude of tolerance that becomes the mode of experiencing and viewing everything, including politics.

The most powerful factor making for this slant is the sheer size of the audience. The press, though less terrorized than the movies, is subject to a variety of pressures brought by groups seeking protection from attack; and these pressures are internalized in the very structure of large media management and distribution.

Again, the larger the scope of the medium, the more likely it is to be edited and produced in a large metropolitan center where the pressures toward other-directed tolerance are greatest. While freer from pressure of advertisers and local cranks than small-town editors and broadcasters, and, in general, often considerably more daring, big-city media with a city-wide audience cannot help being aware of those attitudes that may offend their complex constituencies. Whereas the early nineteenth-century editor could gamble on a crusade that might bring him both a libel suit and a circulation, the twentieth-century publisher often cannot afford to let his editor gamble even on an increased circulation. Like the modern corporation generally, he wants a relatively inflexible demand curve for his product; he cannot risk sharp losses of circulation and often not sharp increases either, since his managers have guaranteed his circulation to the advertisers, planned his paper supply, and committed him to Newspaper Guild contracts and distributive relationships long in advance.

Obviously, moreover, as the one-paper towns and cities grow in number, the owner-monopolist has little to gain by attacking a powerful group. He will prefer the comforts of fair trade, as enshrined in the American Newspaper Publishers' Association or the Broadcasters' Code, to the risks of free trade in punches and ideas. Hence, all other things being equal, the larger the scope of the medium, the more it tends to be produced and consumed in a mood of other-directed tolerance and the less it makes an appeal to the indignants. Indeed, since the chief strategy of the media as tutors of consumption is to introduce and rationalize changes, enrichments, or discontinuities in conventional tastes and styles, the media have a stake in taste tolerance. They cannot afford to have people overcommitted to a taste that they may want to change tomorrow. But it is hardly likely that they are aware of this perhaps most fundamental aspect of their commitment to tolerance.

On the other hand, the very intolerance of some of the older captains of the press and radio, ambitious men with a message, allows them, and the columnistic commissars they encourage, to take a "tough" approach, to find and hold an audience among all those indifferent and maladjusted people who seek not political news but excitement and diversion from their apathy. Hearst, McCormick, Gannett, Shepherd of the Yankee network—such men want power through the press and radio, rather than money or approval. Yet their audiences are made up not primarily

of political indignants but of political new-style indifferents
—would-be inside-dopesters who are attracted by the im-
piety of Hearst, the *Chicago Tribune*, and especially the
New York Daily News, because this sort of news-handling
seems to promise them the unfaked inside story. Having
been trained to associate piety with the official culture of
sermon, school, and print, they take whatever appears by
contrast to be sophisticated, brutal, illegal, or mysterious
as true almost by definition and think the editor sincere
for letting them in on it.

TOLERANCE AND THE CULT OF SINCERITY

The exploration of what is meant by sincerity will take
us far toward understanding the ways in which popular
culture trains its audience in tolerance. We must remind
ourselves that sincerity is one of the qualities by which a
retail store may hold a loyal clientele, according to Mr.
Clements' remarks quoted above.[2]

In a study of attitudes toward popular music we find
again and again such statements as, "I like Dinah Shore
because she's so sincere," or, "that's a very sincere record,"
or, "You can just feel he [Frank Sinatra] is sincere."
While it is clear that people want to personalize their

---

[2] At the University of Chicago a graduate student studying the movement away from craft preoccupations to selling and customer-relation preoccupations among retail
furriers, found the word "sincerity" being used in a similar
way, as in the case of one man who observed, explaining
how he defended himself against competition: "You got
to be able to talk to the customers . . . when a customer
comes in you can turn her one way or the other . . . . the
customers can tell if you're sincere." Success for this man
was defined not in terms of money alone but in terms of
"a personal following" and "a better class of people." See
Louis Kriesberg, "The Relationship of Business Practices
and Business Values among Chicago's Retail Furriers"
(Master's thesis, Department of Sociology, University of
Chicago, 1949).

relationships to their heroes of consumption and that their yearning for sincerity is a grim reminder of how little they can trust themselves or others in daily life, it is less clear just what it is that they find "sincere" in a singer or other performer.[3] One element may be the apparent freedom of the entertainer to express emotions that others dare not or cannot express. Again, sincerity means performance in a style which is not aggressive or cynical, which may even be defenseless, as the question-answering or press-conference technique of some politicians appears to be. The performer puts himself at the mercy of both his audience and his emotions. Thus sincerity on the side of the performer evokes the audience's tolerance for him: it would not be fair to be too critical of the person who has left himself wide open and extended the glad hand of friendliness.

But the popular emphasis on sincerity means more than this. It means that the source of criteria for judgment has shifted from the content of the performance and its goodness or badness, aesthetically speaking, to the personality of the performer. He is judged for his attitude toward the audience, an attitude which is either sincere or insincere, rather than by his relation to his craft, that is, his honesty and skill.

By ignoring what the audience believes itself to lack (ability to perform) and emphasizing the qualities that it believes itself secretly to possess (capacity for sincerity), the audience is enabled, to a degree, to patronize the artist just as it patronizes the bumbling participants in a give-away show. It may well be, too, that the audience that emphasizes an emotional quality of a performer, such as sincerity, escapes from the need for emotional response to the performance itself. Though the

---

[3] I am much indebted to Howard C. Becker for analysis of these interviews. I have profited greatly from the penetrating discussion of sincerity as applied to audience reactions to a Kate Smith War Bond Drive in Robert K. Merton, *Mass Persuasion* (New York, Harper, 1946).

listener likes a star who, as the teen-ager says, can "send me," he does not want to go very far; he has his membership card in the consumers' union to consider. By making sincerity appear as an objective quality, or at least one capable of peer-group discussion, he gets some emotional release while preserving safety in numbers. He can "give the little girl a hand" without committing himself to a judgment on her virtuosity. In this sense the sincere artist is like the artist who tries hard.

Viewing the political scene as a market for comparable emotions, it seems that the appeal of many of our political candidates tends to be of this sort. Forced to choose between skill and sincerity, many in the audience prefer the latter. They are tolerant of bumbles and obvious ineptness if the leader tries hard.[4]

Sincerity and cynicism. The other-directed inside-dopester is far from being simply a cynic. Cynicism is a trait compatible with both inner-direction and other-direction, but it has a different bearing in the two constellations. The inner-directed cynic is or can be an opportunist, ruthless in pursuing his goals. Or he may be a disgruntled idealist, still in practice committed to rectitude. In pursuit of his aims, good or bad, he may be quite ready to exploit others, just as the inner-directed moralizer may be quite ready to force others to be moral, too. However, the other-directed person, cynical as he often seems, is generally too dependent on others to be completely cynical about them: he may keep looking for sincerity—that is, for personalities who, if they exploit his emotions, will also involve their own. The desire for a sincere presidential candidate, such as Eisenhower, is then in part a desire to escape from cynicism and apathy into commitment and enthusiasm—an excuse for the return of repressed qualities. What appears here as cynicism is frequently the readiness of the other-directed person tolerantly to accept the

---

[4] All this, of course, was written before the 1952 election, which offers some good examples of these attitudes.

norms of whatever adult peer-group he is in. But this limp acceptance is rather a source for his cynicism about himself than for his cynicism about others to whom he clings in search of goals. In fact, the other-directed man's cynicism about himself is one of the principal reasons that, while he is willing to say what he likes, he cannot believe in himself enough to know what he wants.

The inner-directed man, when he looks at politics, is likely to be exceedingly cynical about people but not cynical about institutions, constitutions, and, as we saw earlier, the value of politics itself. By contrast, the other-directed man, somewhat sentimental about people, is likely to be quite cynical about legal and political institutions, just as he is about the great game of politics itself. Coupled with this outlook, his concern for sincerity in his political personalities becomes a vice. While the concern for sincerity may imply a refusal to be taken in by any abstract notions of good and bad, along with an insistence that the personal emotional tone of the leader is of decisive importance, there are many situations where this orientation leads one astray.

In the first place, the leader's warmth or sincerity is not always important; that depends on the situation. The structure of politics and of the electorate may be sufficiently firm to make it unlikely that an insincere candidate could bring about great evils even if he wished to. The other-directed person, focused on people as he is, may overlook such institutional hardness of the material. Thus, just as the moralizer romanticizes a government of laws and not of men, the inside-dopester romanticizes a government of men and not of laws.

In the second place, it is obviously most difficult to judge sincerity. While the audience which uses the term sincerity thinks that it is escaping, in its tolerant mood, from the difficulty of judging skills, it is actually moving into a domain of considerably greater complexity. Just because such a premium is put on sincerity, a premium is put on faking it.

Plainly, it is the other-directed person's psychological

need, not his political one, that dictates his emphasis on warmth and sincerity. For leadership, the ability to be disagreeable may often be more important. The man who thinks he is sincere, moreover, may deceive himself and others; the man who knows he is not, may watch himself and be watched.[5]

III. Do the Media Escape from Politics?

Hollywood's discovery of the Negro problem had given the studios a new cycle, and distributors a tough problem: How would the South take to films denouncing racial prejudice? . . . Having already played nine profitable weeks in Manhattan, Home of the Brave opened in Dallas and Houston . . . In Dallas, the Negro elevator operator tried to sum up overheard opinion: "Well, I'll tell you, 99 per cent of the people say it's educational, the other 1 per cent say it's good."

Time, July 18, 1949

Critics of the mass media seem generally to suppose that the media foster political apathy, that they permit and encourage the audience to escape from the political and other realities of life, that, by a kind of Gresham's Law, they drive out the hard money of politics with the soft money of mass entertainment. How can Washington, it is sometimes asked, compete with Hollywood and Broadway?

Actually, however, the much criticized media—especially the press—seem to have maintained a surprisingly inner-directed attitude toward the political. Indeed, they pay more attention to politics than their audience seems to

---

[5] An excellent example of an inner-directed attitude toward the evaluation of sincerity and skill is to be seen in Lincoln's relationships to his wartime generals. As in the case of Grant's drinking, he wanted to know whether these men could do a job, not whether they were nice, or nice to him.

demand. Even tabloids print headlines and, often, news pictures on the front page, not comics. True, this is often "news" of sex, crime, and politically irrelevant or distracting exposé, but a few major political topics figure on occasion. Old Indignant Hearst liked to print "the Chief's" editorials rather than cheesecake on page one. Local radio stations with disk jockeys build their self-esteem (and please the FCC) by broadcasting news every hour, which, like the commercials, people do not bother to switch off. Likewise, newsreels usually begin with shots of some political personage or event, postponing Lew Lehr or the fashion show to the end of the reel. Thus many of the agencies of mass communications give political news a larger play than might be dictated by strict considerations of market research. In this way they help maintain the prestige of politics as a presumed interest on the part of their audience—even though, at the same time, they seldom counter the popular stereotype concerning the disreputability of politicians.

This position of prestige given to politics is especially important for the other-directed person, since he looks to the mass media for guidance in his life plan and hierarchy of values. He is led to assume that other people must rate politics as the mass media themselves do—that they are politically alert moralizers even though he is not. He is also encouraged in this assumption by the polls which the press prints. Save for an "inquiring photographer" here and there, these polls ask many questions and report many answers about public issues and rather few about daily living or sports. The media, far from being a conspiracy to dull the political sense of the people, could be viewed as a conspiracy to disguise the extent of political indifference.

Indeed people in most walks of life are apologetic if they are not up on politics, men especially so. People do not often make the discovery that others are quite as bored or apathetic about politics (or about other things on which the media confer respectability) as they know themselves to be. In the city, where people do not know each other, the "unbelievers" could only be aware of how numerous they are through the mass media, but these are the very channels that give politics priority.[6]

One reason for this is the desire of those who work for the mass media to do what is right or considered to be right by those to whom they look for leadership. Just as publishers want to publish prestige books even though they may lose money on them, under various rationalizations of good will, so newspapermen and broadcasters want to raise themselves above "the lowest common denominator" without fully exploring the potential financial profitability of the latter. The movie king who speaks for mere entertainment feels on the defensive with the bold producer of *Home of the Brave* and similar problem-films.

For in fact, those who work in the mass communications industries are, despite the moralizing style with which they approach politics, typically other-directed. The hypersensitive radar that is their meal ticket is tuned in spare moments not to the audience to whom they sell but to the intellectual strata around and above them. These strata are frequently contemptuous of popular culture.

Doubtless, a hierarchy among the different kinds of entertainment has always existed. But whereas the hierarchy in earlier days was based, at least to some extent, on criteria of artistry, the hierarchy today seems to be based somewhat more on topic than on mode of treatment. As the audience itself is asked to move on a constantly uptilting gradient of topic and taste, from the comics of childhood to the commentators of adulthood, so the makers of the media, in their own combination of social mobility and ethical uplift, are always impatient to get to the point where in addition to entertaining they are, in terms of topic, educating and improving. As the slicks are more high class than the pulps, so politics is more high class than sex. The sports writer wants to become a political colum-

---

[6]Cf. Paul Lazarsfeld and Robert K. Merton, "Mass Communication, Popular Taste and Organized Social Action," *The Communication of Ideas*, ed. Lyman Bryson, p. 95, on the "status-conferral" function of the media.

nist; the night-club broadcaster moves over first into political chitchat, then into political fire; many a newspaper publisher who begins as a "no-nonsense" businessman ends up as a bit of a political moralizer. Just as the new rich are "educated" to philanthropy by their associates, so the new entrants into the mass media are educated away from the "low" commercial motives to ones of more prestige. To take an example, the older pictorial magazines, such as *Life* and *Look* and even some of the less well-known ones, have moved steadily away from pictures, away from cheese-cake toward art, away from Sunday-Supplement sensation toward "serious" reading matter and political exhorting; pictures are only the come-on for social issues.

It seems, therefore, that the mass media, among their highly complex and ambiguous effects, do help prop up the prestige of the political sphere in the United States, and that within this sphere they have the effect of favoring the older, moralizing political styles. This is more true of the press than of the movies and radio, just as within the press it is more true of certain magazines and newspapers than of others. Nevertheless, despite these good intentions the total impact of the mass media on the political attitudes of Americans does more to encourage other-directed tolerance than to preserve inner-directed indignation. The sheer emphasis on consumer skills in the mass media, an emphasis that both encourages and caters to the other-directed, has cumulative effects. One of the most basic of these is that the inner-directed types and their interests are driven out of the media *in every sphere except that of politics itself.*

IV. The Reservoir of Indignation

Outside of politics, indeed, the mass media offer the indignants a rather scanty fare. The moral issues dealt with in the media are posed in increasingly subtle form, and, as we saw in Chapter VII, they reflect problems mainly of personal relationships. Moreover, the pace of the media is too fast, too sophisticated, for many of the readers who remain inner-directed. What are they to make, for instance, of a Billy Rose column about Broadway morals and mores? How are they to translate the specialized lingoes of many comic strips? How can they possibly make sense of the elusiveness and allusiveness of the "A"-grade problem-film? The indignants are apt to find that even horse operas have become pastoral settings for sadism, sex, and social problems, no longer like the old westerns whose chief characters were horses and whose moral problems involved hardly more complicated beings. Soap operas probably seem to casual upper middle-class listeners to be bathed in lachrymose moralizing. But typically their characters are preoccupied with straightening out a complex web of tenuous emotions, often needing the specialized services of the professional or semi-professional helper. The typical curdled indignant, perhaps especially if male, is simply not interested in such things.

We may note the change in popular-culture fare in another medium altogether, by remarking the transformation a few years ago of the new *Scientific American*. The old *Scientific American* used to be read by inner-directed hobbyists of science; now it has become a slick-paper periodical, catering with brilliance and sophistication to the consumer of science, including social science and philosophy; one old subscriber complained that it was no longer edited to be read by men with greasy hands at workbenches—virtually the only hobby column remaining is the astronomy section. Likewise, we might note that Street and Smith, publishers of such moralizing tales as Alger and Nick Carter, in 1948 killed all but one of their remaining pulps, including *Detective Story, Western Story,* etc., to concentrate on their three booming slicks: *Mademoiselle, Charm,* and *Mademoiselle's Living*. What is the barnacled moralizer to do with them?

This gnawing deficit of acceptable mass media would perhaps be less troublesome to the moralizer if the world in which he lived still appeared to be inner-directed, to be governed, that is, by an invisible hand. But his own life experience is often disappointing; he is deprived of a feeling of competence and place. Neither his character nor his work is rewarded. In that situation he tends to turn on both—for he is vulnerable to lack of worldly comprehension even more perhaps than to lack of worldly success—and on the world. In a last desperate effort to turn the country back on its inner-directed course in order to make it habitable for him, he is ready to join a political movement whose basic driving force is indignation. A world that refuses him a place—a world that bombards him with messages that make him feel inadequate—may not appear to him worth saving, though his destructiveness may be rationalized by various ideologies.

The mass media cater to this attitude in politics, even if they no longer cater to it in other fields. We have seen one reason for this: the fact that many media leaders, for prestige and other reasons of their own, espouse a moralizing attitude toward politics rather than an inside-dopesterish one. And we have seen another reason: the fact that the media attract and provide an audience for indignant men with a simple message. While most of their readers are new-style indifferents who are titillated by political excitement, some are indignants who find their responses welcomed on the editorial page and in the commentator's columns if nowhere else.

Moreover, the indignation of the lords of press, comment, and column is not as ineffective with the other-directed readers in their audience as one might suppose at first glance. Many of these have adopted the moralizer's style as their own—many more of course are only marginally other-directed. But even the tolerant other-directed person is often fascinated by the indignant's ire, not because it is compatible with his character structure but because it is not. In commercial sports, for instance, he enjoys a rivalry and temper display—even if he knows in a way that it is cooked up for his benefit—that is vanishing or banished from other spheres of his life. As a result, displays of aggression and indignation in the arena of politics are popular with all types—indignants, inside-dopesters and indifferents. "Pour it on, Harry!" the crowds shouted to President Truman. As Americans, whatever their class or character, can enjoy boxing or a rodeo, so they still look upon a political brawl as very much a part of their American heritage, despite the trend toward tolerance.

This leads us to the important consideration that the nature of the election process encourages the entry of the indignant on his own terms. In campaigning, a tradition of moralizing survives, in competition with the newer search for glamor. The machines, though sensitive to glamor, are also aware, from past defeats, of the political power of the indignants—those who did go fight city hall. Even other-directed men may vote for moralizing inner-directed politicians because the latter present a more familiar, more dramatized, more seemingly appropriate attitude toward politics.

For the indignants have hold of one of the great traditions of American politics, that of asking the government to govern more than it knows how to govern,—as with prohibition—a latter-day survival of the time when a state like Connecticut, to Tocqueville's astonishment, could not justify putting less than the Hebraic law on its statute books but could not justify enforcing its harsh penal provisions either. In line with this tradition, the indignants of today can strive in politics to "get the law" on those movements in culture—in literature, the movies, the universities, the libraries—that symbolize urban sophistication and tolerance. They are resisted in this effort less by tolerant other-directed types than by inner-directed men for whom tolerance is a moral principle, not a character trait. The most fervent defenders of civil liberties in America draw political strength from their principles and firm convictions, not from their knowledge of who's who in politics. In contrast, the tolerant inside-dopester may become "objective" about intolerance: he knows enough about people to doubt the efficacy of reason or to be sure of his own resistance. His vulnerabilities, as well as his abilities, spring from the fact that he has his eye on the others and not on his own principles or wants.

In fact, the other-directed try to defend themselves

against the political onslaughts of the indignants by inside operations rather than by countermoralizing. Disinclined to personal militancy, to "getting out on a limb," they put on pressure through groups and associations that speak in their name. As capable handlers of inside tactics and of the communication process—they are, of course, at home among the mass media, not all of which are controlled by moralizers—they can often put the brakes on what the indignants would like to do. As a clever district attorney can mitigate the fury of a grand jury to whom he has to present an indictment by making a deal with the defendant's lawyer to accept a plea to a lesser offense, so the inside-dopester has often, in national and local politics, been able to hold the indignants off with a concession. He can make concessions, since he does not ask of politics that it straighten out the world for him. Indeed, if the indignant asks too much of politics, the tolerant inside-dopester asks too little.

The moralizers and the inside-dopesters taken together are probably a majority among the better-educated, but surely a minority of the whole population. However, the inside-dopester has little to offer to the indifferents in the way of psychic dividends: His very knowledge leads him to be aware of how little can be accomplished in politics and how fantastic it is to hope to "get rid of politics." But in rousing the indifferents, indignation has great possibilities. Not only does it make for a better show but it also plays on such grievances as the indifferents have. Sometimes these grievances can be brought into the political sphere by an antipolitical summons. The hate-filled promises of the indignant may appeal to many of those whose political indifference rests not on the security of tradition-direction but on incompetence and affectlessness. From similar sources were rallied many of the early Nazis, a large wing of the de Gaullists, and many other groups in various countries who place themselves "above politics," "above parties," and "above opinions." Such groups attack the more traditionally partisan and politically articulate elements of society and demand freedom from politics—

from platforms, principles, and parliaments. Such an attitude toward the American party system and pattern of political discourse is not infrequent. Therefore, if at any time the indignants can make a junction with the indifferents, the former can become very powerful. Internally, indignation can draw on great lower-class reserves of nationalism and xenophobia. Externally, indignation may meet counterindignation, and the congruence of indignants and temporarily aroused indifferents may present the tolerant with a seeming fait accompli. And the tolerant inside-dopesters, as compared with those who are tolerant from inner-directed principle, are men trained to recognize a fait accompli, not resist it.

Long before the tolerant are able to organize politics after their style and their mood, a stampede of the indignant may have brought on an explosion and may have pushed the tolerant cause and the tolerant character into abeyance.

V. "In Dreams Begin Responsibilities"

I would like, in conclusion, to hazard the suggestion that if the media encouraged, and if its audience could permit itself, more genuine escape, "away from it all," Americans would become stronger psychically and more ready to undertake an awakening of political imagination and commitment. By going on with our present course of media performance and media criticism, we make it possible for the media to continue to uphold the prestige of the political even when, as for much of our life at present, the political is devoid of substantial content—for one thing, because this very lack of content could only be glimpsed from a less realistic, more fantasy-oriented outlook. The direct impact of the media on political decision may easily become as thin as the impact of the House of Lords on popular opinion in Britain. The serious press refuses to face this situation, and, far from seeking to explore new emotional currents in American life, it strenuously seeks to present to the Commons of the media—radio, TV, movies, and pulps—a hand-me-down agenda of political debate. Since politics is actually less real than the press lords pretend to themselves and their audience that it is, the consumption of political vituperation may easily become more than ever an escape in the usual invidious sense, rationalized by its high, media-based prestige. Thus, the sources in popular art and culture from which eventual political creation may flow are partially dammed up by false prestige considerations and by the displaced guilts and ethical urges shared by those who control the media and those who, in turn, look to them for a bill of cultural fare.

The probabilities are that the media, in their direct, message-bearing impact, are likely to do less either to help or hurt the audience than the controllers of the media and their critics like to think. Awareness of this fact may permit both the controllers and the critics of the media to reorient their attention. They are free, much freer than they realize, to attend to the medium itself, rather than to the message it purveys or is believed to purvey. The movie producer or critic who is concerned mainly with messages, for instance of ethnic tolerance, may actually despise the movies as an art form. The editorializer or social scientist who is concerned only with arousing the electorate may hate the English language because it has become for him a mere tool. The broadcaster who wants to atone for his big salary and sponsors by slipping in a crack against business may have little respect for the aesthetic resources of his medium.

In these and other ways, the men who work in radio, film, and fiction tend to give politics, as the press and its uplifters see it, a prestige denied to art, and especially the popular art of the media themselves. There is pathos in this for their personal lives, since it leads them to unwarranted contempt for their own craft. There is irony in this for American politics, since it seems to me that a country which produced artistically first-class movies, papers, and broadcasts—no matter what the topic and, indeed, subordinating the whole question of topic—would be, politically as well as culturally, a livelier and happier land. Good mass-media artists are quite as important, and perhaps even scarcer, than responsible, anti-escapist commentators.

X

IMAGES OF POWER

In the United States the more opulent citizens take great care not to stand aloof from the people; on the contrary, they constantly keep on easy terms with the lower classes; they listen to them, they speak to them every day. They know that the rich in democracies always stand in need of the poor, and that in democratic times you attach a poor man to you more by your manner than by benefits conferred.

Tocqueville, DEMOCRACY IN AMERICA

THERE has been in the last fifty years a change in the configuration of power in America, in which a single hierarchy with a ruling class at its head has been replaced by a number of "veto groups" among which power is dispersed. This change has many complex roots and complex consequences, including the change in political mood from moralizing to tolerance. A clear-cut power structure helped to create the clarity of goals of the inner-directed; an amorphous power structure helps to create the consumer orientation of the other-directed.

I. THE LEADERS AND THE LED

There have been two periods in American history in which a sharply defined ruling class emerged. In the late eighteenth and early nineteenth centuries the Federalist leadership—landed-gentry and mercantilist-money leadership—certainly thought of itself as, and was, a ruling group. Long before its leadership was actually dislodged, its power was disputed and, in decisive instances, overruled in the northern and middle states by yeoman farmers and artisans. These latter, having little time or gift for politics, ordinarily left it to their "betters," but they retained a veto on what was done and occasionally, as with Jackson, moved into a more positive command. After the Civil War, however, these farmer and artisan groups lost their capacity to check what was done, and the captains of industry emerged as a ruling class. During their hegemony the images and the actualities of power in America coincided more closely than I think they do today.

CAPTAINS OF INDUSTRY AND CAPTAINS OF CONSUMPTION

According to this view of the matter, the election of 1896 appears as an historical watershed: the high point of oligarchic rule. In terms of political style, there were moralizers for Bryan and moralizers for McKinley. And there were groups that, whether or not they saw their interests in moral terms, had a clear picture of themselves and of their interests; they, too, responded to the election in an innerdirected way. Only a few people like Brooks Adams, who supported Bryan out of his hatred for the "goldbugs," were aware of some of the ambiguities in the positions of both candidates.

Certainly, the victorious leaders—McKinley, Hanna, and Morgan in their several bailiwicks—were not aware of ambiguity. The success of their electoral bid is less important to us than the mood of their undertaking, which was one of conscious leadership, directed by conscious class considerations. This self-conscious leadership took support from the close connection, to which I have already called attention, between politics and work. The world of work was the great world; politics was an extension that could either facilitate work or sabotage it. While bankers and Grangers had different notions as to what work politics should do and what leave undone, they agreed as to the primacy of the production side of life.

Of course, the political sphere was not devoid of entertainment for the inner-directed man: with its opportunity for cracker-barrel argument, beer drinking, and shirt-sleeved good-fellowship by torchlight, it had its occasional uses as a "downward" escape from the dignities of work and the propertied existence. But the great difference from today is that the leaders went into politics to do a job—primarily to assure the conquest of American resources—rather than to seek a responsive audience. As Rockefeller sold his oil more by force or cheapness than by brand, so the late nineteenth-century political leader sold his wares (votes or decisions) to the highest bidder. Either cash or morality might bid— but not "good will" as such.

This situation and these inner-directed motivations gave a clarity to the political and social scene in 1896 that it does not appear to have had in Tocqueville's day and has not had since. The bullet that killed McKinley marked the end of the days of explicit class leadership. Muckraking and savage political cartooning—arts that depend on clarity of line—continued for a time and of course have not quite vanished yet. But as the old-time religion depended on a clear image of heaven and hell and clear judgments of good and evil, so the old-time politics depended on a clear class structure and the clear and easily moralized judgments of good and bad that flow from it. It depended, too, and I cannot emphasize the point too much, on an agreement between leaders and led that the work sphere of life was dominant. And because the goals were clear, the obvious job of the leader was to lead; of the led, to follow. Their political cooperation, like their cooperation in industry and agriculture, was based on mutual interests, whether directly moralized or not, rather than on mutual preferences and likings.

What I have said must be taken as an "ideal-typical" political portrait of the age, useful by way of contrast to our own times. Actually, the changes are, as always, changes in emphasis and degree, and the portrait would be seriously overdrawn if the reader should conclude that no emotional moods, no audience concerns for charisma and glamor, eddied about the relations between leaders and led. These relations were not built entirely out of sober moralizing and well-understood economic interests, but occasionally, as Veblen described matters, the Captain of Industry served to provide the underlying population with personages to admire "to the greater spiritual comfort of all parties concerned."

Ruling-class theories, applied to contemporary America, seem to be spectral survivals of this earlier time. The captain of industry no longer runs business, no longer runs politics, and no longer provides legitimate "spiritual comfort." Here and there, it is true, there are survivals. In the booming Southwest, Texas still produces men like Glenn McCarthy, and California produced an old-style lion of the jungle in A. P. Giannini (who was, significantly enough, from a family which lacked the opportunity to educate him for the newer business motivations). Yet even these types are touched by traits that were not nearly so evident in the earlier captains of industry who fascinated Veblen as Lucifer fascinated Milton. Like Henry Kaiser, they depend much more than did the older magnificoes on public opinion and, as a corollary to public opinion, on the attitude of government. To this end they tend to exploit their personalities, or allow them to be exploited, in a way that makes the elder Rockefeller's Ivy Lee stunt of dime-giving seem as remote as the Fuggers.

Much more than their pre-World War I predecessors, then, these surviving captains stay within the limits as well as the possibilities of the economy of the glad hand. If they enter politics they do so because it is a sport or obligation for the rich; or simply because they are tied in with government at every step in their ramifying enterprises. These latter-day captains neither see themselves nor are recognized as political leaders who, by their presence and by what they stand for, clarify and thereby moralize politics. The elder Morgan and his friends thought it was up to them to stop Bryan and to stop the depression of 1907. No one has taken their place.

In the focus of public attention the old captains of industry have been replaced by an entirely new type: the Captains of Nonindustry, of Consumption and Leisure. Surveys of content in the mass media show a shift in the kinds of information about business and political leaders that audiences ask for.[1] In an earlier day the audience was given a story of the hero's work-minded rise to success. Today, the ladder climbing is taken for granted or is seen in terms of the breaks, and the hero's tastes in dress, food, women, and recreation are emphasized—these are, as we have seen, the frontiers on which the reader can himself compete, while he cannot imagine himself in the work role of the president of the United States or the head of a big company.

What is more, there is a shift in such biographies from an accent on business leaders to an accent on consumption leaders. Proportionately, actors, artists, entertainers, get more space than they used to, and the heroes of the office, hustings, and factory get less. These consumers of the surplus product may, in Veblen's terms, provide "spiritual comfort" by their very skill in consumption. The glamor of such heroes of consumption may reside in their incompetence in the skills of businesslike performance and, as we have seen, in some cases their wholly personal "sincerity" may do duty in place of more objective artistic criteria.

But of course, these captains of consumption are not leaders. They are still only personalities, employed to adorn movements, not to lead them. Yet the actual leaders have much in common with them.

For an illustration we can turn to a recent American leader—undoubtedly a leader—who shared many characteristics of the artist and entertainer: Franklin D. Roosevelt. We are accustomed to thinking of him as a man of great

[1] See the excellent article by Leo Lowenthal, "Biographies in Popular Magazines," Radio Research, 1942–43, ed. Lazarsfeld and Stanton (New York, Duell, Sloan & Pearce, 1944), p. 507. Dr. Lowenthal links the shift from "heroes of production" to "heroes of consumption" to major social changes in American life.

power. Yet his role in leading the country into war was very different from that of McKinley or even of Wilson. Think of McKinley pacing the floor of his study, deciding whether or not to ask for a declaration of war on Spain— when he already knew that Spain would capitulate. McKinley felt it was up to him; so did Wilson. Roosevelt felt he could only maneuver within very narrow limits, limits which came close to leaving the decision to the enemy.

Again, if we compare his activities during the war years with those of Churchill, we can see important differences. Churchill led the British in something like the old-time sense of an explicit relation between the leader and the followers. That he led, moreover, as a moralizing leader and not, despite his great personal charm, as a "personality," appeared in the readiness of the electorate to follow him in war and to dispense with him in peace: they were work-minded rather than consumption-minded about him. Roosevelt on the other hand remained throughout the war, as before, a powerful though tolerant persuader, even conniver and stimulator, of changes in public opinion that he followed with deep concern at all times. Churchill exploited his indignation, Roosevelt his charm.

The admittedly real differences in the military situation of Britain and the United States during this period are not sufficient to explain these differences in the mood and method of leadership. Much more important than the wartime differences between the two countries are the differing shifts in political pattern during the last half century. America in the 90's could be led politically and morally. Since then we have entered a social and political phase in which power is dispersed among veto groups. These groups are too many and diverse to be led by moralizing; what they want is too various to be moralized and too intangible to be bought off for cash alone; and what is called political leadership consists, as we could see in Roosevelt's case, in the tolerant ability to manipulate coalitions.

This means that the men who, at an earlier historical period, were political leaders are now busy with the other-directed occupation of studying the feedback from all the others—their constituencies, their correspondents, and friends and enemies within influential pressure groups. The revolution in communications makes this attention possible in ways that were not available to the equally assiduous client-cultivator of an earlier day, who could buy a few editors if he wanted favorable things said. And those who were once the followers have learned the arts of lobbying and media pressure. The roll call of nineteenth- and early twentieth-century leaders contains many men who refused to follow their flock: Gladstone and Cleveland, Robert Peel and John Stuart Mill (as M.P.), Woodrow Wilson and Winston Churchill. Even today the need to impose unpopular courses brings to the fore inner-directed types: Cripps, for instance, in England; Stimson and Robert Patterson in this country. Of course, political figures in all ages have been dependent on their following, and opportunism and manipulation are not a twentieth-century discovery. The inner-directed leader, however, was quite conscious of discrepancies between his views and those of others; if he shifted his course, it was still *his* course. Moreover, since he was ambitious, he might well prefer later fame to momentary warmth of response; in any event he did not need to have everybody love him, but only those who mattered for his fortunes.

In his autobiography, John Stuart Mill tells the following story:

In the pamphlet, "Thoughts on Parliamentary Reform," I had said, rather bluntly, that the working classes, though differing from those of some other countries, in being ashamed of lying, are yet generally liars. This passage some opponent got printed in a placard which was handed to me at a meeting, chiefly composed of the working classes, and I was asked whether I had written and published it. I at once answered "I did." Scarcely were these two words out of my mouth, when vehement applause resounded through the whole meeting.

It is interesting to compare this incident with the practices of certain American public figures who not only would not think of saying anything that might offend an audience but who frequently depart from a prepared text, carefully designed to please a wide audience, in order to mollify the smaller face-to-face group before whom the speech happens to be delivered.

The old-time captain of industry was also a captain of consumption: what standards were set, were set by him. He was also a captain of politics. The new captain of consumption who has usurped his place in the public eye is limited severely to the sphere of consumption—which itself has of course greatly expanded. Today, the personalities from the leisure world, no matter how much loved, lack the strength and the situation for leadership. If a movie star of today tries to put across a political message, in or out of films, he finds himself vulnerable to all sorts of pressures. The movie producer is no more powerful. The Catholics, the Methodists, the organized morticians, the state department, the southerners, the Jews, the doctors, all put their pressure on the vehicle that is being prepared for mass distribution. Piety or decency protects some minority groups that have no lobbies. The movie maker acts as a broker among these veto groups in a situation much too intricate to encourage his taking a firm, moralizing stance. At best, he or someone in his organization may sneak a moral and political message into the film as Roosevelt or someone in his organization sneaked over an appointment or a new coordinating agency. The message, the appointment, the agency—none of them could get very far in the Alice in Wonderland croquet game of the veto groups.

II. WHO HAS THE POWER?

The Veto Groups. The shifting nature of the lobby provides us with an important clue as to the difference between the present American political scene and that of the age of McKinley. The ruling class of businessmen could relatively easily (though perhaps mistakenly) decide where their interests lay and what editors, lawyers, and legislators might be paid to advance them. The lobby ministered to the clear leadership, privilege, and imperative of the business ruling class.

Today we have substituted for that leadership a series of groups, each of which has struggled for and finally attained a power to stop things conceivably inimical to its interests and, within far narrower limits, to start things. The various business groups, large and small, the movie-censoring groups, the farm groups and the labor and professional groups, the major ethnic groups and major regional groups, have in many instances succeeded in maneuvering themselves into a position in which they are able to neutralize those who might attack them. The very increase in the number of these groups, and in the kinds of interests "practical" and "fictional" they are protecting, marks, therefore, a decisive change from the lobbies of an earlier day. There is a change in method, too, in the way the groups are organized, the way they handle each other, and the way they handle the public, that is, the unorganized.

These veto groups are neither leader-groups nor led-groups. The only leaders of national scope left in the United States today are those who can placate the veto groups. The only followers left in the United States today are those unorganized and sometimes disorganized unfortunates who have not yet invented their group.

Within the veto groups, there is, of course, the same struggle for top places that goes on in other bureaucratic setups. Among the veto groups competition is monopolistic; rules of fairness and fellowship dictate how far one can go. Despite the rules there are, of course, occasional "price wars," like the jurisdictional disputes of labor unions or Jewish defense groups; these are ended by negotiation, the division of territory, and the formation of a roof organization for the previously split constituency. These big monopolies, taken as a single group, are in devastating competition with the not yet grouped, much as the fair-trade economy competes against the free-trade economy.

These latter scattered followers find what protection they can in the interstices around the group-minded.[2]

Each of the veto groups in this pattern is capable of an aggressive move, but the move is sharply limited in its range by the way in which the various groups have already cut up the sphere of politics and arrayed certain massive expectations behind each cut. Both within the groups and in the situation created by their presence, the political mood tends to become one of other-directed tolerance. The vetos so bind action that it is hard for the moralizers to conceive of a program that might in any large way alter the relations between political and personal life or between political and economic life. In the amorphous power structure created by the veto groups it is hard to distinguish rulers from the ruled, those to be aided from those to be opposed, those on your side from those on the other side. This very pattern encourages the inside-dopester who can unravel the personal linkages, and discourages the enthusiast or indignant who wants to install the good or fend off the bad. Probably, most of all it encourages the new-style indifferent who feels and is often told that his and everyone else's affairs are in the hands of the experts and that laymen, though they should "participate," should not really be too inquisitive or aroused.

By their very nature the veto groups exist as defense groups, not as leadership groups. If it is true that they do

---

[2] It should be clear that monopolistic competition, both in business and politics, is competition. People are very much aware of their rivals, within and without the organization. They know who they are, but by the very nature of monopolistic competition they are seldom able to eliminate them entirely. While we have been talking of fair trade and tolerance, this should not obscure the fact that for the participants the feeling of being in a rivalrous setup is very strong. Indeed, they face the problem of so many other-directed people: how to combine the appearance of friendly, personalized, "sincere" behavior with the ruthless, sometimes almost paranoid, envies of their occupational life.

"have the power," they have it by virtue of a necessary mutual tolerance. More and more they mirror each other in their style of political action, including their interest in public relations and their emphasis on internal harmony of feelings. There is a tendency for organizations as differently oriented as, say, the Young Socialists and the 4-H Club, to adopt similar psychological methods of salesmanship to obtain and solidify their recruits.

This does not mean, however, that the veto groups are formed along the lines of character structure. As in a business corporation there is room for extreme inner-directed and other-directed types, and all mixtures between, so in a veto group there can exist complex "symbiotic" relationships among people of different political styles. Thus a team of lobbyists may include both moralizers and inside-dopesters, sometimes working in harness, sometimes in conflict; and the constituency of the team may be composed mainly of new-style political indifferents who have enough literacy and organizational experience to throw weight around when called upon. Despite these complications I think it fair to say that the veto groups, even when they are set up to protect a clear-cut moralizing interest, are generally forced to adopt the political manners of the other-directed.

In saying this I am talking about the national scene. The smaller the constituency, of course, the smaller the number of veto groups involved and the greater the chance that some one of them will be dominant. Thus, in local politics there is more indignation and less tolerance, just as even the *Chicago Tribune* is a tolerant paper in comparison with the community throwaways in many Chicago neighborhoods.

The same problem may be considered from another perspective. Various groups have discovered that they can go quite far in the amorphous power situation in America without being stopped. Our society is behaviorally open enough to permit a considerable community of gangsters a comfortable living under a variety of partisan political regimes. In their lack of concern for public relations these men are belated businessmen. So are some labor leaders who have discovered their power to hold up the economy, though in most situations what is surprising is the moderation of labor demands—a moderation based more on psychological restraints than on any power that could effectively be interposed. Likewise, it is sometimes possible for an aggressive group, while not belonging to the entrenched veto-power teams, to push a bill through a legislature. Thus, the original Social Security Act went through Congress, so far as I can discover, because it was pushed by a devoted but tiny cohort; the large veto groups including organized labor were neither very much for it nor very much against it.

For similar reasons those veto groups are in many political situations strongest whose own memberships are composed of veto groups, especially veto groups of one. The best example of this is the individual farmer who, after one of the farm lobbies has made a deal for him, can still hold out for more. The farm lobby's concern for the reaction of other veto groups, such as labor unions, cuts little ice with the individual farmer. This fact may strengthen the lobby in a negotiation: it can use its internal public relations problems as a counter in bargaining, very much as does a diplomat who tells a foreign minister that he must consider how Senator so-and-so will react. For, no matter what the other-directedness of the lobby's leaders, they cannot bind their membership to carry out a public relations approach. Many labor unions have a similar power because they cannot control their memberships who, if not satisfied with a deal made by the union, can walk off or otherwise sabotage a job.

In contrast, those veto groups are often weaker whose other-directed orientation can dominate their memberships. Large corporations are vulnerable to a call from the White House because, save for a residual indignant like Sewell Avery, their officials are themselves other-directed and because, once the word from the chief goes out, the factory superintendents, no matter how boiling mad, have to fall into line with the new policy by the very nature of the centralized organization for which they work: they can sabotage top management on minor matters but not, say, on wage rates or tax accounting. As against this, the American Catholic Church possesses immense veto-group power because it combines a certain amount of centralized command—and a public picture of a still greater amount—with a highly decentralized priesthood (each priest is in a sense his own trade association secretary) and a membership organization of wide-ranging ethnic, social, and political loyalties; this structure permits great flexibility in bargaining.

These qualifications, however, do not change the fact that the veto groups, taken together, constitute a new buffer region between the old, altered, and thinning extremes of those who were once leaders and led. It is both the attenuation of leaders and led, and the other-oriented doings of these buffers, that help to give many moralizers a sense of vacuum in American political life.

The veto groups, by the conditions their presence creates and by the requirements they set for leadership in politics, foster the tolerant mood of other-direction and hasten the retreat of the inner-directed indignants.

IS THERE A RULING CLASS LEFT?

Nevertheless, people go on acting as if there still were a decisive ruling class in contemporary America. In the postwar years, businessmen thought labor leaders and politicians ran the country, while labor and the left thought that "Wall Street" ran it, or the "sixty families." Wall Street, confused perhaps by its dethronement as a telling barometer of capital-formation weather, may have thought that the midwestern industrial barons, cushioned on plant expansion money in the form of heavy depreciation reserves and undivided profits, ran the country. They might have had some evidence for this in the fact that the New Deal was much tougher with finance capital—e.g., the SEC and the Holding Company Act—than with industrial capital and that when, in the undistributed profits tax, it tried to subject the latter to a stockholder and money-market control, the tax was quickly repealed.

But these barons of Pittsburgh, Weirton, Akron, and Detroit, though certainly a tougher crowd than the Wall Streeters, are, as we saw earlier, coming more and more to think of themselves as trustees for their beneficiaries. And whereas, from the point of view of labor and the left, these men ran the War Production Board in the interest of their respective companies, one could argue just as easily that the WPB experience was one of the congeries of factors that have tamed the barons. It put them in a situation where they had to view their company from the point of view of "the others."

Despite the absence of intensive studies of business power and of what happens in a business negotiation, one can readily get an impressionistic sense of the change in business behavior in the last generation. In the pages of *Fortune*, that excellent chronicler of business, one can see that there are few survivals of the kinds of dealings—with other businessmen, with labor, with the government—that were standard operating practice for the pre-World War I tycoons. Moreover, in its twenty-year history, *Fortune* itself has shown, and perhaps it may be considered not too unrepresentative of its audience, a steady decline of interest in business as such and a growing interest in once peripheral matters, such as international relations, social science, and other accoutrements of the modern executive.

But it is of course more difficult to know whether character has changed as well as behavior—whether, as some contend, businessmen simply rule today in a more subtle, more "managerial" way. In "Manager Meets Union" Joseph M. Goldsen and Lillian Low have depicted the psychological dependence of a contemporary sales manager on the approval of the men under him, his willingness to go to great lengths, in terms of concessions, to maintain interpersonal warmth in his relations with them, and his fierce resentment of the union as a barrier to this emotional exchange.[3] As against this, one must set the attitude of some of the auto-supply companies whose leadership still seems much more craft-oriented than people-oriented and therefore unwilling to make concessions and none too concerned with the emotional atmosphere of negotiations. Likewise, the General Motors-UAW negotiations of 1946, as reported in print, sound more like a cockfight than a Platonic symposium, although in Peter Drucker's *Concept of the Corporation*, a study of General Motors published in the same year, there is much evidence of management eagerness to build a big, happy family.

Power, indeed, is founded, in a large measure, on interpersonal expectations and attitudes. If businessmen *feel* weak and dependent, they do in actuality *become* weaker and more dependent, no matter what material resources may be ascribed to them. My impression, based mainly on experiences of my own in business and law practice, is that businessmen from large manufacturing companies, though they often talk big, are easily frightened by the threat of others' hostility; they may pound the table, but they look to others for leadership and do not care to get out of line with their peer-groupers. Possibly, attitudes toward such an irascible businessman as Sewell Avery might mark a good dividing line between the older and the newer attitudes. Those businessmen who admire Avery, though they might not dare to imitate him, are becoming increasingly an elderly minority, while the younger men generally are shocked by Avery's "highhandedness," his rebuff of the glad hand.

The desire of businessmen to be well thought of has led to the irony that each time a professor writes a book attacking business, even if almost nobody reads it, he creates jobs in industry for his students in public relations, trade association work, and market research! While the Black

---

[3]"Manager Meets Union: a Case Study of Personal Immaturity," *Human Factors in Management*, ed. S. D. Hoslett (Parkville, Missouri, Park College Press, 1946), p. 77.

Horse Cavalry of an earlier era held up businessmen by threatening to let pass crippling legislation desired by anti-business moralizers, today many honest intellectuals who would not think of taking a bribe hold business or trade association jobs because their clients have been scared, perhaps by these very men, into taking cognizance of some actual or imaginary veto group. Since a large structure is built up to woo the group, no test of power is made to see whether the group has real existence or real strength. Understandably, ideologies about who has power in America are relied upon to support these amiable fictions which serve, as we shall see in Chapter XIII, to provide the modern businessman with an endless shopping list, an endless task of glad-handing. This is a far cry, I suggest, from the opportunistic glad-handing of the wealthy on which Tocqueville comments at the chapter head; very likely, what was mere practice in his day has become embedded in character in ours.

Businessmen, moreover, are not the only people who fail to exploit the power position they are supposed, in the eyes of many observers, to have. Army officers are also astonishingly timid about exercising their leadership. During the war one would have thought that the army would be relatively impervious to criticism. But frequently the generals went to great lengths to refrain from doing something about which a congressman might make an unfriendly speech. They did so even at times when they might have brushed the congressman off like an angry fly. When dealing with businessmen or labor leaders, army officers were, it seemed to me, astonishingly deferential; and this was as true of the West Pointers as of the reservists. Of course, there were exceptions, but in many of the situations where the armed services made concessions to propitiate some veto group, they rationalized the concessions in terms of morale or of postwar public relations or, frequently, simply were not aware of their power.

To be sure, some came to the same result by the route of a democratic tradition of civilian dominance. Very likely, it was a good thing for the country that the services were so self-restrained. I do not here deal with the matter on the merits but use it as an illustration of changing character and changing social structure.

All this may lead to the question: well, who *really* runs things? What people fail to see is that, while it may take leadership to start things running, or to stop them, very little leadership is needed once things are under way—that, indeed, things can get terribly snarled up and still go on running. If one studies a factory, an army group, or other large organization, one wonders how things get done at all, with the lack of leadership and with all the featherbedding. Perhaps they get done because we are still trading on our reserves of inner-direction, especially in the lower ranks. At any rate, the fact they do get done is no proof that there is someone in charge.

There are, of course, still some veto groups that have more power than others and some individuals who have more power than others. But the determination of who these are has to be made all over again for our time: we cannot be satisfied with the answers given by Marx, Mosca, Michels, Pareto, Weber, Veblen, or Burnham, though we can learn from all of them.

There are also phenomena in this vast country that evade all of them (and surely, too, evade my collaborators and me). One example is the immense power, both political and economic, possessed by Artie Samish, allegedly the veto-group boss of California. Samish is a new-type lobbyist, who represents not one but scores of interests, often competing ones, from truckers to chiropractors, and who plays one veto group off against others to shake them down and strengthen his own power: he has learned how the other-orientation of the established veto groups will lead them to call still other groups into being through his auspices. Since the old-line parties have little power in California, there is no way of reaching a clear-cut decision for or against a particular veto group through the party system; instead, the state officials have become dependent on Samish for electoral support, or at least nonopposition, through his herded groups of voters and their cash contri-

butions; moreover, he knows how to go directly to the
people through the "democratic" plebiscite machinery.[4]

Carey McWilliams has observed that Samish's power
rests both on the peculiar election machinery of the state
and on the fact that no one industry or allied group of industries, no one union, one ethnic group or region, is dominant. The situation is very different in a state like Montana,
where copper is pivotal, and one must be either for the
union or for Anaconda. It is different again in Virginia
where, as V. O. Key shows in *Southern Politics*, the setup
of the state constitution favors control by the old court-
house crowd. In view of these divergences, rooted in local
legal niceties as well as in major social and economic factors, it is apparent that any discussion of class and power
on the national scene can at best be only an approximation.
Yet I would venture to say that the United States is on the
whole more like California in its variety—but without its
veto boss—than like Montana and Virginia in their partic-
ularity. The vaster number of veto groups, and their greater
power, mean that no one man or small group of men can
amass the power nationally that Artie Samish and, in earlier
days, Huey Long, have held locally.

Rather, power on the national scene must be viewed in
terms of issues. It is possible that, where an issue involves
only two or three veto groups, themselves tiny minorities,

---

[4]Ironically enough, but typically enough, Samish craves
the one power he does not have: social power in the society-
page sense. A poor boy in origin, he can make or break businessmen and politicians but cannot get into the more
exclusive clubs. And while consciously he is said to despise
these social leaders whom he can so easily frighten and
manipulate, he cannot purge himself of the childhood hurts
and childhood images of power that make him vulnerable
to their exclusion of him. In this, of course, he resembles
other and better-known dictators.

I have drawn on Carey McWilliams, "Guy Who Gets
Things Done," *Nation*, CLXIX (1949), 31–33; and Lester
Velie, "Secret Boss of California," *Collier's*, CXXIV (Au-
gust 13, 20, 1949), 11–13, 12–13.

the official or unofficial broker among the groups can be quite powerful—but only on that issue. However, where the issue involves the country as a whole, no individual or group leadership is likely to be very effective, because the entrenched veto groups cannot be budged: unlike a party that may be defeated at the polls, or a class that may be replaced by another class, the veto groups are always "in."

One might ask whether one would not find, over a long period of time, that decisions in America favored one group or class—thereby, by definition, the ruling group or class—over others. Does not wealth exert its pull in the long run? In the past this has been so; for the future I doubt it. The future seems to be in the hands of the small business and professional men who control Congress, such as realtors, lawyers, car salesmen, undertakers, and so on; of the military men who control defense and, in part, foreign policy; of the big business managers and their lawyers, finance-committee men, and other counselors who decide on plant investment and influence the rate of technological change; of the labor leaders who control worker productivity and worker votes; of the black belt whites who have the greatest stake in southern politics; of the Poles, Italians, Jews, and Irishmen who have stakes in foreign policy, city jobs, and ethnic religious and cultural organizations; of the editorial-izers and storytellers who help socialize the young, tease and train the adult, and amuse and annoy the aged; of the farmers—themselves a warring congeries of cattlemen, corn men, dairymen, cotton men, and so on—who control key departments and committees and who, as the living representatives of our inner-directed past, control many of our memories; of the Russians and, to a lesser degree, other foreign powers who control much of our agenda of attention; and so on. The reader can complete the list. Power in America seems to me situational and mercurial; it resists attempts to locate it the way a molecule, under the Heisenberg principle, resists attempts simultaneously to locate it and time its velocity.

But people are afraid of this indeterminacy and amorphousness in the cosmology of power. Even those intellectuals, for instance, who feel themselves very much out of power and who are frightened of those who they think have the power, prefer to be scared by the power structures they conjure up than to face the possibility that the power structure they believe exists has largely evaporated. Most people prefer to suffer with interpretations that give their world meaning than to relax in the cave without an Ariadne's thread.

Let me now summarize the argument in the preceding chapters. The inner-directed person, if he is political at all, is related to the political scene either by his morality, his well-defined interests, or both. His relationship to his opinions is close, not peripheral. The opinions are means of defending certain principles of politics. They may be highly charged and personal, as in the political discussion in the first pages of Joyce's *Portrait of the Artist As a Young Man,* or they may be highly charged and impersonal—a means of defending one's proper Bostonianship or other class position. In either case one's own opinions are felt to matter and to have some direct relationship to the objective world in which one lives.

As against this, the other-directed person, if he is political, is related to the political scene as a member of a veto group. He leaves it to the group to defend his interests, cooperating when called on to vote, to apply pressure, and so on. These pressure tactics seem to make his opinions manifest on the political level, but they actually help make it possible for him to be detached from his opinions. No longer operating as an "independent voter"—mostly an amiable fiction even in the era dependent on inner-direction—his political opinions, as such, are not felt to be related to his political function. Thus, they can serve him as a social counter in his role as a peer-group consumer of the political news-of-the-day. He can be tolerant of other opinions not only because of his characterological tolerance but also because they are "mere" opinions, interesting or amusing perhaps, but lacking the weight of even a partial, let alone a total, commitment to one's political role or action.

They are "mere" opinions, moreover, because so intractable is the political world of the veto groups that opinion as such is felt to be almost irrelevant.

The inner-directed political moralizer has a firm grip—often much too firm—on the gamut of judgments that he is willing to apply anywhere and everywhere. The other-directed inside-dopester is unable to fortify any particular judgment with conviction springing from a summarized and organized emotional tone. It could be argued that the suppressed affect or emotional tone is still there, remaining hidden. Freudian doctrine would predict the return of the repressed. But it seems more likely, social habit being as powerful as it is, that the repeated suppression of such enthusiasm or moral indignation as the inner-directed man would consider natural permanently decreases the capacity of the other-directed man for those forms of response. The other-directed man may even begin as an inner-directed man who plays at being other-directed. He ends up being what he plays, and his mask becomes the perhaps inescapable reality of his style of life.

XI

AMERICANS AND KWAKIUTLS

Moralists are constantly complaining that the ruling vice of the present time is pride. This is true in one sense, for indeed everybody thinks that he is better than his neighbor or refuses to obey his superior; but it is extremely false in another, for the same man who cannot endure subordination or equality has so contemptible an opinion of himself that he thinks he is born only to indulge in vulgar pleasures. He willingly takes up with low desires without daring to embark on lofty enterprises, of which he scarcely dreams.

Thus, far from thinking that humility ought to be preached to our contemporaries, I would have endeavors made to give them a more enlarged idea of themselves and of their kind. Humility is unwholesome to them; what they most want is, in my opinion, pride.

Tocqueville, DEMOCRACY IN AMERICA

THE image of power in contemporary America presented in the preceding chapters departs from current discussions of power which are usually based on a search for a ruling class (for instance, Burnham's discovery of the managers, Mills's of the labor leaders and others). And Americans themselves, rather than being the mild and cooperative people I have portrayed, are, to many observers and to themselves, power-obsessed or money-mad or concerned with conspicuous display. Or, as in the parable I shall use to illustrate my argument, Americans are felt, and feel themselves to be more like rivalrous Kwakiutl Indian chiefs and their followers, than like peaceable, cooperative Pueblo agriculturists. Perhaps by further pursuing these images of power and personality the discrepancies (as they seem to me) between political fact and political ideology may be somewhat better understood.

Ruth Benedict's book, *Patterns of Culture*, describes in vivid detail three primitive societies: the Pueblo (Zuñi) Indians of the southwest, the people of the Island of Dobu in the Pacific, and the Kwakiutl Indians of the northwest coast of America.[1]

The Pueblo Indians are pictured as a peaceable, cooperative society, in which no one wishes to be thought a great man and everyone wishes to be thought a good fellow. Sexual relations evoke little jealousy or other violent response; infidelity is not severely punished. Death, too, is taken in stride, with little violent emotion; in general, emotion is subdued. While there are considerable variations in economic status, there is little display of economic power and even less of political power; there is a spirit of cooperation with family and community.

The Dobu, by contrast, are portrayed as virtually a society of paranoids in which each man's hand is against his neighbor's in sorcery, theft, and abuse; in which husband and wife alternate as captives of the spouse's kin; and in which infidelity is deeply resented. Dobuan economic life is built on sharp practice in inter-island trading, on an intense feeling for property rights, and on a hope of getting something for nothing through theft, magic, and fraud.

The third society, the Kwakiutl, is also intensely rivalrous. But the rivalry consists primarily in conspicuous consumption, typified by feasts called "potlatches," at which chiefs outdo each other in providing food and in burning up the blankets and sheets of copper which are the main counters of wealth in the society; sometimes even a house or a canoe is sent up in flames in a final bid for glory. Indeed, the society is a caricature of Veblen's conspicuous consumption; certainly, the potlatches of the Kwakiutl chiefs serve "as the legitimate channel by which the community's surplus product has been drained off and con-

---

[1] *Patterns of Culture* (Boston, Houghton Mifflin, 1934; reprinted New York, Pelican Books, 1946).

sumed, to the greater spiritual comfort of all parties concerned." Veblen was, in fact, familiar with these north-west-coast "coming-out parties."

I have asked students who have read Ruth Benedict's book which of these three cultures in their opinion most closely resembles the obviously more complex culture of the United States. The great majority see Americans as Kwakiutls. They emphasize American business rivalry, sex and status jealousy, and power drive. They see Americans as individualists, primarily interested in the display of wealth and station.

A minority of students, usually the more politically radical, say that America is more like Dobu. They emphasize the sharp practice of American business life, point to great jealousy and bitterness in family relations, and see American politics, domestic and international, as hardly less aggressive than Hobbes's state of nature.

No students I have talked with have argued that there are significant resemblances between the culture of the Hopi and Zuñi Pueblos and American culture—they wish that there were.

Yet when we turn then to examine the culture patterns of these very students, we see little evidence either of Dobu or Kwakiutl ways. The wealthy students go to great lengths not to be conspicuous—things are very different from the coon-coated days of the 20's. The proper uniform is one of purposeful shabbiness. In fact, none among the students except a very rare Lucullus dares to be thought uppity. Just as no modern Vanderbilt says "the public be damned," so no modern parent would say: "Where Vanderbilt sits, there is the head of the table. I teach my son to be rich."[2]

It is, moreover, not only in the virtual disappearance of conspicuous consumption that the students have abandoned Kwakiutl-like modes of life. Other displays of gifts, native or acquired, have also become more subdued. A lead-

---

[2] The remark is quoted by Justice Oliver Wendell Holmes, Jr., in "The Soldier's Faith," 1895, reprinted in *Speeches* (Boston, Little, Brown, 1934), p. 56.

ing college swimming star told me: "I get sore at the guys I'm competing against. Something's wrong with me. I wish I could be like X who really cooperates with the other fellows. He doesn't care so much about winning."

There seems to be a discrepancy between the America that students make for themselves as students and the America they think they will move into when they leave the campus. Their image of the latter is based to a large extent on legends about America that are preserved in our literature. For example, many of our novelists and critics still believe that America, as compared with other cultures, is a materialistic nation of would-be Kwakiutl chiefs. There may have been some truth in this picture in the Gilded Age, though Henry James saw how ambiguous the issue of "materialism" was between America and Europe even then.

The materialism of these older cultures has been hidden by their status systems and by the fact that they had inherited many values from the era dependent on tradition-direction. The European masses simply have not had the money and leisure, until recent years, to duplicate American consumership patterns; when they do, they are, if anything, sometimes more vulgar, more materialistic.

The Europeans, nevertheless, have been only too glad to tell Americans that they were materialistic; and the Americans, feeling themselves nouveaux riches during the last century, paid to be told. They still pay: it is not only my students who fail to see that it is the turn of the rest of the world to be nouveaux riches, to be excited over the gadgets of an industrial age, while millions of Americans have turned away in boredom from attaching much emotional significance to the consumer-goods frontier.[3]

When, however, I try to point these things out to students who compare Americans with Kwakiutls, they answer that the advertisements show how much emotion is attached to goods consumption. But, when I ask them if they

---

[3] Mary McCarthy's fine article, "America the Beautiful," Commentary, IV (1947), 201, takes much the same attitude as the text.

believe the ads themselves, they say scornfully that they do not. And when I ask if they know people who do, they find it hard to give examples, at least in the middle class. (If the advertisements powerfully affected people in the impoverished lower class who had small hope of mobility, there would surely be a revolution!) Yet the advertisements must be reaching somebody, the students insist. Why, I ask, why isn't it possible that advertising as a whole is a fantastic fraud, presenting an image of America taken seriously by no one, least of all by the advertising men who create it? Just as the mass media persuade people that other people think politics is important, so they persuade people that everyone else cannot wait for his new refrigerator or car or suit of clothes. In neither case can people believe that "the others" are as apathetic as they feel themselves to be. And, while their indifference to politics may make people feel on the defensive, their indifference to advertising may allow them to feel superior. In fact, I think that a study of American advertising during the last quarter century would show that the advertising men themselves at least implicitly realize the consumer's loss of emotional enthusiasm. Where once car and refrigerator advertisements showed the housewife or husband exulting in the new possessions, today it is often only children in the ads who exult over the new Nash their father has just bought. In many contemporary ads the possession itself recedes into the background or is handled abstractedly, surrealistically; it no longer throws off sparks or exclamation points; copy itself has become subtler or more matter of fact.

Of course many old-fashioned enthusiasts of consumption remain in America who have not yet been affected by the spread of other-directed consumer sophistication and repression of emotional response. A wonderful example is the small-town Irish mother in the movie, *A Letter to Three Wives,* whose greatest pride and joy in her dingy railroadside home is the big, shiny, new, not yet paid-for refrigerator. And it may be argued that even middle-class Americans have only covered over their materialism with a veneer of "good taste," without altering their fundamental drives. Nevertheless, the other-directed person, oriented as he is toward people, is simply unable to be as materialistic as many inner-directed people were. For genuine inner-directed materialism—real acquisitive attachment to things —one must go to the Dutch bourgeois or French peasant or others for whom older ways endure.

It is the other-directedness of Americans that has prevented their realizing this; between the advertisers on the one hand and the novelists and intellectuals on the other, they have assumed that other Americans were materialistic, while not giving sufficient credence to their own feelings. Indeed, the paradoxical situation in a stratum which is other-oriented is that people constantly make grave misjudgments as to what others, at least those with whom they are not in peer-group contact, but often also those with whom they spend much time, feel and think.

To be sure, the businessmen themselves often try to act as if it were still possible to be a Kwakiutl chief in the United States. When they write articles or make speeches, they like to talk about free enterprise, about tough competition, about risk-taking. These businessmen, of course, are like World War I Legionnaires, talking about the glorious days of yore. Students and many others believe what the businessmen say on these occasions, but then have little opportunity to watch what they do. Perhaps the businessmen themselves are as much the victims of their own chants and rituals as the Kwakiutls.

Those few students who urge that America resembles Dobu can find little in student life to sustain their view, except perhaps a bit of cheating in love or on examinations. It is rather that they see the "capitalistic system" as a jungle of sharp practice, as if nothing had changed since the days of Mark Twain, Jack London, and Frank Norris. America is to them a land of lynchings, gangsterism, and deception by little foxes and big foxes. Yet, today, only small businessmen (car dealers or furnace repairmen, for instance) have many opportunities for the "wabu-wabu" trading, that is, the sharply manipulative property-pyramiding of the Dobuan canoeists.

If, however, these students turn to social science for their images of power in America, they will very frequently find their own view supported. The scattered remarks on the United States in *Patterns of Culture* are themselves an illustration. My students also read Robert Lynd's chapter on "The Pattern of American Culture" in *Knowledge for What?*[4] While noting contradictory exhortations to amity and brotherhood, Lynd emphasizes business as highly individualistic and politically ruthless; elsewhere he stresses the masterful ambition and conspicuous consumption typified by the older generation of the "X family" of Middletown. Ironically, the outlook of these and other sociological critics of business is confirmed and reflected by those neoclassical economists who construct models for the rational conduct of the firm—wittingly or unwittingly presenting businessmen as dismally "economic men."

Partly as a result of this image of the businessman, many students at privately endowed universities have become reluctant to consider business careers, and, as more and more young people are drawn into the colleges, these attitudes become increasingly widespread. The abler ones want something "higher" and look down their noses at the boys at Wharton or even at the Harvard Business School. Business is thought to be dull and disagreeable as well as morally suspect, and the genuine moral problem involved in career choice—namely, how best to develop one's potentialities for a full existence—is obfuscated by the false, over-dramatized choice of making money (and losing one's soul) in business versus penury (and saving one's soul) in government service or teaching. The notion that business today, especially big business, presents challenging intellectual problems and opportunities and is no more noticeably engaged in Dobuan sharp practice and Kwakiutl rivalry than any other career, seems not to exist even in the minds of

---

[4] Robert S. Lynd, *Knowledge for What?* (Princeton, Princeton University Press, 1939), pp. 54–113.

students whose fathers are (perhaps woefully inarticulate) businessmen.

It is likely, then, that the students' image of business, and of American life generally, will have some self-confirming effects. Business will be forced to recruit from the less gifted and sensitive, who will not be able to take advantage of the opportunities for personal development business could offer and who, therefore, will not become models for younger men. Moreover, people who expect to meet hostility and calculation in others will justify an anticipatory hostility and calculation in themselves.

To be sure, there are plenty of unlovely, vicious, and mean Americans, in and out of business life; plenty of frightening southern mobs, northern hoodlums, dead-end kids with and without tuxedoes. There are many cultural islands in the United States where Dobu ways abound, just as there are survivals of late nineteenth-century Kwakiutl patterns. But these islands and survivals do not make a system of power, nor are they linked by any conspiracy, fascist or otherwise.

Now, of course, to show that Americans are neither like Kwakiutls nor Dobuans does not prove they are like Zuñi and Hopi Indians. Obviously, in any case, the comparisons must be very rough; from the standpoint of my character types all three tribes, as long as they are in the phase of high population growth potential, would be more or less dependent on tradition-direction. My purpose is to present a parable, not a description. There is evidence, though it is perhaps somewhat understressed by Ruth Benedict, that the Pueblo Indians are actually not so bland and amiable as they seem, that they are, to a degree, antagonistic cooperators, with a good deal of repressed hostility and envy that crops up in dreams and malicious gossip. But this only strengthens the analogy with the middle-class Americans, whose other-directed cooperativeness is also not completely mild but contains repressed antagonistic elements.

Indeed the whole emotional tone of life in the Pueblos reminds me strongly of the American peer-group, with its insulting "You think you're big." While the Kwakiutls pride themselves on their passions that lead them to commit murder, arson, and suicide, the Pueblos frown on any violent emotion.

Ruth Benedict writes:

A good man has . . . "a pleasing address, a yielding disposition, and a generous heart." . . . He should "talk lots, as they say—that is, he should always set people at their ease—and he should without fail co-operate easily with others either in the field or in ritual, never betraying a suspicion of arrogance or a strong emotion."

The quotation brings to mind one of the most striking patterns from our interviews with young people. When we ask them their best trait they are hard pressed for an answer, though they sometimes mention an ability to "get along well with everybody." When we ask them, "What is your worst trait?" the most frequent single answer is "temper." And when we go on to ask, "Is your temper, then, so bad?" it usually turns out that the interviewee has not got much of a temper. If we ask whether his temper has gotten him into much trouble, he can cite little evidence that it has. What may these answers—of course no proper sample—mean? My impression is that temper is considered the worst trait in the society of the glad hand. It is felt as an internal menace to one's cooperative attitudes. Moreover, the peer-group regards rage and temper as faintly ridiculous: one must be able to take it with a smile or be charged with something even worse than temper, something no one will accuse himself of even in an interview—lack of a sense of humor. The inner-directed man may also worry about temper, for instance, if he is religious, but his conscience-stricken inhibitions and reaction-formations leave the emotion still alive, volcano-like, within him—often ready to erupt in political indignation—whereas the other-directed man allows or compels his emotions to heal, though not without leaving scars, in an atmosphere of enforced good fellowship and tolerance.

Many young people today also set themselves an ideal in

their sex lives not too different from the Zuñi norm. They feel they ought to take sex with little interpersonal emotion and certainly without jealousy. The word of the wise to the young—"Don't get involved"—has changed its meaning in a generation. Once it meant: don't get, or get someone, pregnant; don't run afoul of the law; don't get in the newspapers. Today the injunction seeks to control the personal experiencing of emotion that might disrupt the camaraderie of the peer-group.

The chief worry of the Pueblo Indians is directed not to each other's behavior but to the weather, and their religious ceremonies are primarily directed toward rain-making. To quiet their anxiety the Indians go through rituals that must be letter perfect. American young people have no such single ritual to assure personal or tribal success. However, one can see a similarity in the tendency to create rituals of a sort in all spheres of life. People make a ritual out of going to school, out of work, out of having fun, out of political participation as inside-dopesters or as indignants, as well as out of countless private compulsions. But the rituals, whether private or public, have usually to be rationalized as necessary; and since this is not self-evident and since the sign of success is not so explicit as a downpour of rain, the American young people can hardly get as much comfort from their rituals as the Pueblo Indians do from theirs.

The young people who express the views I have described have begun to pass out of the adolescent peer-groups; they have not yet taken their places in the adult patterning of American life. What will be the effect of the discrepancy between their picture of the United States as a place led by Kwakiutl chiefs, leading Kwakiutl-style followers, and the reality of their progress along the "Hopi Way"? Will they seek to bring about changes, through social and political action, that will make America more comfortable for the tolerant, other-directed types? Or will they seek to adopt more ruthless, Kwakiutl-like behavior as supposedly more compatible with real life? Or, perchance, will they admit that they, too, are Americans, after all not so unique, which might require a revision of their images of power, their images of what Americans in general are like?

Doubtless, all these things can occur, and many more. But there is perhaps one additional factor which will shape both changing ideology and changing character. The students, aware of their own repressed competitiveness and envy, think that others may try to do to them what they themselves would not dare to do to others. The society *feels* to them like Kwakiutl or even Dobu, not only because that is the ideology about America they have learned but also because their own cooperativeness is tinged with an antagonism they have not yet completely silenced. And perhaps this gives us an answer to a puzzle about other-directed tolerance: why, if the other-directed person is tolerant, is he himself so afraid of getting out of line? Can he not depend on the tolerance of others? It may be that he feels his own tolerance precarious, his dreadful temper ready to let fly when given permission; if he feels so irritable himself, no matter how mild his behavior, he must fear the others, no matter how amiable they, too, may appear.

These students would prefer to live in the Pueblo culture, if they had to choose among the three described by Ruth Benedict. And, while this choice is in itself not to be quarreled with, the important fact is that they do not know that they already are living in such a culture. They want social security, not great achievements. They want approval, not fame. They are not eager to develop talents that might bring them into conflict; whereas the inner-directed young person tended to push himself to the limit of his talents and beyond. Few of them suffer, like youth in the earlier age, because they are "twenty, and so little accomplished." Whereas the inner-directed middle-class boy often had to learn after twenty to adjust, to surrender his adolescent dreams and accept a burgher's modest lot, the other-directed boy never had such dreams. Learning to conform to the group almost as soon as he learns anything, he does not face, at adolescence, the need to choose between his family's world and that of his own generation or between his dreams and a world he never made.

Since, moreover, his adjustment to this group reality begins earlier, it becomes more a matter of conforming character and less a matter of conforming behavior. The popular song, "I don't want to set the world on fire," expresses a typical theme. The Kwakiutl wanted to do just that, literally to set the world on fire. The other-directed person prefers "love" to "glory." As Tocqueville saw, or foresaw: "He willingly takes up with low desires without daring to embark on lofty enterprises, of which he scarcely dreams."

There is a connection between the feeling these students and other young people have about their own fates and the contemporary notions of who runs the country. We have seen that the students feel themselves to be powerless, safe only when performing a ritual in approving company. Though they may seek to preserve emotional independence by not getting involved, this requirement is itself a peergroup mandate. How, then, as they look about them in America, do they explain their powerlessness? Somebody must have what they have not got: their powerlessness must be matched by power somewhere else. They see America as composed of Kwakiutls, not only because of their own residual and repressed Kwakiutl tendencies but even more because of their coerced cooperativeness. Some big chiefs must be doing this to them, they feel. They do not see that, to a great extent, it is they themselves who are doing it, through their own character.

The chiefs have lost the power, but the followers have not gained it. The savage believes that he will secure more power by drinking the blood or shrinking the head of his enemy. But the other-directed person, far from gaining, only becomes weaker from the weakness of his fellows.

PART III: AUTONOMY

XII

ADJUSTMENT OR AUTONOMY?

*Among the works of man, which human life is rightly em-
ployed in perfecting and beautifying, the first in importance
surely is man himself. Supposing it were possible to get
houses built, corn grown, battles fought, causes tried, and
even churches erected and prayers said, by machinery—by
automatons in human form—it would be a considerable
loss to exchange for these automatons even the men and
women who at present inhabit the more civilized parts of
the world, and who assuredly are but starved specimens of
what nature can and will produce. Human nature is not a
machine to be built after a model, and set to do exactly the
work prescribed for it, but a tree, which requires to grow
and develop itself on all sides, according to the tendency of
the inward forces which make it a living thing.*

John Stuart Mill, ON LIBERTY

IF THE leaders have lost the power, why have the led not
gained it? What is there about the other-directed man and
his life situation which prevents the transfer? In terms of
situation, it seems that the pattern of monopolistic competition of the veto groups resists individual attempts at
power aggrandizement. In terms of character, the other-
directed man simply does not seek power; perhaps, rather,
he avoids and evades it. If he happens to be an inside-
dopester, he creates a formula that tells him where the
power exists, and he seeks to make all the facts thereafter
conform to this formula. In a sense, this means that he
would rather be right than be president. His need to be in
the know, his need for approval, his need in the upper
strata for marginal differentiation, may lead to actions that
look like a drive to get or hold power. But the fact is that

the further away the inside-dopester is from inner-direction, the less is he ambitious, exploitative, and imperialistic. He expects some "others"—some Kwakiutl or Dobuan types —to be doing the exploiting. He fits himself as a minor manipulator, and self-manipulator, into the image he has of them.

If the other-directed person does not seek power, then what does he seek? At the very least, he seeks adjustment. That is, he seeks to have the character he is supposed to have, and the inner experiences as well as outer appurtenances that are supposed to go with it. If he fails to attain adjustment, he becomes *anomic*—a term I shall define in a moment. At most, the other-directed man occasionally seeks to be *autonomous*.

His opportunity to become autonomous lies precisely in the disparity that exists between the actual, objective pressures for conformity that are inescapable and the ritualistic pressures that spring not from the Kwakiutl-like institutions of America but from the increasingly other-directed character of its people. In other words, I do not believe that the social character evoked by today's social structure, namely, the other-directed character, is a perfect replica of that social structure, called into being by its demands.

I. THE ADJUSTED, THE ANOMIC, THE AUTONOMOUS

How, one may well ask, is it possible that a large group of influential people in a society should develop a character structure more constricted than the society's institutions require? One answer is to look at history and to see that earlier institutional inevitabilities tend to perpetuate themselves in ideology and character, operating through all the subtle mechanisms of character formation discussed in the earlier chapters of Part I. By the same token, disparities between social character and adult social role can be among the important leverages of social change. It is too simple to say that character structure lags behind social structure: as any element in society changes, all other elements must also change in form or function or both. But in a large society such as the American there is room for disparities, and hence for individuals to choose different modes of reconciliation. In the upper-income strata in America, many of the pressures which individuals feel spring from their shared interpretations of what is necessary to get along. As soon as one or two in a group emancipate themselves from these interpretations, without their work or their world coming to an end, others, too, may find the courage to do so. In that case, character will change in consonance with the altered interpretations of conditions.

In asking where the one or two innovators may come from, we must remember that social character is not all of character. The individual is capable of more than his society usually asks of him, though it is not at all easy to determine this, since potentialities may be hidden not only from others but from the individual himself.

Of course, social structures differ very much in the degree to which they evoke a social character that in the process of socialization fills up, crushes, or buries individuality. We may take, as extreme cases, the primitive societies of Dobu or Alor. People there seem to be so crushed from infancy on by institutionalized practices that, while they manage to do what their culture asks of them in the emotional tone which the culture fosters, they cannot do much more. The Rorschach tests taken of the Alorese, for instance, indicate that there is a good deal of characterological uniformity among individuals and that few reserves of depth or breadth exist beyond the cultural norm or what Kardiner calls the basic personality type. Such a society might die out as a result of its apathy and misery, especially when further disorganized by white contact, but it is hard to conceive of an internal rejuvenation led by the more autonomous members of the group. Caught between social character and rigid social institutions, the individual and his potentialities have little scope. Nevertheless, even in such a society there will be deviants; as Ruth Benedict has pointed out, we know of no cultures without them. However, before turning to see whether the extent of deviation may be related to population phase, it is necessary to understand more precisely what is meant by deviation.

The "adjusted" are those whom for the most part we have been describing. They are the typical tradition-directed, inner-directed, or other-directed people—those who respond in their character structure to the demands of their society or social class at its particular stage on the curve of population. Such people fit the culture as though they were made for it, as in fact they are. There is, characterologically speaking, an effortless quality about their adjustment, although as we have seen the mode of adjustment may itself impose heavy strains on the so-called "normal" people. That is, the adjusted are those who reflect their society, or their class within the society, with the least distortion.

In each society those who do not conform to the characterological pattern of the adjusted may be either anomic or autonomous. Anomic is English coinage from Durkheim's *anomique* (adjective of *anomie*) meaning ruleless, ungoverned. My use of anomic, however, covers a wider range than Durkheim's metaphor: it is virtually synonymous with maladjusted, a term I refrain from using because of its negative connotations; for there are some cultures where I would place a higher value on the maladjusted or anomic than on the adjusted. The "autonomous" are those who on the whole are capable of conforming to the behavioral norms of their society—a capacity the anomics usually lack —but are free to choose whether to conform or not.

In determining adjustment, the test is not whether an individual's overt behavior obeys social norms but whether his character structure does. A person who has the appropriate character for his time and place is "adjusted" even when he makes mistakes and does things which deviate sharply from what is expected of him—to be sure, the consequences of such mistakes may eventually produce maladjustment in character. (Much in the same way, a culture may be a going concern even if it behaves "irrationally" vis-à-vis its neighbors or material environment.) Conversely, just as nonconformity in behavior does not necessarily mean nonconformity in character structure, so utter conformity in behavior may be purchased by the individual at so high a price as to lead to a character neurosis and anomie: the anomic person tends to sabotage either himself or his society, probably both.[1] Thus, "adjustment," as the term is used here, means socio-psychological fit, not adequacy in any evaluative sense; to determine adequacy either of behavior or character we must study not only the individual but the gear box which, with various slips and reversals, ties behavior in with institutional forms. The person here defined as autonomous may or may not conform outwardly, but whatever his choice, he pays less of a price, and he has a choice: he can meet both the culture's definitions of adequacy and those which (to a still culturally determined degree) slightly transcend the norm for the adjusted.

These three universal types (the adjusted, the anomic, the autonomous), like our three historical types (tradition-directed, inner-directed, and other-directed) are, in Max Weber's sense, "ideal types," that is, constructions necessary for analytical work. Every human being will be one of these types to some degree; but no one could be completely characterized by any one of these terms. To put it in the extreme, even an insane person is not anomic in every sphere of life; nor could an autonomous person be completely autonomous, that is, not irrationally tied in some part of his character to the cultural requirements of his existence. Nevertheless, we can characterize an individual by the way in which one mode of adaptation predominates, and, when we study individuals, analysis by such a method provides certain helpful dimensions for descriptive and comparative purposes. We can also characterize a society by examining the relative frequency with which the three modes of adaptation occur in it, and the relative importance of the three types in the social structure.

---

[1] See Robert K. Merton, "Social Structure and Anomie," in *Social Theory and Social Structure* (Glencoe, Illinois, The Free Press, 1949).

About the anomics who arise as by-products, so to speak, of the attempt to create inner-direction and other-direction, a good deal has been suggested in the foregoing pages. Even a society depending on tradition-direction will have a certain number of anomics, those constitutionally and psychologically unable to conform or feel comfortable in the roles such a society assigns to its regularly recurring deviants. Some of these people can exploit the kinship system to keep going, but in a society of any size there will be some who are pushed out of that tight web. To these somewhat idiosyncratic and accidental outcrops of anomic character, more complex societies add the people who, once capable of adjustment, are thrust aside by the emergence of a new dominant type. Types brought up under a familial regime of tradition-direction may later find themselves misfits in a society by then dependent on inner-direction; likewise, the rise of other-direction may drive inner-directed as well as tradition-directed types into anomie. Reference has already been made to some of the possible political consequences of such anomic character types in America, how their political indifference can be mobilized by a crusade appealing to their inability to cope with the social demands of modern urban culture.

The anomics include not only those who, in their character, were trained to attend to signals that either are no longer given or no longer spell meaning or success. They also may be, as has just been said, those who are overadjusted, who listen too assiduously to the signals from within or without. Thus we have seen that in a society dependent on inner-direction there may be oversteered children and oversteered adults, people of too tight superego controls to permit themselves even the normal satisfactions and escapes of their fellows. Likewise, among those dependent on other-direction, some may be unable to shut off their radar even for a moment; their overconformity makes them a caricature of the adjusted pattern—a pattern that escapes them because they try too hard for it.

We have seen, for example, the effort of the other-directed person to achieve a political and personal style of tolerance, drained of emotion, temper, and moodiness. But, obviously, this can go so far that deadness of feeling comes to resemble a clinical symptom. The psychoanalyst Ralph Greenson, observing soldiers hospitalized for apathy in World War II, writes of them:

The most striking characteristic of the apathetic patient is his visible lack of emotion and drive. At first glance he may seem to be depressed; closer scrutiny, however, reveals lack of affect. He appears slowed up in the psychic and motor responses; he shows an emptiness of expression and a mask-like facies . . . They behave very well in the ward, complying with all the rules and regulations. They rarely complain and make no demands . . . these patients had no urge to communicate their sufferings and no insight into their condition.[2]

My own belief is that the ambulatory patients in the ward of modern culture show many analogous symptoms of too much compliance and too little insight, though of course their symptoms are not as sudden and severe. Their lack of emotion and emptiness of expression are as characteristic of many contemporary anomics as hysteria or outlawry was characteristic of anomics in the societies depending on earlier forms of direction.

Taken all together, the anomics—ranging from overt outlaws to "catatonic" types who lack even the spark for living, let alone for rebellion—constitute a sizable number in America. Quite a little is known about them in terms of personality type, social class, "preference" in illness, and so on. In fact, social science and psychiatry have until recently been preoccupied with understanding the anomic and suggesting therapies, just as medicine has been concerned with fighting the external agents that make people sick rather than with understanding the internal mysteries that keep them well. Indeed, it is usually not too difficult to explain

---

[2] "The Psychology of Apathy," Psychoanalytic Quarterly, X (1949), 290; see also Leites, "Trends in Affectlessness," American Imago, Vol. IV (April, 1947).

why someone is anomic, since the tragedies and warpings of life, like germs, are omnipresent, and any personal disaster can be traced back to its "cause."

We obviously know much less about those whom I call autonomous. Many will even deny that there are such people, people capable of transcending their culture at any time or in any respect. Those who become autonomous in our own society, for instance, seem to arise in a family background and class or regional setting that have had quite different consequences for others. In fact, autonomous, adjusted, and anomic types can be brothers and sisters within the same family, associates on the same job, residents in the same housing project or suburb. When someone fails to become autonomous, we can very often see what blockages have stood in his way, but when someone succeeds in the same overt setting in which others have failed, I myself have no ready explanation of this, and am sometimes tempted to fall back on constitutional or genetic factors— what people of an earlier era called the divine spark. Certainly, if one observes week-old infants in a hospital crèche, one is struck with the varieties in responsiveness and aliveness before there has been much chance for culture to take hold. But, since this is a book about culture and character, I must leave such speculations to others.

It seems reasonable to assume that a decisive step in the road toward autonomy is connected with the social shifts I have linked to the curve of population. To put this in the negative, it is difficult, almost impossible, in a society of high population growth potential, for a person to become aware of the possibility that he might change, that there are many roles open to him, roles other people have taken in history or in his milieu. As the philosopher G. H. Mead saw, this taking the role of the other leads to becoming aware of actual differences and potential similarities between the other and the self. That is why culture contact alone does not lead people to change when their interpretations of the contact spring out of a tradition-directed mode of life. High population growth potential, tradition-direction, and the inability of the individual to change roles —to think of himself as an individual capable of such change—these, as we saw, go together.

For centuries the peasant farmers of Lebanon suffered from invasions by Arab horsemen. After each invasion the peasants began all over again to cultivate the soil, though they might do so only to pay tribute to the next marauder. The process went on until eventually the fertile valleys became virtual deserts, in which neither peasants nor nomads could hope for much. The peasants obviously never dreamed they could become horsemen; the marauders obviously never dreamed that they too might become cultivators of the soil. This epic has the quality not of human history but of animal life. The herbivores are unable to stop eating grass though they eat only to be devoured by the carnivores. And the carnivores cannot eat grass when they have thinned out the herbivores. In these societies dependent on tradition-direction there is scarcely a notion that one might change character or role.

If Arabs could imagine becoming cultivators, and vice versa, it would not necessarily follow that the symbiotic ecology of the two main groups would change. These tradition-directed types might still go on doing what they realized they need not do. Nevertheless, once people become aware, with the rise of inner-direction, that they as individuals with a private destiny are not tied to any given ecological pattern, something radically new happens in personal and social history. Then people can envisage adapting themselves not only within the narrow confines of the animal kingdom but within the wide range of alternative possibilities illustrated—but no more than illustrated—by human experience to date. Perhaps this is the most important meaning of the ever renewed discovery of the oneness of mankind as a species: that all human experience becomes relevant.

The Arab who can see himself as a peasant, even though he would be, for reasons of temperament or other factors,

unable to make so radical a shift, has already gained a new
perspective on the relation: Arab-peasant. He may conceive
of structuring it in some other way, by manipulation rather
than by force, for instance. But if he did that, he would
change, and so would the peasant: their relations could
never again have the old animal-like simplicity.

The more advanced the technology, on the whole, the
more possible it is for a considerable number of human beings to imagine being somebody else. In the first place, the
technology spurs the division of labor, which, in turn, creates a greater variety of life experiences and human types.
In the second place, the improvement in technology permits sufficient leisure to contemplate change—a kind of
capital reserve in men's self-adaptation to nature—not on
the part of a ruling few but on the part of many. In the
third place, the combination of technology and leisure
helps to acquaint people with other historical solutions—to
provide them, that is, not only with more goods and more
experiences but also with an increased variety of personal
and social models.

How powerful such an influence can be the Renaissance
indicates. Then, a richer picture of the past made it possible to live toward a more open future. Italians, newly rich
and self-conscious, tried to imitate Greeks; and northern
peoples, such as the Elizabethan English, tried to imitate
Italians. The inner-directed character type emerged as the
dominant type from the new possibilities created at this
period; he built both those possibilities and the limits he
put on them into his character. From the masses of the
tradition-directed there arose many mobile ones who decided that they could be "horsemen" and no longer had to
be "cultivators"; and the new technology and new lands
beyond the sea gave them the necessary physical and intellectual store for the shift, while at the same time making it
possible for the cultivators to support more noncultivators.
Ever since, in the countries of transitional population
growth, men have robbed the earth of its fruits and the
farmer of his progeny in order to build the industrial civilization (and the lowered birth rate) of today. In this process

the farmer's progeny had to learn how to become something other than cultivators.

Today again, in the countries of incipient population decline, men stand on the threshold of new possibilities of being and becoming—though history provides a less ready, perhaps only a misleading, guide. They no longer need limit their choices by gyroscopic adaptation but can respond to a far wider range of signals than any that could possibly be internalized in childhood. However, with the still further advance of technology and the change of frontiers from production to consumption, the new possibilities do not present themselves in the same dramatic form of passing from one class to another, of joining one or another side—the exploiting or the exploited—in the factory and at the barricades. In fact, those, namely the Communists, who try to structure matters according to these older images of power, have become perhaps the most reactionary and most menacing force in world politics.

In a society of abundance that has reached the population phase of incipient decline, the class struggle alters as the middle class expands until it may number more than half of the whole population in occupational terms, with an even larger proportion, measured in terms of income, leisure, and values. The new possibilities opening up for the individual are possibilities not so much for entering a new class but rather for changing life style and changing character within the middle class.

Under these conditions autonomy will not be related to class. In the era dependent on inner-direction, when character was largely formed for work and at work, it made a great deal of difference whether one owned means of production or not. Today, however, the psychological advantages of ownership are very much reduced in importance; character is increasingly formed for leisure and during leisure—and both leisure and means of consumption are widely distributed. Thus, adjusted, autonomous, and anomic outcomes are often the result of very impalpable variations in the way people are treated by and react to their education, their consumer training, and, generally, their encounters with people—all within the broad status band of the middle class.

To be sure, there may be correlations, as yet unnoticed, between autonomy and occupation. Work is far from having lost its relevance for character even today. And occupational status affects leisure status. Those who are potentially autonomous may select some occupations in preference to others; beyond that, the day-by-day work experiences of members of different occupational groups will shape character. On the whole, however, it seems likely that the differences that will divide societies in the phase of incipient population decline will no longer be those between back-breaking work on the one hand and *rentier* status on the other, between misery and luxury, between long life and short life—those differences that dominated the thinking of men as varied as Charles Kingsley, Bellamy, Marx, and Veblen during the era of transitional population growth. Most people in America today—the "overprivileged" two thirds, let us say, as against the underprivileged third—can afford to attend to, and allow their characters to be shaped by, situational differences of a subtler nature than those arising from bare economic necessity and their relations to the means of production.

II. The Autonomous among the Inner-directed

The autonomous person, living like everyone else in a given cultural setting, employs the reserves of his character and station to move away from the adjusted mean of the same setting. Thus, we cannot properly speak of an "autonomous other-directed man" (nor of an "anomic other-directed man") but only of an autonomous man emerging from an era or group depending on other-direction (or of an anomic man who has become anomic through his conflict with other-directed or inner-directed patterns or some combination of them). For autonomy, like anomie, is a deviation from the adjusted patterns, though a deviation controlled in its range and meaning by the existence of those patterns.

The autonomous person in a society depending on inner-direction, like the adjusted person of the same society, possessed clear-cut, internalized goals and was disciplined for stern encounters with a changing world. But whereas the adjusted person was driven toward his goals by a gyroscope over whose speed and direction he had hardly a modicum of control and of the existence of which he was sometimes unaware, his autonomous contemporary was capable of choosing his goals and modulating his pace. The goals, and the drive toward them, were rational, nonauthoritarian and noncompulsive for the autonomous; for the adjusted, they were merely given.

Obviously, however, as long as tight despotic or theocratic controls of conduct existed, it was difficult to "choose oneself" either in work or play. For, while it is possible to be autonomous no matter how tight the supervision of behavior as long as thought is free—and thought as such is not invaded effectively until modern totalitarianism—in practice most men need the opportunity for some freedom of behavior if they are to develop and confirm their autonomy of character. Sartre, I believe, is mistaken in his notion that men—other than a few heroic individuals—can "choose themselves" under conditions of extreme despotism.

The autonomous are not to be equated with the heroes. Heroism may or may not bespeak autonomy; the definition of the autonomous refers to those who are in their character capable of freedom, whether or not they are able to, or care to, take the risks of overt deviation. The case of Galileo illustrates both points. In order to accomplish his work, Galileo needed some freedom, such as the freedom to exchange astronomical texts and instruments, to write down results, and so on. Yet he chose a nonheroic course. In the Soviet Union and its satellites today he could not make this choice, since the choice between martyrdom or secrecy is not available under the grisly regime of the NKVD.

The four centuries since the Renaissance have seen the rise and fall of many periods when theocratic, royal, or other authoritative controls were not as tight as in Soviet Russia today; periods also when economic life for many was raised above mere subsistence, thus providing opportunities for autonomy. And there were loopholes for autonomy even in the earlier despotic periods, since the despots were inefficient, corrupt, and limited in their aims. Modern totalitarianism is also more inefficient and corrupt than it is often given credit for being, but its aims are unlimited and for this reason it must wage total war on autonomy—with what ultimate effectiveness we do not yet know. For the autonomous person's acceptance of social and political authority is always conditional: he can cooperate with others in action while maintaining the right of private judgment. There can be no recognition whatever of such a right under totalitarianism—one reason why in the Soviet Union artistic works and scientific theories are so relentlessly scrutinized for "deviationism," lest they conceal the seeds even of unconscious privacy and independence of perception.

Fortunately for us, the enemies of autonomy in the modern democracies are less total and relentless. However, as Erich Fromm has insisted in *Escape from Freedom*, the diffuse and anonymous authority of the modern democracies is less favorable to autonomy than one might assume. One reason, perhaps the chief reason, is that the other-directed person is trained to respond not so much to overt authority as to subtle but nonetheless constricting interpersonal expectations. Indeed, autonomy in an era depending on inner-direction looks easier to achieve than autonomy today. Autonomy in an inner-directed mode is, however, no longer feasible for most people. To understand why this is so requires a glance at the powerful bulwarks or defenses for autonomy that an era dependent on inner-direction provided and that are no longer so powerful today. These include, in the Protestant lands, certain attitudes toward conscience, and everywhere, the bulwarks of work, property, class, and occupation as well as the comforting possibilities of escape to the frontier.

In the first place, a Protestant or secular-Protestant society of adjusted inner-directed types expects people to conform, not by looking to others but by obedience to their internal gyroscopes or consciences. This affords privacy, for while society may punish people more or less for what they *do*, it lacks the interest and psychological capacity to find out what they *are*. People are like the yachts in a Bermuda race, attentive not to each other but to the goal in view and the favoring winds.

In the second place, there was always available a line of defense in the existence of frontiers of settlement and the right of asylum. The power to move around the globe in the days before passports placed limits on the tyrants' reach and gave reality to the concept of inalienable rights.[3] Roger Williams lighting out for himself; Voltaire shuttling back and forth over Europe; Karl Marx finding refuge in the British Museum; Carl Schurz fleeing to America—these are scenes from an almost vanished past.

In the third place, the autonomous in the era dependent on inner-direction had available to them the defenses provided by work itself, in a period when the adjusted people also were mainly work-oriented. Though it was hard to admit that one found joy in one's work in the puritan countries, it was permissible to regard it as an end in itself, as well as a means to other ends. The "hardness of the material" attracted the autonomous, indeed—again, like their less autonomous fellows—often hardened them to all other considerations. The following passage from Claude Bernard's *Experimental Medicine*, first published in 1865, expresses this outlook:

After all this, should we let ourselves be moved by the sensitive cries of people of fashion or by the objections of

---

[3] For fuller discussion of this now dormant freedom, see my article, "Legislative Restrictions on Foreign Enlistment and Travel," *Columbia Law Review*, XL (1940), 793–835.

men unfamiliar with scientific ideas? All feelings deserve respect, and I shall be very careful never to offend anyone's. I easily explain them to myself, and that is why they cannot stop me. . . . A physiologist is not a man of fashion, he is a man of science, absorbed by the scientific idea which he pursues; he no longer hears the cry of animals, he no longer sees the blood that flows, he sees only his idea and perceives only organisms concealing problems which he intends to solve. Similarly, no surgeon is stopped by the most moving cries and sobs, because he seeks only his idea and the purpose of his operation. . . . After what has gone before we shall deem all discussion of vivisection futile or absurd. It is impossible for men, judging facts by such different ideas, ever to agree; and as it is impossible to satisfy everybody, a man of science should attend only to the opinion of men of science who understand him, and should derive rules of conduct only from his own conscience.[4]

Such a man as Claude Bernard looked to his scientific colleagues, not for approval of himself as a person but for the validation of his objective work. He had less need for people, for warm interpersonal response, than the autonomous man who arises among the groups dependent on other-direction.

---

[4] Claude Bernard, *An Introduction to the Study of Experimental Medicine*, trans. Henry C. Greene (New York, Macmillan, 1927), pp. 102–103. Freud, whose attitude was remarkably similar, gives us as one of his favorite quotations, a similar passage from Ferdinand Lassalle: "A man like myself who, as I explained to you, had devoted his whole life to the motto 'Die Wissenschaft und die Arbeiter' (Science and the Workingman), would receive the same impression from a condemnation which in the course of events confronts him as would the chemist, absorbed in his scientific experiments, from the cracking of a retort. With a slight knitting of his brow at the resistance of the material, he would, as soon as the disturbance was quieted, calmly continue his labor and investigations." See Freud, *Wit and Its Relations to the Unconscious*, trans. Brill (New York, Moffat, Yard, 1916), p. 115.

In the fourth place, property and class were substantial defenses for those who strove for autonomy. They protected not only the crazy millionaire's conspicuous consumption but the irreverence of the secluded Bentham and the integrated double life of that fine horseman and industrialist of Manchester, Friedrich Engels. People were protected, too, not only by their work and their property but by their position, be it elevated or humble. If people could manage to fulfill their occupational role, what they did in their off hours was more or less up to them. Charles Lamb as a petty official could write in his spare time. Hawthorne, and many other nineteenth-century American writers, held posts that did not require them to give much of themselves—certainly not the self-exploitation on and off the job asked of far better paid writers who hold hack jobs today. The hierarchical chain of occupations, once one achieved a position in it, held people in place with some degree of security, while permitting sufficient tether for the autonomous. Within certain given limits of property and place, one could move without arousing shocked antagonism, traumatic either in terms of one's feelings or one's worldly fate.

Many of these same defenses, however, operated far more frequently as barriers to autonomy than as defenses for it. A society organized in terms of class, private property, and occupation resisted autonomy with all the weapons of family, wealth, religion, and political power: the complaints and protests of political and religious reformers, artists, and artisans against this type of largely bourgeois social organization, now vanishing, were true and just enough. But we must never forget that these barriers could frequently be organized as defenses of the individual; once their flanks were turned by energy and talent, they provided the freedom in which autonomy as well as *rentier* complacency could flourish.

In biographies and memoirs of the last several hundred years, we can reconstruct, as it were, the way in which individuals begin their struggle for autonomy within the despotic walls of the patriarchal family. The family operated, much more than the state, as the "executive committee" of the inner-directed bourgeois class, training the social character both of future members of that class and of future servants to it. Print, however, as we have seen, might succor a child in his lonely battle with parents, teachers, and other adult authorities—though a book might also disorient him and increase the pressure on him. But with good luck a book, like a sympathetic teacher or relative, might break the solid front of authority in the home.

Not until adolescence were other children likely to be of much help, though then, especially when adolescent youth groups later took institutional form, they might assist the break from home. Adolescence, in fact, was usually the period of crisis for the boy or girl who sought autonomy. While even the adjusted had to make the passage from home, they moved thence into a social system that still held them fast, finding such authoritative parent surrogates as were necessary to calibrate their already internalized parental signals. However, the would-be autonomous youth, in breaking with parents, were breaking with authority as such, internalized as well as external. One can trace this process in all its poignancy in the development of John Stuart Mill, who got out from under his father only when well along in life, or of Franz Kafka, who never did.

Once out in the world, the person struggling for autonomy faced directly the barriers of property—if he was without it; of hierarchy—if he sought to climb or oppose it; of religion—if he contravened its controls on expression. In strongly Protestant communities in particular, one's discreet overt behavior could not assure to oneself the freedom Erasmus or Galileo had made use of. The result was that between the oversteered and the understeered there was little room for autonomy. The struggle to turn these obstacles into defenses was often too tough, and the individual was scarred for life, as were Marx, Balzac, Nietzsche, Melville, E. A. Robinson, and many other great men of the era dependent on inner-direction. Still others, however—John Dewey, wiry Vermonter, was a magnificent example and so, in a very different way, is Bertrand Russell—more favored by fortune, could live lives of personal and intellectual collision and adventure with little inner conflict.

III. The Autonomous among the Other-directed

Lawyers and lawmakers have a technique called "incorporation by reference"; by means of it they can refer in one statute or document to another without full quotation. In the same way I would like to incorporate by reference here the writings of Mill which deal with individuality: the *Autobiography*, the essays *On Liberty* and *On Social Freedom*, and *The Subjection of Women*. These writings represent an extraordinary foreshadowing of the problems of the autonomous individual when, with the decline of the older barriers to freedom, the newer and far more subtle barriers of public opinion in a democracy arise. Indeed, in reading modern writers, such as Sartre, Simone de Beauvoir, Erich Fromm, José Ortega y Gasset, and Bertrand Russell, who deal with similar themes, one is struck by the degree to which, underneath differences in idiom, their philosophic outlook resembles Mill's in many important respects.

Mill wrote: "In this age the mere example of nonconformity, the mere refusal to bend the knee to custom, is itself a service." But his interest was more in the individual than in the service. He observed two tendencies that have grown much more powerful since he wrote. He saw, as many others did, that people no longer took their cues "from dignitaries in Church or State, from ostensible leaders, or from books" but rather from each other—from the peer-group and its mass-media organs, as we would say. He saw, as few others did, that this occurred not only in public matters but also in private ones, in the pursuit of pleasure and in the development of a whole style of life. All that has changed, perhaps, since he and Tocqueville wrote, is that the actions they saw as based on the fear of what people might say—on conscious opportunism, that is—are today the more automatic outcome of a character structure governed, not only from the first but throughout life, by signals from outside. In consequence, a major difference between the problems of Mill's day and ours is that someone who today refuses "to bend the knee to custom" is tempted to ask himself: "Is this what I really want? Perhaps I only want it because . . ."

This comparison may overstate historical changes; the autonomous at all times have been questioners. The autonomous among the inner-directed, however, were partially shaped by a milieu in which people took many psychological events for granted, while the autonomous among the other-directed live in a milieu in which people systematically question themselves in anticipation of the questions of others. More important, in the upper socioeconomic levels in the western democracies today—these being the levels, except for the very highest, most strongly permeated by other-direction—the coercions upon those seeking autonomy are not the visible and palpable barriers of family and authority that typically restricted people in the past.

This is one reason why it is difficult, as an empirical matter, to decide who is autonomous when we are looking at the seemingly easy and permissive life of a social class in which there are no "problems" left, except for persons striving for autonomy. These latter, in turn, are incapable of defining the "enemy" with the relative ease of the autonomous person facing an inner-directed environment. Is the inside-dopester an enemy, with his sympathetic tolerance, but veiled disinterest, and his inability to understand savage emotions? Are they enemies, those friends who stand by, not to block but to be amused, to understand and pardon everything? An autonomous person of today must work constantly to detach himself from shadowy entanglements with this top level of other-direction—so difficult to break with because its demands appear so reasonable, even trivial.

One reason for this is that the autonomous person of today is the beneficiary of the greater sensitivity brought into our society, at great personal cost, by his autonomous predecessors of the era of inner-direction. The latter, in rejecting the Philistine norm, were frequently very much preoccupied with taste, with what they liked; in their sensuous openness to experience, their awareness of personal nuance, many of the Romantic poets and other artists of the nineteenth century were strikingly "modern." What they put into their poems and other works, in refinement and subjectivity, is part of their legacy to the emotional vocabularies of our own day. These precursors, moreover, had no doubt as to who their enemies were: they were the adjusted middle-class people who aggressively knew what they wanted, and demanded conformity to it—people for whom life was not something to be tasted but something to be hacked away at. Such people of course still exist in great numbers but, in the better educated strata of the larger cities, they are on the defensive; and opposition to them is no longer enough to make a person stand out as autonomous.

Autonomy, I think, must always to some degree be relative to the prevailing modes of conformity in a given society; it is never an all-or-nothing affair, but the result of a sometimes dramatic, sometimes imperceptible struggle with those modes. Modern industrial society has driven great numbers of people into anomie, and produced a wan conformity in others, but the very developments which have done this have also opened up hitherto undreamed-of possibilities for autonomy. As we come to understand our society better, and the alternatives it holds available to us, I think we shall be able to create many more alternatives, hence still more room for autonomy.

It is easier to believe this than to prove or even illustrate it. Let me instead point to a number of areas in which people today try to achieve autonomy—and to the enormous difficulties they meet.

Bohemia. As has just been indicated, among the groups dependent on inner-direction the deviant individual can escape, geographically or spiritually, to Bohemia; and still remain an "individual." Today, whole groups are matter-of-factly Bohemian; but the individuals who compose them are not necessarily free. On the contrary, they are often zealously tuned in to the signals of a group that finds the meaning of life, quite unproblematically, in an illusion of attacking an allegedly dominant and punishing majority of Babbitts and Kwakiutl chiefs. That is, under the aegis of the veto groups, young people today can find, in the wide variety of people and places of metropolitan life, a peer-group, conformity to which costs little in the way of search for principle.

The nonconformist today may find himself in the position unanticipated by Mill, of an eccentric who must, like a movie star, accept the roles in which he is cast, lest he disappoint the delighted expectations of his friends. The very fact that his efforts at autonomy are taken as cues by the "others" must make him conscious of the possibility that the effort toward autonomy might degenerate into other-directed play-acting.

Sex. What is here the autonomous path? Resistance to the seemingly casual demand of the "sophisticated" peer-group that one's achievements be taken casually, or acceptance of this "advanced" attitude? What models is one to take? One's forefathers, who were surrounded by chaste and modest women? Or the contemporary Kinsey athletes who boast of "freedom" and "experience"? And, as women become more knowing consumers, the question of whether or when to "assume the initiative" becomes a matter for anxious speculation. Perhaps even more difficult roles are forced upon women. Also pioneers of the sex frontier, they must foster aggressiveness and simulate modesty. They have less chance to escape the frontier even temporarily through their work, for, if they have a profession, both men and women are apt to think that their skill detracts from their sexual life or that their sexual life detracts from their skill. Many middle-class women appear to have turned back, in a futile effort to recapture the older and seemingly more secure patterns.

Tolerance. Tolerance is no problem when there is a wide gap between the tolerant and the tolerated. The mere expression of good will, and perhaps a contribution now and then, is all that is demanded. But when the slaves become freed men, and the proletarians self-respecting workers, tolerance in this earlier sense must be replaced by a more subtle and appropriate attitude. Again, the would-be autonomous individual is hard put to it to approximate this.

One frequently observes that, in emancipated circles, everything is forgiven Negroes who have behaved badly, because they are Negroes and have been put upon. This sails dangerously close to prejudice in reverse. Moral issues are befogged on both sides of the race line, since neither whites nor Negroes are expected to react as individuals striving for autonomy but only as members of the tolerating or the tolerated race. Plainly, to sort out what is valid today in the mood of tolerance from what is suspect requires a high level of self-consciousness.

This heightened self-consciousness, above all else, constitutes the insignia of the autonomous in an era dependent on other-direction. For, as the inner-directed man is more self-conscious than his tradition-directed predecessor and as the other-directed man is more self-conscious still, the autonomous man growing up under conditions that encourage self-consciousness can disentangle himself from the adjusted others only by a further move toward even greater self-consciousness. His autonomy depends not upon the ease with which he may deny or disguise his emotions but, on the contrary, upon the success of his effort to recognize and respect his own feelings, his own potentialities, his own limitations. This is not a quantitative matter, but in part an awareness of the problem of self-consciousness itself, an achievement of a higher order of abstraction.

As we know all too well, such an achievement is a difficult thing; many of those who attain it cannot manage to mold it into the structure of an autonomous life but succumb to anomie. Yet perhaps the anomie of such processes is preferable to the less self-conscious, though socially supported, anxiety of the adjusted who refuse to distort or reinterpret their culture and end by distorting themselves.

The characterological struggle that holds the center of the stage today is that between other-direction and inner-direction, as against a background in which tradition-direction gradually disappears from the planet. Now we already discern on the horizon a new polarization between those who cling to a compulsive adjustment via other-direction and those who will strive to overcome this milieu by autonomy. But it seems to me unlikely that the struggle between those striving for autonomy and those other-directed persons not capable of becoming autonomous or not desirous of allowing others so to become could be a ferocious one. For other-direction gives men a sensitivity and rapidity of movement which under prevailing American institutions provide a large opportunity to explore the resources of character—larger, as I shall try to show in the following chapters, than is now generally realized—and these suggest to me at least the possibility of an organic development of autonomy out of other-direction.

XIII

FALSE PERSONALIZATION: OBSTACLES TO AUTONOMY IN WORK

> *Only man can be an enemy for man; only he can rob him of the meaning of his acts and his life because it also belongs only to him to confirm it in its existence, to recognize it in actual fact as a freedom . . . my freedom, in order to fulfill itself, requires that it emerge into an open future: it is other men who open the future to me, it is they who, setting up the world of tomorrow, define my future; but if, instead of allowing me to participate in this constructive movement, they oblige me to consume my transcendence in vain, if they keep me below the level which they have conquered and on the basis of which new conquests will be achieved, then they are cutting me off from the future, they are changing me into a thing. . . .*

> Simone de Beauvoir, THE ETHICS OF AMBIGUITY

I. CULTURAL DEFINITIONS OF WORK

THE character reserves of the other-directed are the possible sources of increased autonomy. But it should be clear from the discussion of the work, the play, and the politics of the other-directed man that his reserves, while perhaps more flexible than those of the inner-directed man, are constantly exhausted by his social organization. These reserves are especially exhausted by our current cultural definitions of work and play and the relations between them—definitions which, as we saw, introduce much strenuous "play" into the glad handers' work and much group-adjustive "work" into their play. All of us are forced, to a degree, to accept these cultural definitions of work and play, just as we are forced to accept certain cultural definitions of class, sex, race, and occupational or social role. And the definitions are forced on us by the ways of the culture and by the socialization process we undergo, whether they happen to be timely or anachronistic, useful for or destructive of our character reserves and of our fundamental humanity.

Work has the greater prestige; moreover, it is thought of as alien to man—it is a sort of disciplined salvage operation, rescuing a useful social product from chaos and the disorders of man's innate laziness. The same era, that of transitional growth of population, that saw the most astounding increase in man's mastery over nature, took it as axiomatic, echoing a series of writers from Malthus to Sumner and Freud, that people had to be driven to work by economic necessity. Today, knowing more about the nature of man and of work, we still nevertheless tend to accept the psychological premise that work and productivity are disciplines exerted against the grain of man's nature. We do not quite see, though we are close to seeing, that what looks like laziness may be a reaction against the kind of work people are forced to do and the way in which they are forced to define it.

Because work is considered more important than play, it has been traditional to take most seriously the work that looks least like play, that is, the more obviously physical or physically productive work. This is one of the reasons why the prestige of the tertiary occupations, particularly the distributive trades, is generally low.

Our definitions of work also mean that the housewife, though producing a social work-product, does not find her work explicitly defined and totaled, either as an hour product or a dollar product, in the national census or in people's minds. And since her work is not defined as work, she is exhausted at the end of the day without feeling any right to be, insult thus being added to injury. In contrast, the workers in the Detroit plant who finish their day's production goal in three hours and take the rest of the day off in factory loafing, are defined as eight-hour-per-day workers by themselves, by their wives, by the census.

These cultural definitions of work have curious implications for the health of the economy as a whole and, therefore, derivatively for the chances of autonomy in living. We tend to emphasize the importance of expanding those parts of the economy that have prestige and to overlook economic opportunities in the parts closer to play. For example, in the days of the CCC camps, it was widely assumed that CCC work on fire trails was more important than CCC work on recreational areas, just as the WPA Federal Theater was considered as less important economically than the stalwart Georgian public buildings of the PWA.

In our society, consumption is defined as a means rather than an end. This implies we consume in order to achieve full employment—and we look for full employment through more production of production rather than through an increased production of the enormous variety of recreational resources our leisure, our training in consumption, and our educational plant allow us to develop. However, by thinking of expansion of consumption in terms of the market for durable and semi-durable consumer goods—with the skies eagerly scanned for such new gadgets as television to hurl into the Keynesian multiplier formula—we are left open to an antiquated set of economic habits and assumptions. By clinging to them, one heavy-draft, politically feasible outlet remains for the overexpanded primary and secondary spheres: a war economy.

Indeed, the struggle for autonomy, for a personally productive orientation[1] based on the human need for active participation in a creative task, has become more exigent because we live in a period when the solution of the technical problems of production is in sight. The institutions and character of the inner-directed man combined to

---

[1]The term "productive orientation" is that used by Erich Fromm in *Man for Himself* for the type of character that can relate itself to people through love and to objects and the world generally through creative work. I have drawn freely on his discussion for my concept of autonomy.

prevent him from choosing his work, and made him accept it as a Malthusian necessity. Both the institutions and character of the other-directed man give him a potentially greater degree of flexibility in redefining and restructuring the field of work. Objectively, the new situation concerning work permits a reduction of hours; subjectively, it permits a withdrawal of the concern work demanded in the earlier era and the investment of this concern in non-work. Instead of attempting to undertake this revolution, however, other-directed man prefers to throw into work all the resources of personalization, of glad handing, of which his character is capable, and just because he puts so much energy and effort into work, he reaps the benefit of being able to continue thinking it important.

II. Glamorizers, Featherbedders, Indispensables

We turn now to the first of a pair of twin concepts that will concern us in this and the following chapter. The one, I shall call "false personalization"; the other, "enforced privatization." We have met false personalization in this book before, in the form of the spurious and effortful glad hand. I see false personalization as a principal barrier to autonomy in the sphere of work: it is this, more than such technical problems of production as still remain, that exhausts the character reserves of the other-directed man. Enforced privatization is a principal barrier to autonomy but, as we shall see, by no means the only one in the sphere of play. Privatization will be our generic term for the restrictions—economic, ethnic, hierarchical, familial—that keep people from adequate leisure opportunities, including friendship. To some degree those who suffer most from false personalization at work also suffer most from enforced privatization at play.

There is a dialectic of social and individual advance that makes it likely that, if these barriers to autonomy should be overcome, we would then be privileged to become aware of still others. Man's freedom, since it must be won anew in each generation, is only slightly a cumulative growth. Yet it makes sense to point to some apparent major difficulties which block autonomy today by draining energies that could be more productively used, even while granting that we scarcely know what autonomy will look like, or require, with these blockages removed.

WHITE-COLLAR PERSONALIZATION: TOWARD GLAMOR

The inner-directed manager never "saw" his secretary. The latter, as a member of a different class and, often, a different ethnic group, also seldom "saw" the boss as an individual. Brought together by the invisible hand, both were concentrated on the work, not on each other, save as a benevolent but insensitive paternalism bridged the social gap. By contrast, the other-directed manager, while he still patronizes his white-collar employees, is compelled to personalize his relations with the office force whether he wants to or not because he is part of a system that has sold the white-collar class as a whole on the superior values of personalization. The personalization is false, even where it is not intentionally exploitative, because of its compulsory character: like the antagonistic cooperation of which it forms a part, it is a mandate to manipulation and self-manipulation for those in the white-collar ranks and above.

We can see the change in comparing the attitudes toward women's office work signified by two Chicago dailies. One, the *Tribune*, stands by the older values of job-mindedness; the other, the *Sun-Times*, speaks implicitly for the newer values of personalization. The *Tribune* conducts a regular daily column called "White Collar Girl," which preaches the virtues of efficiency and loyalty. Its tone suggests that it is written for the office girl who wants a paternalistic response from a somewhat distant boss but does not expect much more. It is beamed at readers who on the whole accept the classic inner-directed pattern of office management—though just the same they would not mind if the boss personalized a bit more, while staying definitely boss.

The *Sun-Times* speaks to a presumably somewhat more

liberal and progressive group in the same occupational stratum but under the general classification of the "career girl." The career girl is appealed to not in a single column focused on the employee relationship but in a variety of columns emphasizing careers, successful self-entrepreneurships by glamorous women, and articles on the psychology of office relationships. These articles project the sense of a personnel-managed economy in which most executives are dutifully other-directed and, whether male or female executives, interested in the girls as more than the "help," in fact, as glamor-exuding personalities.

The *Sun-Times* makes a much closer connection between styles of leisure sociability and styles of relationship to a working group than the *Tribune* does. It conveys the idea that the boss is personalizing all the time, and as well as he knows how, and that the problem—virtually the only problem—for the white-collar girl is to determine the style in which to respond to the boss and to make him responsive. The *Tribune*, far less interested in what we may call "mood engineering," retains respect for the nonglamorous skills of shorthand and typing.

Where there is apathy about politics, we expect to find an appeal to glamor. So here, where there is apathy about work, the appeal is again to glamor, which depends less on the work itself than on whom one does it for. Most unpopular of all is work in a pool, which minimizes glamor, or work for a woman boss, which inhibits it. It appears that the women actually wish to throw their emotional reserves into the office situation, rather than to protect them for the play situation. And we must conclude from this that neither their work nor their play is very meaningful in itself.

This puts the boss, in effect, in the position of having to satisfy an almost limitless demand for personalization that is partly based on the unsatisfactory nature of the white-collar girls' life outside the office. There enforced privatization often prevails: despite an urban milieu, white-collar girls seldom have the resources, educational, financial, simply spatial, to vary their friendship circle and their recreations. Grasping at glamor, these women are driven to find it in their work time, in the boss and in the super-structure of emotions they weave into the office situation. That the other-directed manager helped start this chain of personalization because he, too, holds skill in disrepute is not much comfort to him when he must personalize, not only as a banker selling bonds, a statesman selling an idea, or an administrator selling a program, but also simply as a boss or customer surrounded by white-collar girls.

This new sensitivity, moreover, to those of lower status makes it difficult for people to extricate themselves from chains of false personalization by wearing a completely alien work mask. Some inner-directed people can do this: they simply do not see the others as people, or as highly differen-tiated and complicated people. But the other-directed man-agers, professionals, and white-collar workers cannot so easily separate coercive friendliness on the job from a spontaneous expression of genuine friendliness off the job.

THE CONVERSATION OF THE CLASSES: FACTORY MODEL

The white-collar worker imitates, even caricatures, the style of the other-directed upper middle class. The factory worker, on the other hand, is from Missouri: he has to be sold on the virtues of the glad hand. And to date, he has not been. On the whole, the manager has an uphill fight in getting factory workers in large unionized plants to ac-cept the proffered glad hand, and this very resistance fur-nishes him with a virtually unlimited agenda for the devour-ing of his own work energies. As we saw earlier, he can go on endlessly adding people to the management group—training directors, counselors, and other morale builders—and he can also become involved in arranging research on morale to test the efficacy of these men and measures.

Just as the factory worker, when he was at school, re-garded the teachers as management and went on strike or slowdown against their well-intentioned or class-biased efforts, so in the factory he does not take the glad hand held out by the personnel department. Indeed, while the manager believes that high production attests high morale, the opposite may be the case: high morale can coexist with low production via featherbedding. For if the workers feel united in solidarity and mutual understanding—which they would define as "high morale"—the conditions exist for facilitating slowdowns and the systematic punishing of rate-busters.

There are many managers, however, who do not content themselves with allowing top management and the personnel department to tell workers that they have a stake in the output and that their work is important and glamorous—whether it is or not. Many sincerely seek to put plans into operation that give workers an actually greater share by rearrangement of ownership, production planning, and control. One aim of these proposals is to introduce emotional vitality, or a gamelike spirit, into the factory. Both results, along with higher productivity, are often attained.

But the harmony of feelings among manager, worker, and work process often matters more to the manager than it matters to the worker or the work process, partly because, as we have seen, the other-directed manager cannot stand hostility and conflict; partly, as we have also seen, because trying to eliminate hostility and conflict keeps him busy; more important, perhaps, because contemporary American ideology cannot conceive of the possibility of hostility or indifference between members of the "work-team" not adversely affecting production. The achievement of harmony sometimes becomes not a by-product of otherwise agreeable and meaningful work but an obligatory prerequisite. The consequence in some cases may even be to slow down the work because people have been led to expect harmony of mood, and need to be persuaded and repersuaded constantly that it exists.

This does not deny that much can and needs to be done to reduce the monotony of the production line and the tactlessness of the supervisors. When the morale engineers have power to move people from job to job and to change team patterns, they accomplish a great deal. But, as I have said, it is often the psychological needs of the managers that determine the emphasis and priority of factory reorganization.

Meanwhile, two groups stand out against the better integration of the workers into the "work-team": the "isolates" who, while doing their production job, refuse to involve themselves in the harmony of feelings of the factory workers and, on the other hand, the much larger group of featherbedders who involve themselves all too well. Both these groups seek to retain their emotional freedom against the efforts of the factory to force them to mix work and play. The isolate does not want to be involved in emotional planning and factory-group dynamics. The featherbedders simply resist what they consider the boss's exploitation.

Obviously, in the face of such resistance it will be a long time before the factory worker follows the example of the white-collar worker and, in imitation of the boss, puts pressure on him to personalize still more and better. But perhaps we see here one source for the envy of the working class that many middle-class people feel: they envy not only its greater freedom in overt aggression but also the very refusal to get involved in the work situation and the consequent ability to save reserves for play even where the work is monotonous, physically tiring, or sweated.

THE CLUB OF INDISPENSABLES

Responding to the personalizations of the secretary or trying to give mood leadership to the factory floor—these occupations do not alone account for the manager's keeping himself busy. He is busy because he is more than busy: he is indispensable. He clings to the notion of scarcity that was so thoroughly elaborated in the official American culture of the school, the church, and politics. He needs to combat the notion that he himself might not be so scarce —that he might be dispensable. And surely, in the world as it is now, this fear of being considered surplus is understandably frightening.

Yet the other-directed man buys his feeling of being

scarce at the expense of failing to see how little work, and much less teamwork, is needed in many productive sectors to keep the society rolling.[2] It is of the very nature of false personalizing to conceal this fact. And of course the cultural definitions of work also play a part in building up the notion of indispensability—for instance, by making paid work an ideal expression of man's effortfulness—and in providing the indispensables with secondary gains, such as sympathy from wives and children and exculpation from leisure demands and possibilities.

III. THE OVERPERSONALIZED SOCIETY

One of the possibilities for opening up channels for autonomy then, is to de-personalize work, to make it less strenuous emotionally, and to encourage people to decide for themselves whether and how much they want to personalize in what the culture inescapably requires in the way of work. But of course there are psychological obstacles in the way of any institutional changes. The character of the other-directed man is elicited by contemporary institutions, and then, as an adult, he demands that the institutions exploit the character he has come to assume as his. Consequently, if the institutions should no longer employ him in the way he expects to be employed, will he not feel empty emotionally?

Percival and Paul Goodman asked themselves this same

---

[2]Hanns Sachs, *Freud, Master and Friend* (Cambridge, Massachusetts, Harvard University Press, 1945), pp. 46-47, tells one of Freud's favorite stories, which seems as relevant to social as to individual structure: "Many years ago an old professor of medicine died who had ordered in his will that his body should be dissected. The autopsy was performed by a renowned pathological anatomist and I functioned as his assistant. 'Look here,' the anatomist said to me, 'these arteries! They are as hard and thick as ropes. Of course the man couldn't live with them.' I answered him: 'All right. But it is a fact that the man did live till yesterday with these blood vessels.' "

question in *Communitas*, a book which includes one of the most imaginative discussions of work and play in any contemporary writing.[3] They portray a utopia in which people could earn their living by a minimum of effort and would then be faced with the really shocking problem of how to get through the day:

Suddenly, the Americans would find themselves rescued from the physical necessity and social pressure which alone, perhaps, had been driving them to their habitual satisfactions: they might suddenly find the commercial pleasures flat and unpalatable, but they would not therefore suddenly find any resources within themselves.

Like that little girl in the progressive school, longing for the security of the grownup's making her decisions for her, who asks: "Teacher, today again do we have to do what we want to do?"

There appear to be two major ways of reducing the demands of work, one through automatization, which would release the attention of many of us from productive processes entirely, and the other through making use of the potentialities for impersonality in our productive and distributive processes. Both these developments are strenuously resisted, and not only by men who find work as a machine tender, boring as it sometimes is, less boring than the alternatives; in fact, I believe we would now be much further on the road to the wholly automatic factory if management did not harbor residual—and surely understandable—fears that without work we would be lost. This fallacy is characteristic of the proposals for introducing joy and meaning into modern industrialism that come from the schools of De Man, Mayo, and many other recent writers. These men, like some of the syndicalists and those who put their faith in the cooperatives, want to restore the personal relations at work characteristic of a society dependent on tradition-direction as well as of the

---

[3]*Communitas: Means of Livelihood and Ways of Life* (Chicago, University of Chicago Press, 1947), p. 120.

earlier stages of inner-direction. They would like, in a fallacy of misplaced participation, to personalize, emotionalize, and moralize the factory and white-collar worlds at every point. At least in America they make the mistake of seeing our civilization as an "impersonal" society and bemoaning it. For the long run, I think it makes more sense to work with rather than against the grain of impersonality in modern industry: to increase automatization in work—but for the sake of pleasure and consumption and not for the sake of work itself.

For many white-collar workers, as we have seen, false personalization is the only personalizing that they meet. For many factory workers featherbedding is the only sociability they get. Work, when it has these overtones for people, still remains real, important, and magnetic. This was one lure that during the last war drew many women of the middle and lower middle classes into the factories and held them there despite poor working conditions, inadequate transportation, and pressure from spouses. Escaping from domestic lives of extreme privatization, they were willing, even eager, to accept the most monotonous-seeming jobs. Any effort, therefore, further to automatize work must take account not only of temporary technological unemployment but of the situation of those overly privatized ones who still suffer from the residual barriers of family, poverty, and hierarchy we have inherited from the era dependent on inner-direction. But surely we can think of better things for them than the factory as a refuge from home, just as we can think of better ways of giving poverty-stricken people security and good medical care than shutting them up in prison or mental hospitals.

THE AUTOMAT VERSUS THE GLAD HAND

In the present state of our social and economic accounting, I find it impossible to say where necessary personalization ends and unnecessary personalization begins. Nor have I the indices to separate profitably productive effort from busy work. I cannot tell, for example, how much the slow progress toward automatization in the tertiary trades is due to low wages, engaging Negro laundresses and pressers in a muscular race with existing mechanical power, how much to failure to invent the necessary machinery, how much to consumer demand to buy personalization along with a product, and how much to the needs of the work force itself to personalize, for reasons already given, whether the consumer asks for it or not.

It is also hard to judge how much the consumer's demand for individual attention inevitably conflicts with the producer's right to freedom from unnecessary personalization. Retail trade offers a particularly difficult problem in this connection. The growth of the consumer and luxury market in the United States, coupled with the rise of other-direction, make the salesperson's work harder than it was in 1900. Then, for example, the salesgirl in the Fifth Avenue store sold her limited stock to the carriage trade at a pace set for her by the relative slowness of the trade itself. To be sure, "shopping" was a pastime even then. But the customer was not in a hurry, nor, within the range of her class-based style, was she too anxious about her choice. Moreover, the salesgirl, serving only a few customers, could recall their requirements and therefore be of some assistance where assistance was in order. Today the salesgirl in the department store, a typical figure in the distributive chain of personalization, faces a mass clientele huge in size, nervous in motion, and unsure in taste. She is asked to respond in a hurry to a series of vaguely specified wants.

These observations suggest that much of the pathos of our current stage of industrialism resides in the fact that we need rapidly to expand the tertiary trades that cater to leisure, while these are the very trades which may today combine the greatest difficulty and tediousness of physical work—there is much of this, for instance, in the department store—along with the severest emotional demands. The problem of where to automatize is generally looked at by economists as a problem in investment and reinvestment, and also in labor mobility. Yet perhaps a national capital goods budget should include in its forecasts a guess as to the degree of false personalization that it may evoke or eliminate.

What we very much need is a new type of engineer whose job it is to remove psychic hazards springing from false personalization, as safety engineers now remove hazards that endanger life and limb. For instance, such an engineer might seek a way of making gas pumps automatic like slot machines and of turning service stations into as nearly automatic form as some of the most up-to-date roundhouses for engines now are. In factories and offices, an effort could be made, by careful layout engineering, to eliminate working conditions and locations that coerce the emotions—making sure meanwhile that other jobs are available for those displaced by automatization. Some imagination and ingenuity will be required to construct indexes by which to measure the amount of false personalization required by a given job under normal conditions and to set ceilings beyond which such personalization would not be allowed to go.

It would be interesting to review from this perspective the present trend in America to get rid of private offices and have everybody work "democratically" in a single accessible and well-lighted room. For many, I would guess, the dual requirement that one be sociable and get the work done has the same consequences that it does in school and college, of leading to censure of those who too obviously like their work, and of anxiety on the part of those who cannot simultaneously orient themselves to the task at hand and to the human network of observers. For others, there must be a reduction in the anxiety of isolated work, and a net gain in friendliness.

In the distributive trades, where the salesperson is confronted at every turn by customers, there can be no solution through private offices, but only through further automatization. Bellamy saw some of the possibilities quite lucidly, and in *Looking Backward* he made consumer purchasing take the form of giving an order "untouched by human hands" to merchandising centers much like the local depots in which one today can make out orders to Sears or Montgomery Ward. Clearly, if most vending could be made automatic, both consumers and salespeople would be saved from much motion and emotion. The supermarket, the Automat, the mail order house, all dependent on colorful, accurate display and advertising, are the technical inventions that widen the interstices of the distribution system where autonomy can thrive.

Bellamy also suggests to us how we may reduce some of the guilt many of us feel at living a relatively easy life while others are engaged in the irreducible minimum of hard and unpleasant jobs—a guilt which is certainly far more widespread in an era of other-direction, and which may deepen rather than not with an increase in autonomy. His plan, requiring all youth to serve a three-year term in the "industrial army," was designed by him to facilitate national industrial organization and to guide the young in their final vocational choices. When the CCC gave us something of the same sort, it was, like so many of the good things we do, only for "relief"; the well-off were excluded. Something like a combination of Bellamy's army and the CCC would perhaps serve all of us as an initiatory alleviation of guilts about later "unproductive" work, pending the arrival of our new definitions of productiveness. Once people had done an arduous stint in the late adolescent years of strong energies and, for some, of strong idealisms, they might feel entitled to the life of Riley. Certainly, many veterans, studying or loafing in an interesting way under the GI Bill of Rights—the phrase is exceedingly important—would feel guilty about pulling down a check from Uncle Sam had they not suffered their share of deprivation.

These are suggestions for social solutions: but we need not wait on them. Those seeking autonomy might simply refuse to take the cultural definitions of what constitutes "work" for granted—a kind of strike, not against work as such but against the requirement that all recruitable emotional energies be harnessed to work by an endless reciprocal chain.

Thoreau was a first-class surveyor; he chose this occupation—a near-vanished craft-skill par excellence—as a well-paying one that would give him a living if he worked one day a week. Dr. William Carlos Williams is a popular general practitioner in Rutherford, New Jersey. Charles Ives "worked" by heading an agency that sold half a billion dollars' worth of insurance, and he "played" by composing some of the more significant, though least recognized, music that has been produced. Ives felt, and feels, not in the least guilty about the money he made or about the fact that he lived a "normal" American life, rather than a Bohemian one. Yet many men are unwilling to do what these men have done or what Charles Lamb or Hawthorne or many others did in the nineteenth century: to justify their work primarily by its pay check, especially if the work is short and the pay check large. Instead as we have seen they try by false personalization, by mood leadership, by notions of indispensability, and by countless similar rituals and agendas, to fill up the vacuum created by high productivity. Yet people's real "work"—the field into which, on the basis of their character and their gifts, they would like to throw their emotional and creative energies—cannot now conceivably coincide, perhaps in the majority of cases, with what they get paid for doing.

XIV

ENFORCED PRIVATIZATION: OBSTACLES TO AUTONOMY IN PLAY

I may remark . . . that though in that early time I seem to have been constantly eager to exchange my lot for that of somebody else, on the assumed certainty of gaining by the bargain, I fail to remember feeling jealous of such happier persons—in the measure open to children of spirit. I had rather a positive lack of the passion, and thereby, I suppose, a lack of spirit; since if jealousy bears, as I think, on what one sees one's companions able to do—as against one's falling short—envy, as I knew it at least, was simply of what they were, or in other words of a certain sort of richer consciousness supposed, doubtless often too freely supposed, in them.

Henry James, A Small Boy and Others

BECAUSE the distribution of leisure in America has been rapid as well as widespread, leisure presents Americans with issues that are historically new. At the same time part of the promise of leisure and play for the other-directed man is that it may be easier in play than in work to break some of the institutional and characterological barriers to autonomy. Play, far from having to be the residue sphere left over from work-time and work-feeling, can increasingly become the sphere for the development of skill and competence in the art of living. Play may prove to be the sphere in which there is still some room left for the would-be autonomous man to reclaim his individual character from the pervasive demands of his social character.

Admittedly, we know very little about play, partly as the

result of the cultural definitions that give priority to work. Research has been concerned mainly with the "social character" of the producer; only recently has the same attention been paid to the consumer; we have still to discover the player. Yet is it sensible to suggest research into play when it is possible that it would lead to increasing public and systematic interference with an area that ideally deserves privacy and lack of system? Perhaps a conspiracy of silence about leisure and play is its best protection.

Rather than speaking about how one should play, or what the play of man seeking autonomy should be, which is in any case beyond me, I turn to a consideration of restrictions on freedom in the field of play generally.

I. The Denial of Sociability

In the previous chapter we noted the excess of sociability, in the form of false personalization, which is forced on many people in our economy. Nevertheless, I do not deny that for the other-directed man a deficit of sociability is even more serious than an excess. The presence of the guiding and approving "others" is a vital element in his whole system of conformity and self-justification. Depriving him of the sociability his character has come to crave will not make him autonomous, but only anomic—resembling in this the cruelty of depriving the addict of liquor or drugs by a sudden incarceration. Moreover, if the other-directed man is seeking autonomy, he cannot achieve it alone. He needs friends.

The other-directed man is socialized in a peer-group of children who resemble him in such visible indexes as age, color, and class but who may not resemble him at all in his more private temperament, interests, and fantasies. He has learned, if he is adjusted, to look like those others with whom he has been brought up, with whom he has learned cooperation, tolerance, and restraint of temper. In this process he has learned to forget aspects of his character that are not "social," not other-directed. As long as he continues to remain in a peer-group of his happenstance neighborhood, his occupational colleagues, his status equals or would-be equals, the chances are that he may not notice, or notice only in boredom and other vague unrest, any discrepancies between his image of himself and his image of the "others." Conversely, if he should begin to find himself among people who welcome and appreciate or at least do not punish expression and exploration of these buried parts of the self, he may be able to move toward greater autonomy.

To make this move, however, requires the ability, psychological and institutional, to find one's way to the new friends, the new or overlapping peer-group.

As matters stand, however, greater freedom in friendship choice is not by any means the most fashionable remedy offered today for the sociability problems of modern urban people. Many critics of contemporary life would move in the exactly opposite direction, on the assumption that people have not too little freedom but too much. Some of these critics speak from a religious platform, others out of a preoccupation with urban anomie. Greatly troubled by the fact that Americans move their households every few years, they do not seek to make this movement easier by developing, for example, trailers or Buckminster-Fuller-type houses that possess a relative freedom from particular sites. Rather, they would like to freeze people into communities in which friendship will be based largely on propinquity. They are apt to share the outlook of the city planner who said that he thought the ideal communities in America were to be found among the rural Negroes of the deep South and the French Canadians of the Quebec villages. It was disclosed later in the conversation that his own friends were scattered over two continents. Here we find the classes attempting to root down the masses just as the Dobuans try by magical incantations to keep their yam tubers in place!

We might term those critics the neotraditionalists. They seem to want to deny to others the privileges of modern society which, however, they themselves take as a matter of course. Their own choice is for French food one day and Italian the next; they select their ideas from all ages and their friends from all places; they enjoy primitive African and Renaissance Italian sculpture and read books in four languages. These are felt as advantages, not liabilities; and it is ironic that many sophisticated other-directed people, out of fear, impatience, fashion, and boredom, express nostalgia for a time in the past in which they could not have had such choices. Mark Twain's *Connecticut Yankee in King Arthur's Court* indicates a greater awareness of the irony; and Twain, with all his bitterness, expresses a sounder sentiment about the road back.

Despite such critical voices, however, American sociability or the friendship market, like the American goods market, is in many ways the freest and largest in the world. Parents can monitor their children's social relations only at the class and ethnic fringe, and this they are still free to do assiduously. In adolescence, however, the automobile frees many Americans from parentally supervised sociability. By adulthood ease of transport, unity of language, and plenty of spending money release people for vacations, parties, and trips in search of many and varied friends.

Nevertheless the friendship market is beset with many "tariffs," economic, political, and cultural. First of all, there are the grosser inequities in income distribution that limit individual access to consumer goods, leisure, and play. Although floors are built under the consumption of some farmers and workers, many of them fancy featherbedders, other farmers and workers remain unprotected by subsidies or wage contracts and are therefore excluded from the "4-H Club Culture" or "UAW Culture" variants of taste, sociability, and play. These exclusions and privatizations have complex results for the excluders and, in general, for the more privileged groups. In particular, the other-directed may find their paths to autonomy twisted by guilt for the excluded, by the limitation of their own choices that exclusion entails, and by the over-all reduction of the play potentialities of the economy that is the consequence of such reduction in any of its subsectors.

On the other hand, sociability is sometimes subtly and

paradoxically limited by the very efforts undertaken, in the name of tolerance, to cross the tariff walls and to establish associations that the general culture may still call "guilty" ones. The other-directed man, moving with a tolerant peer-group, is not permitted to expand his friendships to wider social strata at his own pace. He may be asked suddenly to drop not only one barrier at a time— say, the caste barrier—but two—say, the class barrier as well. For example he may be asked to meet Negroes of a class position lower than his own, while the moral issue is posed for him simply in terms of color. This can happen to him at precisely the time when he has cut himself off from the customary sources of his morality and, thereby, from the personal forcefulness he needs in order to live up to his new equalitarian values. One possibility here is that he will feel sudden panic at the forcible dropping of tariffs on the friendship market to which his psychic economy has grown accustomed, and react violently in favor of his older standards.

II. Sociability and the Privatization of Women

As with other "minorities," the education and partial emancipation of women puts the "majority" (in this case, the men) in an ambiguous position. They are no longer protected against women by a rigid etiquette or other formal arrangements. Moreover, as we saw earlier, women make sexual demands and offer sexual potentialities that their mothers would never have dreamed of, or would only have dreamed of. By the same token, they make demands for understanding and companionship. But men, already anxious among the antagonistic cooperators of their own sex, do not always welcome the "cooperation" and companionship from the opposite sex that the dropping of an older tariff permits and in a way requires. While the inner-directed man, who could still patronize women, complained to his mistress that his wife did not understand him, the other-directed man in effect complains that his women understand him all too well.

These uneasinesses among the newly liberated are one source of the current attempts to re-privatize women by redefining their role in some comfortably domestic and traditional way. Many people, both men and women, are troubled by the so-called disintegration of the family and look longingly back to the family structure of societies at an early point on the curve of population. They usually fail to see that the current divorce rate is, in part, an index of the new demands made upon marriage for sociability and leisure by sensitive middle-class couples; that these demands not only begin high, in the choice of a mate, but, as Margaret Mead has observed, include the expectation that each partner grow and develop at approximately the same rate as himself.[1]

To be sure, many divorces are the result of wildcatting on the sex frontier that our leisure society has opened up for exploitation by others than aristocrats and bums, and by women as well as men. Yet clearly, any effort by the neo-traditionalists to close the sex frontier, while it might help restore the glamor sin had in the earlier era, would be irrelevant to the problems created by the greater demands a leisure-oriented people put upon their choice in companionship, sexual and otherwise. What is obviously demanded is the development of a new model of marriage that finds its opportunity precisely in the choices that a free-divorce, leisure society opens up. Because women are less privatized than they have traditionally been, marriage offers more for millions of people than ever before in its long history.

Nevertheless, we have quite a way to go before women can associate with men at work and play on any footing of equality. Today men who find it easy and natural to get along with women and prefer mixed company both at

[1]Margaret Mead, *Male and Female* (New York, William Morrow, 1949); see also the very perceptive observations in the article by Talcott Parsons, "Age and Sex in the Social Structure of the United States," *American Sociological Review*, VII (1942), 604–616; reprinted in *Personality in Nature, Society, and Culture*, ed. Kluckhohn and Murray.

work and play have to fight the residues of the older privatization. For one thing, they are hardly able to avoid many stag occasions, into which some men retreat from the liberations forced on them by the new intersex ethics. As the latency period in childhood gets shorter and shorter, so that boys can be boys only from six to ten, adult males try to create or retain artificial latency periods in which they will not be under pressure from women—or, worse, from male judgments as to how they are succeeding with women. Thus, both sexes experience the limits, pressures, and guilts of emancipation.

Hence, we should not be surprised to see in the social strata where other-direction prevails that very considerable privatization even of the women of higher economic status still goes on, and that these women, often compulsory players and consumers, have not solved the problems of competence in play. The heroine of "Let's Go Out To-night," for example, is frozen into her suburban cottage, cut off from the whole friendship market of both men and women—except those she can meet socially with her husband. Many suburbanites, not to speak of farm wives, are much worse off. The husband drives to work in the only car and leaves his wife a prisoner at home with the small children, the telephone, and the radio or television. Such women can easily become so uninteresting that they will remain psychological prisoners even when the physical and economic handicaps to their mobility are removed. And this privatization in turn limits the friendship choices and increases the guilts of everyone else.

As we saw earlier, the war helped deprivatize many women who welcomed work in industry or other war work as a real increase in their sociability. Even in those cases where earnings are not vital to the established living standards of a family, the working woman frequently does find her way to an independence that would hardly be recognizable by the middle-class woman of the nineteenth century. This independence lays the groundwork for some autonomy in play, even when the work remains, as it does for most working women, routine.

Of course, some middle- and upper middle-class women do have time to play. Such women can move into the peer-groups of the bridge players, the garden clubbers, any of the other groups of pastimers. The transition sounds easy. The difficulty is that women are being driven out of many of the areas in which they formerly occupied their leisure with amateur competence. For example, they are no longer welcome as ladies bountiful; the social workers have so professionalized the field of helping people that any intrusion by benevolent amateurs is deeply resisted and resented. Likewise, amateurs can no longer help sick people, unless they are willing, as nurse's aids, to help registered nurses be professionals by doing all the dirty work for them. They cannot help others enjoy themselves, because settlement work and recreational activities have also been professionalized. While they can discuss politics and race relations in the League of Women Voters and the YWCA, they can do so only under the packaged and, in fact, quite excellent programs provided from central headquarters.

Thus everywhere they turn to put their part time energies to work, they face a veto group and its insistence that, to participate, they must "go through channels" or become slaveys and money-raisers for those who control the channels. And money-raising itself is now increasingly professionalized, with only the money-giving left to the "participants." Reacting to this situation, the women either sink back into indifference or conclude, like their working-class sisters, that only through a job, a culturally defined job, will they be liberated. Instead of moving toward autonomy in play, an autonomy toward which they could also help their men, they often simply add to their own domestic problems all the anxieties men endure at work.

III. Packaged Sociabilities

These culturally defined tariffs that crisscross the friendship market among the American peer-groups severely limit the choices any given individual has for finding those who can help him become autonomous. Perhaps one other example should be mentioned, namely the tendency toward self-privatization on the part of the various not quite assimilated ethnic groups. For we encounter here a rather paradoxical development, which results from a change in the meanings read into the otherwise admirable doctrine of "cultural pluralism."

What has happened is that the older pressures toward forcible Americanization which we associate with the settlement house have receded. Only recent groups of poverty-stricken immigrants, like the Mexicans and Puerto Ricans, are steadily subjected to such pressures. The lower-class Negro, Italian, Jew, or Slav is permitted to approach the American middle-class norm at more or less his own pace. Under the practice of cultural pluralism this means that the ethnic groups are no longer urged to accept the whole package of work and play as "the Americans" define it. On the contrary, the ethnics are invited to add to the variety of the nation by retaining the colorful flavors of their "racial heritages." As we saw in discussing food, these are precisely the heritages that are combed over by the dominant groups in search of gastronomical differentiations.[2] So far, so good. But at the same time the middle-

---

[2] Food, of course, is only a symbol or instance of the way in which American play styles are greatly dependent on the post-Protestant (Jew or Catholic) and pre-Protestant (Negro) immigration. From the 1880's to the 1920's, for example, the white Protestant majority waged an increasingly unsuccessful war to maintain its dominance not only in the work sphere, where it was well skilled, but also in the play sphere, where it was constantly having to fight for a precarious competence. Hence it resisted any new consumption potentialities offered by the work-disfranchised ethnics, ranging from Italian food to the borsch-circuit comedy and the Negroid Charleston. Prohibition was the last major battle in that war. Its bad effects were blamed on the "Sicilian gangster." Now obviously the fact that Jews and Negroes could climb, and even avoid the ethnic affronts, most easily in the arts and entertainments, put them in a good position of leadership when the larger society itself shifted to embrace consumption values. Thus it is that

and upper-class Negro, Italian, Jew, or Slav is not quite assimilated; he remains identifiably, or in his own feeling, an ethnic. He is kept from complete social participation in the dominant groups by subtle and not so subtle barriers. Meanwhile veto-group leaders in his own ethnic group come along to urge him to welcome the autarchy thus partially forced on him from outside, to confine his sociability "voluntarily" to his "own" group, and to obey the leisure styles of that group. This, too, is called cultural pluralism, though for the individual it operates to restrict him to a single culture.

Thus, for example, while lower-class Negroes in the big northern cities are immobilized by poverty and segregation, the upper middle-class Negroes are subject to their race leaders' definitions of what it means to be a Negro, especially in those fields, like leisure, which, more than the field of work, are under race control. Sociability with whites runs risks not only from the side of the newly liberated whites but from the pressures of the race leaders, who may for instance interpret friendliness as Uncle Tomism.

Other leisure pursuits may similarly become tainted by race considerations. In some circles middle-class Negroes are forbidden to like jazz because there are whites who patronize Negroes as the creators of jazz; other Negroes may be compelled to take pride in jazz or in Jackie Robinson, as Jews may be required to take pride in Israel or Einstein. Still other middle-class Negroes cannot enjoy watermelon or other foods that are part of the traditional Negro diet and certainly are not allowed to enjoy popular-culture portrayals such as those of Rochester or Amos and Andy. Similarly, while the lower-class Jew is not much bothered by metaphysical definitions of Jewishness, the almost but not wholly assimilated Jew is subservient to the Jewish

---

the ethnics are the ones who liberate the majority. Increasingly, America's play patterns may suffer from the lack of a customary though under-recognized stimulus and élan when there are no more immigrants or people close to immigrant culture.

cultural compartmentalizers who tell him what his leisure style and friendship practice should be. Sociability in these groups is thus limited by a combination of external pressure and small-time culture dictators. Play and sociability are then consumed in guilty or anxious efforts to act in accordance with definitions of one's location on the American scene, a location which, like a surviving superstition, the individual cannot fully accept or dare fully to reject.

XV

THE PROBLEM OF COMPETENCE:
OBSTACLES TO AUTONOMY IN PLAY
(Continued)

For as soon as labor is distributed each man has a particular and exclusive sphere from which he cannot escape. He is a hunter, fisherman, a shepherd, or a critical critic, and must remain so if he does not want to lose his means of livelihood; while in a communist society, where nobody has one exclusive sphere of activity, but each can become accomplished in any branch he wishes, society regulates the general production and thus makes it possible for one to do one thing today and another tomorrow—to hunt in the morning, to fish in the evening, to criticize after dinner just as I have in mind, without ever becoming hunter, fisherman, shepherd, or critic.

Karl Marx, on the amateur

I can play the lute and the pipe, the harp, the organistrum, the bagpipe and the tabor. I can throw knives and catch them without cutting myself. I can tell a tale against any man and make love verses for the ladies. I can move tables and juggle with chairs. I can turn somersaults and stand on my head.

Medieval entertainer, on the professional

I. The Play's the Thing

PRIVATIZATION as an obstacle to play can be thought of as primarily a relic of previous eras of status-dominated leisure; indeed, the immobilization of women, children, and the lower classes harks back to the earlier days of the industrial revolution. Wealth, transport, and education are the great liberators here. But we have also inherited obstacles to leisure from the puritan wing of inner-direction, which succeeded in destroying or subverting a whole historic spectrum of gregarious fun-making: sport, drama, feast days, and other ceremonial escapes. Even those ceremonies that survive, or have been newly invented, such as the Fourth of July or Halloween, have had to meet, if not the critique of puritan asceticism, then the critique of puritan rationalism, from which young children have been precariously exempted. For many adults our holidays make work out of fun-making or gift-giving which we have neither the wit to welcome nor the courage to refuse; we know holidays are calculated steps in the distributive economy and that new holidays, e.g., Mother's Day, are foisted on us—there are more commercially sponsored "Weeks" than there are weeks in the year. Here puritanism has proved an Indian giver: it not only gives priority to work and distribution but, what is more, takes back the niggardly holidays it gives us. The scars that puritanism has left on the American, and not only on the Philadelphian, Sunday are well known.

It may take a long time before the damage done to play during the era depending on inner-direction can be repaired. In the meantime other-direction has added new hazards. The other-directed man approaches play, as he approaches so many other areas of life, without the inhibitions but also without the protections of his inner-directed predecessor. Beset as he is with the responsibility for the mood of the play-group, he might like to fall back on fixed and objective play ceremonials, and to some extent he does so—it is a common mistake to assume that American city-dwellers are wholly without rituals. Our various drinks, our various card and parlor games, our various sports, and our public entertainments—all can be arranged in a series from the less to the more intimate, the less to the more fluctuating, innovational, and subjective. Even so, the responsibility of all to all, that each join in the fun and involve himself at a similar level of subjectivity, interferes with spontaneous sociability in the very effort to invoke it. Above all, perhaps, this groupiness shuts off the privacy which the other-directed man, engaged in personalizing in his work, requires (without often knowing it) in his play. Just because he feels guilty if he is not contributing to the fun of the group, he needs to learn to distinguish between the loneliness he understandably fears and the privacy he might occasionally choose.

We have seen that children learn early in their lives that they must have no secrets from companionable peers and adults; and this includes their use of leisure. This is perhaps to be expected from the other-directed, who care more for the mood and manner of doing things than for what is done, who feel worse about an exclusion from others' consciousness than about any violation of property or pride, and who will tolerate almost any misdeed so long as it is not concealed from them. Presumably, parents who want their children to become autonomous may help them very much by letting them learn they have the right to make their choices (by lying if necessary) between those leisure situations in which they wish to be intimate with others and those in which intimacy is merely the demand of an authority, parental or groupish. Obviously an individual who needs, for the autonomous use of leisure, both play which is private, reverie-filled, and fantasy-rich, and play which is sociable, even ceremonial, has a hard time combating all at once the privatizations we have inherited and the personalizations we have newly elaborated.

These are very general considerations, and they must be supplemented by reminding ourselves of the continuing consequences, both for work and play, of the Great Depression. The depression did not lead to a redefinition of work but on the contrary made work seem not only precious but problematic—precious because problematic. It is significant that we have now taken full employment, rather than full nonemployment, or leisure, as the economic goal to which we cling in desperation. This is not surprising when we realize how stunted were the play opportunities for the man unemployed in the depression. We could see then, in the clearest form, how often leisure is defined as a permissive residue left over from the demands of work-time. Even financially adequate relief could not remove this moral blockage of play, any more than retirement pay can remove it for the forcibly retired oldsters. For the prestige of work operates as a badge entitling the holder to draw on the society's idleness fund. Even the adolescent who is engaged in "producing himself" suffers emotional discomfort if he cannot demonstrate that he is at work or training assiduously for narrowly defined work aims. In sum, taking together the young, the unemployed, the postemployment old, the housewife, and the guilty featherbedders, not to speak of the "idle rich," we may have a great number who more or less unconsciously feel some uneasiness in play—because by cultural definition the right to play belongs to those who work.

The same industrial advance which has given us a some-times intolerable freedom from work has also operated to introduce unprecedented specialization into the area of play, with similar ambiguous consequences for many technologically unemployed players. The varied capacities of the medieval entertainer whose boast is quoted at the chapter head include some amiable virtuosities. But they would hardly get him a billing on the RKO circuit or television today, and he would certainly not be good enough for Ringling Brothers. The amateur player has to compete with professionals who are far more professional than ever before—can he tell Laurence Olivier how to play *Hamlet*, as Hamlet himself could get away with telling the professional players how *not* to do it? We saw in Part I that, while the inner-directed man held on tenaciously to his competence as a player at least in his downward escapes, the other-directed man is faced with and oppressed by virtuosity from the omnipresent media wherever he turns.

Thus it looks as if the task of restoring competence to play is almost, if not quite, as difficult as that of restoring it to work. While a change in income relations, or even in the organization of industry, might make for fairer distribution of leisure and a lessening of guilts, it could not of itself teach men how to play who have historically forgotten how and who have turned the business over to professionals. Are we right, then, in supposing that play offers any easier channels to autonomy than work; are not both equally "alienated"?

I think it is not unreasonable to believe that various types of competence, as yet hardly recognized, are being built up in the play of the other-directed, in the face of all the obstacles we have listed. Some of these skills, such as craftsmanship, have old foundations; others, such as consumership, have new aspects. Even taste-exchanging, that intangible product of the play-work of the other-directed peer-groups, can be seen as a training ground for leisure skills. Perhaps there is more competence at play than meets the eye—less passivity, less manipulation, less shoddiness than is usually charged.

II. The Forms of Competence

CONSUMERSHIP: POSTGRADUATE COURSE

The mass media serve as tutors in consumption style, and if we are looking for straws in the wind, we can begin there. To my mind, it is symptomatic that a number of recent movies can be interpreted as encouraging new leisure and domestic styles among men—with the implication that freedom from their peers will help them to increase their own competence as consumers and encourage their development toward autonomy. In *Letter to Three Wives* and *Everybody Does It* the hero (Paul Douglas) is represented as a power seeker with hair on his chest who is making the "one-class jump"—the jump from lower-middle class to upper-middle class which still propels much of our economic and social life. The one-class jumper, caught as he is between a peer-group he has left and another he has not quite achieved, is usually too insecure, too driven, to be a good candidate for autonomy. Douglas begins with a stereotyped, inner-directed tone of toughness and insensitivity but ends up by discovering new angles in his own complex emotions when he learns (in *Everybody Does It*) that the singing talent being sought by his socialite would-be canary wife is actually his own. This discovery may constitute a commentary on the fact that men need no longer delegate artistic sensibilities to wives seeking culture as status or as career, but can if they wish enjoy them as part of their own competence—a new twist (and one that James M. Cain and the scenarists must have been perfectly aware of) in the old comedy-dilemma of the man who meets and surpasses the leisure ideals of his new, upper-class peer-group.

Still other comedies of manners of recent years tackle a similar theme of peer-free competence from a different perspective. They portray with sympathy the style of a man who allows himself the luxury of being a "generalist" at life, self-educated, eccentric, near-autonomous. In the *Mr. Belvedere* series, for instance, Clifton Webb is a thinly disguised intellectual and social deviant who is an expert at anything he cares to turn his hand and brain to. Yet, like Beatrice Lillie, he attains his range of skill and competence only in situations where society permits a high degree of individualism; and he is allowed to create his breath-taking personal style only because of his astonishing dexterity. On one level the "message" of the Belvedere movies is quite different from that of the Douglas movies, where a heightened expressiveness is suggested as an attractive "extra" in life to the ordinary upper-middle-class man and not to the nonconformist. But on another level the two types of pictures are very much alike. Both seem to be saying, among all the other amusing things they have to say, that the power of the peers can be overcome. Both characterizations give the individual the right to explore and elaborate his own personality and sensitivity with a work-leisure competence that goes beyond the requirements of the peers.

Surely the great mass-media artists, including the directors, writers, and others behind the scenes who "create" and promote the artists, make an important contribution to autonomy. The entertainers, in their media, out of their media, and in the never-never land between, exert a constant pressure on the accepted peer-groups and suggest new modes of escape from them. The sharpest critics of American movies are likely to forget this too easily. In their concentration on the indubitable failures of quality in Hollywood movies, they sometimes miss the point that the movies have multiplied the leisure styles available to millions. Even the fan who imitates the casual manner of Humphrey Bogart or the fearless energetic pride of Katharine Hepburn may in the process be emancipating himself or herself from a narrow-minded peer-group. Or, to take another instance, it seems likely that the wild, fantastic suspiciousness of W. C. Fields may have served many in his audience as a support to their own doubts concerning the unquestioned value of smooth amiability and friendliness. I believe that the movies, in many conventionally unexpected ways, are liberating agents, and that they need defense against indiscriminate highbrow criticism as well as against the ever-ready veto groups who want the movies to tutor their audiences in all the pious virtues the home and school have failed to inculcate.

One of these virtues is "activity" as such, and much current rejection of the movies symbolizes a blanket rejection of our allegedly passive popular-culture consumership. By contrast, the critics are likely to place their bets on leisure activities that are individualistic and involve personal participation. For instance, craftsmanship.

THE POSSIBILITIES OF CRAFTSMANSHIP

The "Belvedere" movies happen to be flashing satire on competence and craftsmanship, in much the way that *The Admirable Crichton* is a satire on competence and class. Today the craftsman often seems eccentric because of his fanatical devotion to his craft or hobby; Mr. Belvedere uses his various craft-skills to flaunt and enjoy his eccentricity, to rub it in. In this sense his life style is a new commentary on the question whether craft competence in leisure is on the decline in America. Certainly many people have the leisure and encouragement to pursue crafts who never did before. We are told that the employees at the Hawthorne plant of the Western Electric Company include thousands of active, eager gardeners; that they run an annual hobby show of considerable size and style; that the factory helps bring together amateur photographers, woodcarvers, model builders—the whole countless range of modern hobbyism —in addition, of course, to the usual sports, music, and dramatic groups. But there are no statistics to show whether hobbies that were once privately pursued are now simply taken over as part of the program of the active, indeed world-famous, industrial relations department. Beyond a few careful exploratory works such as the Lundberg, Komarovsky, and McInerny book, *Leisure: a Suburban Study*, we do not even begin to know whether craftsmanlike leisure has developed new meanings in modern America.

It seems plausible to assume that the craftsmanlike use of leisure has certain compatibilities with the whole way of life of men dependent on inner-direction: their attention to the hardness of the material, their relative unconcern and lack of training for the more complex forms of peer-group taste-exchanging. Moreover, the inner-directed man who carries into his hobby some of his surplus work impulses might find the maintenance of his technical skill playing directly back into his value on the job, making him, for instance, a better and more inventive gadgeteer. Even today, among many skilled workmen, such interchange between the home hobby shop and the plant suggestion box is not by any means a forgotten folkway. But the craft-skill is valued more than ever before for its own sake, as in the case of the Sunday painter.

The dramatic turn toward craftsmanlike hobbies in an advanced economy, in which it pays to cater to the desires of those reacting against mass production, has its own peculiar problems. The conservatism of the craftsman—in this aspect, part of the conservatism of play itself—finds its ideals of competence constantly threatened by a series of power tools and hobby products that make it possible for the dub to appear like a professional. The home craftsman of real craft aspirations is better off with a power tool than without one. But how many can retain the spontaneous craft aspiration in the face of the temptation to have the machine do it better?

Some of the ambiguities of contemporary craft hobbyism dependent on a power tool are illustrated by a study of automotive hobbyists—especially the hot rodders.[1] In this field, a wide range of standards of technique and design gives room to both the green amateurs and the semi-professional car racers, while all the hobbyists have the comfort of working within an old American tradition of high-level tinkering. Competence and imagination are on the scene in force among the youths who race their quasi-Fords and quasi-Chevrolets on the Dry Lakes of the Far West, in a continuous competition with the mass-produced standards of Detroit. Among these groups there exists an active and critical attitude toward the Detroit car as it is now built, or as it was built until recently. Here, astonishingly enough, the top commercial product of the country, the Detroit car, far from driving out amateur performance, has only stimulated, perhaps even provoked it. Moreover, the individual who remakes cars according to standards of his own devising is obviously not exploiting any questionable social dividend in his pursuit of leisure but is "doing for himself" with what parts and help he can muster on a small bankroll. The very economy of his means helps give the procedure its atmosphere of high competence and high enjoyment.

But this field too is becoming professionalized and standardized. *The Hot Rod*, a magazine founded to cater to the growing number of auto hobbyists (at the same time standardizing their self-image), reports that the business of supplying the amateurs with parts and tools is becoming a big business—some $8,000,000 in 1948. In the meantime Detroit has found its way to many of the hot-rodder powerplant notions, if not stripped-down body notions.

_____

[1] See "The Hot-Rod Culture," by Eugene Balsley, in the *American Quarterly*, II (1950), 353.

We see looming upon the horizon of the hot rodder much the same fate that has overtaken other forms of amateur competence, not only in the area of crafts and hobbies but, as we shall see below in the instance of jazz, in the area of taste-exchange and criticism. Those who seek play autonomy in a craft must keep an eye on the peer-groups (other than their own immediate one) and on the market, if only to keep out of their way. But this in turn may involve them in a steady search for difficulties in execution and privacies in vocabulary (in some ways, like the "mysteries" of medieval craftsmen) in order to outdistance the threatening invasion of the crowd. Then what began more or less spontaneously may end up as merely effortful marginal differentiation, with the roots of fantasy torn up by a concern for sheer technique. The paradox of craftsmanship, and of much other play, is that in order to attain any importance as an enlivener of fantasy it must be "real." But whenever the craftsman has nourished a real competence he also tends to call into being an industry and an organization to circumvent the competence or at least to standardize it.

The man whose daily work is glad handing can often rediscover both his childhood and his inner-directed residues by serious craftsmanship. An advertising man, involved all day in personalizing, may spend his week ends in the craftsmanlike silences of a boatyard or in sailboat racing—that most inner-directed pursuit where the individual racers independently move toward the goal as if guided by an invisible hand! And yet it is clear that these "players" may locate themselves in the craftsmanship pattern for reasons that have nothing to do with the search either for competence or for the more distant goal of autonomy.

It is important to see the limitations of the answer of craftsmanship, because otherwise we may be tempted to place more stock in it than is warranted. This temptation is particularly strong among those who try to deal with the challenge of modern leisure by filling it with play styles drawn from the past in Europe or America. Indeed, there

is a widespread trend today to warn Americans against re-
laxing in the featherbed of plenty, in the pulpy recreations
of popular culture, in the delights of bar and coke bar, and
so on. In these warnings any leisure that looks easy is suspect, and craftsmanship does not look easy.

The other-directed man in the upper social strata often
finds a certain appeal in taking the side of craftsmanship
against consumption. Yet in general it is a blind alley for
the other-directed man to try to adapt his leisure styles to
those which grew out of an earlier character and an earlier
social situation; in the process he is almost certain to become a caricature. This revivalist tendency is particularly
clear in the type of energetic craft hobbyist we might term
the folk dancer. The folk dancer is often an other-directed
urbanite or suburbanite who, in search of an inner-directed
stance, becomes "artsy and craftsy" in his recreations and
consumer tastes. He goes native, with or without regional
variations. He shuts out the mass media as best he can. He
never wearies of attacking from the pulpit of his English
bicycle the plush and chrome of the new-model cars. He is
proud of not listening to the radio, and television is his
bugbear.

The vogue of the folk dancer is real testimony to people's
search for meaningful, creative leisure, as is, too, the revival of craftsmanship. The folk dancer wants something
better but does not know where to look for it. He abandons
the utopian possibilities of the future because, in his hatred
of the American present, as he interprets it, he is driven to
fall back on the vain effort to resuscitate the European or
American past as a model for play. Like many other people
who carry the ancestor within of an inner-directed character and ideology, he fears the dangerous avalanche of
leisure that is coming down on the Americans.

In this fear the folk dancer is near-cousin to a number of
other contemporary critics who, though genuinely concerned with autonomy, have no hope of finding it in play—
not even, for the most part, in the hard play of crafts or
sports. These critics go the folk dancer one better; they look
to experiences of enforced hardship in work, or even to

social and individual catastrophe, as the only practicable source of group cohesion and individual strength of character. They see men as able to summon and develop their resources only in an extreme or frontier situation, and they would regard my program for the life of Riley in a leisure economy as inviting psychological disintegration and social danger. Hating the "softness of the personnel"—not seeing how much of this represents a characterological advance—they want to restore artificially (in extreme cases, even by resort to war[2]) the "hardness of the material."

That catastrophes do sometimes evoke unsuspected potentialities in people—potentialities which can then be used for further growth toward autonomy—is undeniable. A serious illness may give a man pause, a time for reverie and resolution. He may recover, as the hero, Laskell, does in Lionel Trilling's novel, *The Middle of the Journey*. He may die, as does the Russian official in Tolstoy's short story, "The Death of Ivan Ilyitch," who near death, confronts himself and his wasted life honestly for the first time. And the swath of the last war does offer repeated evidence that not only individuals but whole groups and communities can benefit from hardship, where not too overwhelming. An example is reported by Robert K. Merton, Patricia Salter West, and Marie Jahoda in their (unpublished) study of a warworkers' housing community in New Jersey.

---

[2] The war experience seemed to establish that there was little "practical" need for such hardship therapies in the interests of production or warmaking. It turned out that characterological other-direction and political indifference did not imply an inability to stand physical hardships. Efforts were made to treat the soldier as if he were in America, with cokes, radio programs, and entertainments from home. Apparently such "softness" did not impede fighting power. The tractability of Americans made it possible to build an army less on hierarchy than on group-mindedness. The tractability, the familiarity with machines, the widespread social skills, and the high educational level made it possible to train men quickly for the fantastically varied services and missions of modern warfare.

The warworkers found themselves living in a jerry-built morass, without communal facilities, without drainage, without a store. Challenged by their circumstances, they responded by energetic improvisation and managed, against all kinds of obstacles, to make a decent, livable, even a lively community for themselves. The dispiriting sequel is familiar: the community, its major problems of sheer existence surmounted, became less interesting to live in, its cooperative store, built by so much energetic and ingenious effort, folded up.

When one reflects on such instances, one realizes that emergencies in a modern society help recreate social forms into which people can with justification pour their energies. People need justification and, as inner-direction wanes, look for it in the social situation rather than within themselves. European and Asian visitors tell Americans that we must learn to enjoy idleness; they criticize alternately our puritan idealism and the so-called materialism which is a by-product of it. This is not too helpful: for if we are to become autonomous, we must proceed in harmony with our history and character, and these assign us a certain sequence of developmental tasks and pleasures. What we need, then, is a reinterpretation which will allow us to focus on individual character development the puritan demands no longer needed to spur industrial and political organization. We need to realize that each life is an emergency, which only happens once, and the "saving" of which, in character terms, justifies care and effort. Then, perhaps, we will not need to run to a war or a fire because the daily grist of life itself is not felt as sufficiently challenging, or because external threats and demands can narcotize for us our anxiety about the quality and meaning of individual existence.

THE NEWER CRITICISM IN THE REALM OF TASTE

Craftsmanship, whatever part it may play in the leisure of an individual or a group, is obviously not a complete solution to the problems of leisure among the would-be autonomous. While the inner-directed man could solace himself in these pursuits, the other-directed man in search of autonomy has no choice but to pass into and through— to transcend—taste-exchanging—that characteristic process by which the other-directed person relates himself to the peer-groups. Once he has traversed this stage successfully he may be able to value and develop his own standards of taste, even to criticize the taste-making operations in the society as a whole.

We have already discussed the negative side of this process: the fact, for example, that the other-directed man feels a mistake in taste as a reflection on his self, or at least on what he conceives to be the most vital part of his self, his radar, and that taste-exchanging is consequently often harried and desperate. But now we must look at the positive side of taste-exchanging: the fact that it is also a tremendous experiment, perhaps the most strategic one, in American adult education. The taste of the most advanced sections of the population is ever more rapidly diffused—perhaps *Life* is the most striking agent in this process—to strata, formerly excluded from all but the most primitive exercise of taste, and who are now taught to appreciate, and discriminate between varieties of, modern architecture, modern furniture, and modern art—not to speak of the artistic achievements of other times.[3]

Of course, all the other-directed processes we have described play a central role in this development, but I am convinced that real and satisfying competence in taste also increases at the same time. It is interesting to note how "old-fashioned" American movies of only twenty years ago appear to a contemporary audience. In part, again, this is caused only by changes in film conventions; but in far greater measure, it is the product of an amazingly rapid growth of sophistication as to human motivation and behavior among movie-makers and their audience.

---

[3]Charles Livermore, formerly a CIO official, recently called my attention to the extremely rapid disavowal by Detroit auto workers of overstuffed, Grand Rapids furniture. Many in the last several years have gone in for modern design.

The speed with which the taste gradient is being climbed has escaped many critics of the popular arts who fail to observe not only how good American movies, popular novels, and magazines frequently are but also how energetic and understanding are some of the comments of the amateur taste-exchangers who seem at first glance to be part of a very passive, uncreative audience. One of the most interesting examples of this is jazz criticism. I speak here not of such critics as Wilder Hobson and Panassié but of the large number of young people who, all over the country, greeted jazz affectionately and criticized it fondly, on a level of discourse far removed from the facile vocabulary of "sincerity" or "swell." These people found in jazz, as others have found in the movies or the comic strips, an art form not previously classified by the connoisseurs, the school system, or the official culture. They resisted, often violently, and occasionally with success, the effort of the popular-music industry itself to ticket its products: in the very form of their choices—preference for combos over star soloists, preference for improvisation, distrust of smooth arrangers —they set up their own *standards* in opposition to *standardization*. Much like the hot rodders, they developed their own language and culture to go with their new skill.

Here again, as with the hot rodders, the verbal craftsmanship of jazz lovers' taste-exchange could not long continue to develop among isolated peer-groups. Jazz has long since been parceled out by a cult or a series of cults using increasingly exacting aesthetic criteria which have often become ends in themselves.

Unwilling to see that taste-exchanging in popular audiences often is the basis for increasing competence in criticism, writers on popular culture generally view jazz, soap opera, the movies, and television with the same horror with which the inner-directed man was urged to view the brothel and burlesque. Essentially this critique of mass culture is the same as the critique of mass production. But what the critics often fail to observe is that, while in its earlier stages mass production did drive out fine handicrafts and debase taste, we have now a situation better termed *class*-mass production where our industrial machine has become flexible enough to turn out objects of even greater variety and quality than in the handicraft era. Likewise, the critics of the mass media may fail to observe that, while their first consequences were often destructive of older values, we have today a situation in which it is economically possible for the first time in history to distribute first-class novels and nonfiction, paintings, music, and movies to audiences that can fit them into leisure patterns of great individuality.

It is these developments which suggest to me that the process of taste-exchanging holds the promise of transcending itself and becoming something quite different, and of signally contributing to the development of autonomy in other-directed man.

III. THE AVOCATIONAL COUNSELORS

To bring the individual into unfrightening contact with the new range of opportunities in consumption often requires some guides and signposts. In our urban, specialized society it may demand "avocational counselors."

"Avocational counseling" may seem like a rather clinical term with which to describe the activities undertaken by a number of relatively rapidly growing professions in the United States, including travel agents, hotel men, resort directors, sports teachers and coaches, teachers of the arts, including dancing teachers, and so on. But there are also many counselors who supply advice on play and leisure as a kind of by-product of some other transaction. The interior decorator, for instance, seems at first glance to belong in a different occupational group from the dude-ranch social director. To be sure, most clients of the interior decorator may be looking for the correct design for conspicuous display. But beyond these functions may lie a realm in which the interior decorator is looked to for more basic domestic rearrangements that can facilitate a more comfortable leisure life, more "colorful" literally and figuratively. The sale of the decorating service may conceal the sale of this significant intangible.

This function is perhaps even more evident in the work of the domestic architect for the upper middle-class client. True, like the decorator, he still counsels his clients in providing the correct public façade. But a generation ago he would not have dreamed of counseling his clients about the functional interior relationships in the dwelling in terms of anything more than "gracious living." Today, however, the architect, by interior and exterior planning, can lead as well as follow the play patterns of his clients. Through him and his views there filters a variety of tastes, inclinations, social schemes (as in easily rearranged living rooms), leisure-time ecologies that scarcely existed a generation ago. The architect—and, beyond him, the city planner—brings together play opportunities that might otherwise remain subdivided among a score of specialists.

Another set of avocational counselors is clustered around the chronological center of American leisure habits, the vacation. The vacation itself, frequently involving the meeting of others who are not members of one's own peer-group and who may be located outside one's own experience with the social structure, may be considered as dramatic a symbol of the encounters among people in the population phase of incipient decline as the market place was in the population phase of transitional growth. To be sure, with high wages millions of Americans spend their vacations hunting animals rather than people; other millions putter about that restorative residue of earlier eras—the house-and-garden. But increasingly the vacation serves as a time and place for bringing those who have leisure and money to buy in contact with those who have a leisure skill to sell—riding, swimming, painting, dancing, and so on. But of course avocational counseling here, except perhaps for ship and shore recreational directors, is usually trying to sell a commodity or a service rather than to help the individual find what he wants and might want.

It is easy to foresee, in the next decades, a great expansion among the avocational counselors. The objection remains that to turn the other-directed man over to an avocational counselor to teach him competence in play is merely to increase the very dependence which keeps him other-directed rather than autonomous. Will not any effort at planning of play rob him of such spontaneity and privacy as he may still retain? This is certainly one possible effect. We can counter it by doing our best to make the avocational counselors as good and as available as possible. The avocational counselor might stimulate, even provoke, the other-directed person to more imaginative play by helping him realize how very important for his own development toward autonomy play is.

IV. Freeing the Child Market

Up to now we have talked of what might be done to increase the competence at play of adults, and quite ignored the realities and possibilities of play for children. Yet it is quite clear that it is childhood experience that will be most important in making possible true adult competence at play. Without any intention of exhausting the subject, I want to suggest a more or less fantastic model to stimulate thinking about what might be done, here and now, to alter some of those aspects of children's play which, as we pointed out in Chapter III, now so often serve to inhibit autonomy. The proposal I want to make should interest producers and advertisers addressing themselves to a child market. I would like to suggest that they set up a fund for the experimental creation of model consumer economies among children.

For example, scrip might be issued to groups of children, allowing them to patronize some central store—a kind of everyday world's fair—where a variety of "luxury" goods ranging from rare foods to musical instruments would be available for their purchase. At this "point of sale" there would stand market researchers, able and willing to help children make their selections but having no particularly frightening charisma or overbearing charm or any interest on the employers' side in pushing one thing rather than another. The point of these "experiment stations" would be to reveal something about what happens to childhood taste when it is given a free track away from the taste gradients and "reasons," as well as freedom from the financial hobbles of a given peer-group. In precisely such situations children might find the opportunity to criticize and reshape in their own minds the values of objects. In the "free store" they would find pivate alcoves where they might enjoy books and music, candy and comics, in some privacy.[3] It would be interesting to see whether children who had had the luck to express themselves freely in consumption preferences, released from ethnic and class and peer-group limitations, might develop into much more imaginative critics of the leisure economy than most adults of today are.

One can conceive of other such model "economies of abundance" in which every effort would be made, on an experimental basis, to free children and other privatized people from group and media pressure. Indeed, market research has for many years seemed to me one of the most promising channels for democratic control of our economy. Market researchers know as well as anyone that their methods need not be used simply to manipulate people into buying the goods and cultural definitions that already exist or to dress them up in marginal differentiations, but can be employed to find out not so much what people want but what with liberated fantasy they might want.[4] Without

---

[3]The closest existing analogy to this "commodity library" is perhaps the neighborhood librarian, who can help children find their way to books because she seems to be out of the direct line of school and home authority, because her interest often actually is in helping rather than in forcing children, and because being typically of an inner-directed background, she does not insist on personalizing the relationship with the child.

[4]My emphasis throughout on the mass media and the commodities turned out by mass production should not be taken as an implicit denial of the importance of the more traditional fine arts. My effort rather has been directed to closing the gap generally believed to exist between high culture and mass culture. The relation between high cul-

"mock-ups" and pilot models people rarely enough make this leap of the imagination.

ture and popular culture seems to me filled with hopeful possibilities in spite of the fear, snobbery, and anti-intellectualism that now so often operate to inhibit easy movement between them.

XVI

AUTONOMY AND UTOPIA

Time, events, or the unaided individual action of the mind will sometimes undermine or destroy an opinion, without any outward sign of the change. It has not been openly assailed, no conspiracy has been formed to make war on it, but its followers one by one noiselessly secede; day by day a few of them abandon it, until at last it is only professed by a minority. In this state it will still continue to prevail. As its enemies remain mute or only interchange their thoughts by stealth, they are themselves unaware for a long period that a great revolution has actually been effected; and in this state of uncertainty they take no steps; they observe one another and are silent. The majority have ceased to believe what they believed before, but they still affect to believe, and this empty phantom of public opinion is strong enough to chill innovators and to keep them silent and at a respectful distance.

Tocqueville, DEMOCRACY IN AMERICA

IN THESE last chapters I have set forth some thoughts about the middle-class world of work and play, in the hope of finding ways in which a more autonomous type of social character might develop. I cannot be satisfied that I have moved very far along these lines. It is difficult enough to consider how we may remove the barriers of false personalization and enforced privatization. It is enormously more difficult to descry, after these barriers are overcome, what in man may lead him to autonomy, or to invent and create the means that will help him to autonomy. In the end, our few suggestions are paltry ones, and we can only conclude our discussion by saying that a vastly greater stream of creative, utopian thinking is needed before we can see more clearly the goal we dimly suggest by the word "autonomy."

The reader who recalls our beginnings with the large, blind movements of population growth and economic and technological change may ask whether we seriously expect utopian thinking, no matter how inspired, to counter whatever fate for man these movements have in store. Indeed, I believe that only certain ideas will be generated and catch on, under any given socioeconomic conditions. And character, with all its intractabilities and self-reproducing tendencies, will largely dictate the way ideas are received. But despite the massed obstacles to change inherent in social structure and character structure, I believe that ideas can make a decisive historical contribution. Marx, who himself denied that ideas are very important and dismissed the utopian speculations of his predecessor socialists, himself supplied an irrefutable example of the power of ideas in history. As we all know, he did not leave the working class to be emancipated only by events. In his alternate role as propagandist, he tried himself to shape the ideological and institutional environment in which workers would live.

I think we need to insist today on bringing to consciousness the kind of environments that Marx dismissed as "utopian," in contrast to the mechanical and passive approach to the possibilities of man's environment that he helped, in his most influential works, to foster. However, since we live in a time of disenchantment, such thinking, where it is rational in aim and method and not simply escapism, is not easy. It is easier to concentrate on programs for choosing among lesser evils. We are well aware of the "damned wantlessness of the poor"; the rich as well, as I have tried to show in this book, have inhibited their claims for a decent world. Both rich and poor avoid any goals, personal or social, that seem out of step with peer-group aspirations. The politically operative inside-dopester seldom commits himself to aims beyond those that common sense proposes to him. Actually, however, in a dynamic political context, it is the modest, commonsensical goals of the insiders and the "constructive" critics that are unattainable. It often seems that the retention of a given status quo is a modest hope; many lawyers, political scientists, and economists occupy themselves by suggesting the minimal changes which are necessary to stand still; yet today this hope is almost invariably disappointed; the status quo proves the most illusory of goals.

Is it conceivable that these economically privileged Americans will some day wake up to the fact that they overconform? Wake up to the discovery that a host of behavioral rituals are the result, not of an inescapable social imperative but of an image of society that, though false, provides certain "secondary gains" for the people who believe in it? Since character structure is, if anything, even more tenacious than social structure, such an awakening is exceedingly unlikely—and we know that many thinkers before us have seen the false dawns of freedom while their compatriots stubbornly continued to close their eyes to the alternatives that were, in principle, available. But to put the question may at least raise doubts in the minds of some.

Occasionally city planners put such questions. They comprise perhaps the most important professional group to become reasonably weary of the cultural definitions that are systematically trotted out to rationalize the inadequacies of city life today, for the well-to-do as well as for the poor. With their imagination and bounteous approach they have become, to some extent, the guardians of our liberal and progressive political tradition, as this is increasingly displaced from state and national politics. In their best work, we see expressed in physical form a view of life which is not narrowly job-minded. It is a view of the city as a setting for leisure and amenity as well as for work. But at present the power of the local veto groups puts even the most imaginative of city planners under great pressure to show that they are practical, hardheaded fellows, barely to be distinguished from traffic engineers.

However, just as there is in my opinion a greater complexity of leisure response in contemporary America than appears on the surface, so also the sources of utopian political thinking may be hidden and constantly changing, constantly disguising themselves. While political curiosity and interest have been largely driven out of the accepted sphere of the political in recent years by the "crisis" mood of the press and of the more responsible sectors of public life, people may, in what is left of their private lives, be nurturing newly critical and creative standards. If these people are not strait-jacketed before they get started—by the elaboration and forced feeding of a set of official doctrines—people may some day learn to buy not only packages of groceries or books but the "larger package" of a neighborhood, a society, and a way of life.

If the other-directed people should discover how much needless work they do, discover that their own thoughts and their own lives are quite as interesting as other people's, that, indeed, they no more assuage their loneliness in a crowd of peers than one can assuage one's thirst by drinking sea water, then we might expect them to become more attentive to their own feelings and aspirations.

This possibility may sound remote, and perhaps it is. But undeniably many currents of change in America escape the notice of the reporters of this best-reported nation on earth. We have inadequate indexes for the things we would like to find out, especially about such intangibles as character, political styles, and leisure uses. America is not only big and rich, it is mysterious; and its capacity for the humorous or ironical concealment of its interests matches that of the legendary inscrutable Chinese. By the same token, what my collaborators and I have to say may be very wide of the mark. Inevitably, our own character, our own geography, our own illusions, limit our view.

But while I have said many things in this book of which I am unsure, of one thing I am sure: the enormous potentialities for diversity in nature's bounty and men's capacity to differentiate their experience can become valued by the individual himself, so that he will not be tempted and coerced into adjustment or, failing adjustment, into anomie. The idea that men are created free and equal is both true and misleading: men are created different; they lose their social freedom and their individual autonomy in seeking to become like each other.

INDEX